FLEI

AND L

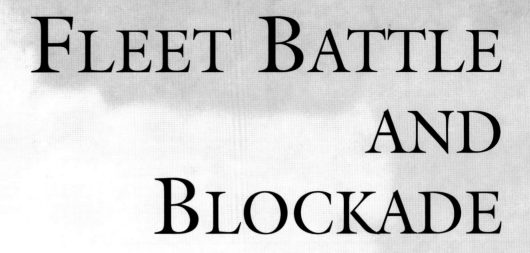

FLEET BATTLE AND BLOCKADE

The French Revolutionary War 1793 – 1797

General Editor
ROBERT GARDINER

MERCURY BOOKS

In association with
The National Maritime Museum

FRONTISPIECE
The meaning of close blockade: the Inshore Squadron,
under Nelson's command, off Cadiz in the summer of
1797, water-colour by Thomas Buttersworth (1768-1842).
NMM neg 3841

Copyright © Chatham Publishing 1996

First Published in Great Britain in 1996 by
Chatham Publishing.

This soft back edition published in 2005 by
Mercury Books, 20 Bloomsbury Street, London WC1B 3JH
ISBN 1845600 11 8

Cover Design: Open Door Limited

Library of Congress Catalog Card No. 96-71388

Print and bound by C.T.P.S. Hong Kong.

Contributors

Nicholas Tracy
Introduction
Part I: Home Waters 1793-1795
Part II: War on Trade
Part III: Mediterranean Theatre 1793-1797
Part IV: Ireland and the Channel 1795-1797
Postscript

Stephen Chumbley
The Nootka Sound crisis 1789-1790
The Low Countries 1793
The West Indies 1793-1794
Capture of the Cape 1795
East Indies 1793-1796
The West Indies 1795-1797
The Corsican Campaign 1794
Santa Cruz de Tenerife
The Great Mutinies of 1797

Robert Gardiner
First shots of the naval war
Ships of the Royal Navy: the First Rate
The Glorious First of June: preliminary skirmishes
The Glorious First of June: the battle
A ship of the line in action
The Glorious First of June: aftermath
The Glorious First of June: the prizes
'Dangers of the sea': fire
The Channel Fleet 1794-1795
Bridport's action, 23rd June 1795
The Channel frigate squadrons
Ship of the Royal Navy: the 18pdr frigate
Commerce warfare in the West Indies
The Cruise of a frigate
Occupation of Toulon
Political tangles
The original Martello tower
Evacuation of Toulon
Ships of the Royal Navy: fireships
Ships of the Royal Navy: flush-decked ship sloops
The Mediterranean Fleet under Hotham
Britain withdraws from the Mediterranean
Battle of Cape St Vincent, 14 February 1797
Nelson's Patent Bridge
The naval officer: recruitment and advancement
Blockade of Cadiz
Close Blockade
The Irish Guard
Inshore warfare in the Channel
The Black Legion invades Wales
'Dangers of the sea': grounding
A global war

David Lyon
French naval bases: Brest
French naval bases: Cherbourg
Droits de l'Homme, 13-14 January 1797
The North Sea Squadron
The Battle of Camperdown, 11 October 1797
Camperdown: end of the battle

Julian Mannering
Notes on artists

Roger Morriss
London: commercial capital of the world
The naval officer: duties and privileges
The naval: life at sea
Portsmouth – key to the Channel

CONTENTS

Thematic pages in italic

PREFACE

THIS IS the second contribution to a new series begun with *Navies and the American Revolution,* and those who are familiar with the earlier volume will have to forgive me for repeating the rationale for the series.

Although the eighteenth century lacked the kind of mass, and instantaneous, media so familiar in the late twentieth, the earlier age was just as interested in news and current affairs. This was largely satisfied by the written word—at increasing chronological distance from the events themselves, newspapers, journals and books. But even in the 1700s, the written medium was not the only source of information. A sophisticated printselling industry evolved, producing relatively cheap, and sometimes tasteless images of a nature that even modern tabloids would eschew, purporting to depict recent happenings of public interest. However, among them were also to be found fine engravings based on the works of well known artists, including remarkably detailed maps and charts of land and sea engagements, which often stand up in point of accuracy to modern research.

In this fashion the public was provided with an image of the great occurrences of the time, and the 'Chatham Pictorial Histories' are intended to recreate this impression in the naval sphere, which for an island nation like Britain was a paramount concern right down to recent decades. Of course, besides the public prints, there were also more formal representations like the oil paintings commissioned by those involved, but by their very nature they are celebratory and, although often the result of the most meticulous research by the artist, they lack immediacy. They are also quite well known, and another of our concerns has been to seek out the less familiar, and in some cases the never previously published, so while we do use some finished paintings, we have preferred the artist's own sketchbooks where available; they reveal not only the lengths the painters went to get details correct, but often cover occurrences that are not otherwise represented, or where the art world has lost track of the finished work.

In the search for original and, if possible, eyewitness depictions, we have also dipped into some of the logs, journals and contemporary manuscripts. Naval officers, in particular, were encouraged to observe closely, and part of the training process involved making sketches of everything from coastal features to life on board. To a lesser extent, this was true of army officers, who were often fine mapmakers—especially those in the technical branches like the engineers and the artillery (today most people in Britain are unaware of why the best official mapping of the country is called the Ordnance Survey).

However, the series was inspired by the Prints and Drawings collection of the National Maritime Museum at Greenwich, on the outskirts of London. Reckoned to comprise 66,000 images, it is a surprisingly under-used resource, despite the fact that an ongoing copying programme has made three-quarters of it available on microfilm. While this forms the core of the series, we have also had recourse to the Admiralty Collection of ship draughts—itself running to about 100,000 plans—as well as some reference to the charts collection in the Navigation Department and logs and personal journals kept by the Manuscripts Department. This last is a very substantial holding with no easy mode of access to any illustrations it may contain, so although some work has been done in this area, it must be said that there is probably far more to discover if only time were available for the task.

The series is intended first and foremost to illustrate the great events of maritime history, and we have made little attempt to pass artistic judgement on any of the images, which were chosen for content rather than style. The pictures are grouped, as far as practical, to show how events were presented at the time. Since this is not primarily a work of art history, for the technical credits we have relied on the Maritime Museum's extant indexing, the product of a massive and long-running documentation programme by many hands with some inevitable inconsistencies, depending on the state of knowledge at the time each item was catalogued. We have reproduced what information there is, only correcting obviously wrong attributions and dates, and quoting the negative number or unique reference number of each illustration for anyone wishing to obtain copies of these from the museum or archive concerned.

Unlike *Navies and the American Revolution,* which was a stand-alone volume, *Fleet Battle and Blockade* is intended to form the first of five titles covering the whole of the period of the great French wars from 1793 to 1815, including America's 'Quasi-War' with France and the conflict with the Barbary states. The series runs chronologically, except that the War of 1812 fills a single volume of its own, and each otherwise covers its period completely. However, the thematic spreads are cumulative in their coverage, because we are keen to illustrate many general aspects of the weapons and warfare of the period which stand outside the chronological structure. Therefore, we devised a single programme of such topics and simply positioned each at an appropriate point in the series. The best example is provided by the many features on individual ship types and their roles, which will add up to a complete analysis of the function of the Navy's order of battle by the end of this five-volume set. Similarly, *Fleet Battle and Blockade* looks at the life of commissioned officers, while later volumes will do the same for warrant officers and seamen; and there will be ongoing picture essays on themes like the perils of the sea, and on individual ports and harbours. This, we believe, avoids predictability and gives every volume variety and additional interest.

Acknowledgements

My intellectual and emotional debts for this volume are much the same as for *Navies and the American Revolution* and I am happy to repeat my thanks.

The project would have been impossible without the co-operation of those at the National Maritime Museum's publications division, initially David Spence and latterly Pieter van der Merwe, who negotiated and set up a workable joint venture. I received generous and friendly advice from Clive Powell on logs and journals and from Brian Thynne on charts, while the staff of the library were endlessly patient with demands for myriads of photocopies and frequent requests to put right snarl-ups in the microfilm readers. Karen Peart organised the crucially important visit to the outstation where the original prints and drawings are stored, and Nick Booth was a tower of strength in hauling out and reshelving more than sixty boxes that I needed to investigate.

However, our greatest thanks must be reserved, as previously, for Chris Gray, Head of Picture Research, who organised and executed the massive programme of photography that we demanded within a very unreasonable timescale. He and David Taylor of the same division remained cool under considerable pressure, coping with whatever was asked of them, and smoothed the path of a vast number of prints through a photographic studio struggling to keep up with an avalanche of work.

Robert Gardiner
London, October 1996

Introduction

FRENCH intervention in the American Revolutionary War, which had ended in 1782, had been decisive in the achievement of American independence, but the French Treasury had been severely hurt by the expense of the war. The need to obtain national support for new taxes, and the intoxicating example of a people rallying to the cause of 'The Rights of Man', proved to be the catalysts of revolution in France. In May 1789, for the first time since 1614, the Estates General were summoned. The bourgeois 'Third Estate' forced the establishment of a National Assembly in which it could dominate the political process. This moderate constitutional development was rapidly eclipsed by revolutionary activity. In July the Paris mob stormed the Bastille prison, peasant risings during the summer began to drive the aristocracy into exile, in December Admiral d'Albert de Rions, commandant at the naval dockyard at Toulon, was imprisoned by the mob when he tried to deal with mutiny and in July 1790 Louis XVI was forced to agree to a liberal constitution. In June 1791 he attempted to go into exile himself but was stopped before he reached the frontier.

Under pressure from French *emigrés* to intervene in support of royal government and of Louis's Austrian wife Marie-Antoinette, Frederick William II of Prussia and Emperor Leopold II of Austria agreed that they would only do so with the unanimous consent of the powers. This, however, was seen in Paris as a threat. In February 1792 Prussia and Austria allied, and in response, the Assembly forced the King to declare war. During the summer of 1792 constitutional government broke down altogether, and was replaced by the Paris Commune and the extremist Jacobin clubs. In September war was declared against Sardinia, and a French army entered the territory of Savoy. A French squadron under Rear-Admiral Laurent-Jean-François Truguet landed soldiers at Nice, Montalban, Villefranche and Oneglia which was taken by assault.

Confident of an easy victory, Austria and Prussia began military operations against the debilitated French state. However, the weakness of French finances, and the disruption of the institutions of the state by emigration, was soon shown to be offset by revolutionary ardour. Early defeat was followed on 20 September 1792 by a victory over a Prussian army at Valmy in a heavy fog. Although a minor action, it was psychologically important in reviving French military morale.

In September 1792 the French monarchy was abolished, and in November the army, having pushed the Prussians back across the Rhine, occupied Brussels. The Scheldt, which had been closed to navigation for two centuries because it threatened Dutch commerce and the safety of the English south coast, was now opened. In the south, Savoy and Nice were annexed to France. In January 1793 Louis XVI was executed, and the British government under the leadership of William Pitt the younger expelled the French Ambassador, M. Chauvelin, as the representative of a regicide regime. In response, the French National Convention, successor to the Assembly, declared war against Britain, the Netherlands and Spain, and they, with Sardinia, allied with Prussia and Austria in what became known as 'The First Coalition'. In fact, the French had already commenced hostilities against Britain when on 2 January fire had been opened from the Brest batteries at the 16-gun brig *Childers*. Letters of Marque against Spanish shipping had also been issued prior to the declaration of war. The new French Republic had set out to conquer all the powers of Europe, and nearly succeeded.

The *Marine de la Républic Française* entered the war with a strong fleet constructed during the last years of the *ancien régime*, first under Charles-Eugène de La Croix, Marquis de Castries, who was appointed Minister of Marine in October 1780, and then by his successor César-Henri, Comte La Luzerne. According to William James, whose *Naval History of Great Britain 1793-*

1820 was first published in 1822, at the outbreak of war the French fleet possessed eighty-two ships of the line, including three 120-gun ships, five 100-gun ships, ten two-decker 80-gun ships, and sixty-four 74-gun ships. The Atlantic fleet was divided among three dockyards. At Brest was the largest squadron of thirty-nine ships of the line and thirty-four frigates. At Lorient were stationed ten 74-gun ships and six frigates, and at Rochefort another twelve 74-gun ships and the only 64-gun ship in the French Marine, with sixteen frigates. In the Mediterranean based at Toulon were two ships of 120 guns, three 80s, nineteen 74s, and twenty-two frigates.

This numerical strength, however, was a symptom of the underlying weakness of the French state. The ships had been built at a cost which precipitated revolution, not only by its pressure on the central treasury, but also because it became impossible to pay the wages of seamen and dockyard workers. This stimulated local revolt and mutiny in the dockyards. Insolvency was to persist into the war years and precluded the effective supply of ships with sound equipment and adequate provisions. Throughout the war, the fleet was forced to sail under-canvassed because of the weakness of its equipment, and shortage of supplies was to prove operationally disastrous.

The effect of the Revolution on naval discipline and leadership was even more debilitating. The French Marine's command under the *ancien régime* had been divided among the closed naval elite of the *Grand Corps* which provided most of the executive officers, the *Officiers Bleu* who in wartime were transferred from the merchant marine, and the *Officiers de la Plume* who handled the accounts. An inefficient system, efforts had been begun by Castries between 1781 and 1786 to strengthen the professional element in the fleet. These, however, were overtaken by the Revolution. The central concern of the Marine Committee of the Constituent Assembly was not fighting effi-

9

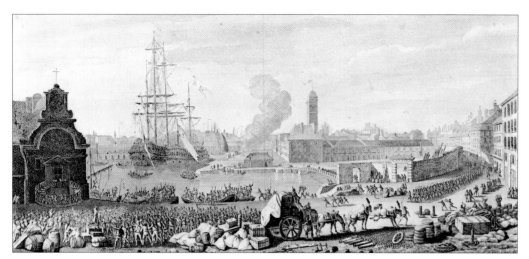

'Port de Brest. Insurrection des vaisseaux de Leopard et l'America en Septembre 1790', etching by Berthault from an original by Prieur. A contemporary French depiction of the Brest mutinies of 1790.   NMM ref PAD1498

ciency, but the need to ensure that the navy did not become an instrument of Royalist reaction. During the 1790 crisis over Spanish eviction of British traders from Nootka Sound on Vancouver Island the Constituent Assembly issued a new code of naval discipline, but when the fleet at Brest mutinied and were support by the municipal authorities, the Assembly agreed to review the provisions of the code. This marked the end of the efforts to reform the navy within the context of an effective Royal administration, and La Luzerne resigned the ministry.

The failure of central government to support the authority of the officer corps led to its disintegration. Officers sought leave, and failed to return, or deserted and went into exile. In 1790 only 40.5 per cent of the 212 officers given leave at Brest ever returned to their duty, and in 1791 only 18.5 per cent of 237 officers. The places of these experienced officers were taken by relatively junior officers or seamen, sometimes drawn from the administrative branch, or from the merchant marine, promoted to high command. The navy was all but paralysed by the assertion of popular sovereignty by the municipalities of Brest and Toulon and by the sailors. The commandant of the dockyard at Toulon, Joseph Marquis de Flotte, struggled to work within the concept of popular sovereignty, but in September 1792 he was dragged from his home and murdered by a Jacobin mob. When the revolutionary government turned to terror in 1793 and 1794 to re-establish authority, the guillotine further reduced the French officer corps. When in April 1794 Admiral d'Estaing, who was too loyal to emi-

grate and favoured moderate reform, was condemned to death for testifying in her defence at the trial of Marie Antoinette, he scornfully exclaimed: 'Send my head to the English: they will pay well for it.'

The army had also, figuratively but also quite literally, been decapitated, but new tactics were eventually developed to make use of the enthusiasm of men fighting for the new social order. The navy was not able to make a similar transformation. It took time for the new men to learn the technical skills of the naval profession, and there was less latitude for the development of new tactics to replace technical skill with *élan*. For that matter, men conscious of their technical limitations, and aware that vocal rabble-rousers, the *pistols*, had gained power over the professionals, showed little if any *élan*. Inevitably, awareness of technical inadequacy, and uncertainty about the social relationships within the navy, undermined morale. Even the professional corps of seamen-gunners was abolished as inconsistent with the revolutionary spirit. The use of army gunners crippled the fleet's armament. The breakdown of discipline, exacerbated by the collapse of the *inscription maritime* which had ensured a fair sharing of the burden of naval duty, extended from topmen who refused to go aloft to craftsmen who produced inferior cordage and sails.

The creative developments in ship design, signalling, and tactics which had occurred in the middle of the century, and had led to unparalleled success during the American Revolutionary War, found no sequel during the war against the 'First Coalition'. Du

Pavillion's system of tabular signals, which had been adopted by the fleet at the beginning of the American Revolutionary War, remained in use throughout the coming struggle. In one respect only was the French Marine more capable than had been that of the *ancien régime*: in 1792 lines of shutter telegraph stations had been constructed connecting the French dockyards with Paris. In clear weather, the naval ministry could pass simple messages to fleet commanders while they were in port or close off-shore in a matter of hours.

The Royal Navy, in contrast, was in good shape. The mobilisations of 1787 in support of William of Orange against the Patriot Party in the Netherlands, and that of the 1790 Nootka Sound crisis, had ensured that needed repairs were undertaken. William Pitt firmly supported Vice-Admiral Sir Charles Middleton, navy Comptroller from 1778 to 1790 and later a member of the Admiralty Board between 1794 and 1795, who built thirty-three new sail of the line. The appointments of Sir William Rule in 1784, and of Sir John Henslow in 1793 as surveyors, led to the building of larger warships than had been British practice. A 74-gun ship ordered in 1785, *Brunswick*, was 176ft long, the largest yet built in Britain. The Netherlands crisis had led to five ships being ordered in 1788, the largest of which was the 110-gun *Ville de Paris,* named after Admiral de Grasse's flagship which had been captured at the Battle of the Saintes. The 98-gun *Dreadnought* and 80-gun *Foudroyant* were each 3ft longer than earlier designs. *Mars* and *Centaur* were each built to *Brunswick*'s dimensions. Another 110-gun ship, *Hibernia*, was ordered in 1790. At the beginning of 1793 there were twenty-six ships of the line in commission, and another eighty-seven laid up 'in ordinary', or under repair. There were also another 191 ships in the fleet too small to take a place in the line of battle. A further twenty-eight ships and fifty-eight smaller vessels were on the list, but were too old for service except as harbour auxiliaries.

The defeats of the American Revolutionary War had stimulated reform. The use of a numerical signalling system, first introduced by Lord Howe on the North American station, had become general in the fleet, and was to be made the official system in 1799. In 1796 the British copied the French shutter telegraph, constructing two chains which joined Dover with London, and London with Portsmouth and Plymouth. Middleton had adopted the administrative plan in 1783 of reserving in the dockyards under each ship's name a large proportion of the imperishable stores needed for service. The result was that in material terms, mobilisation was able to take place faster than in any previous war. At the end of 1793 there were eighty-five ships of the line in commission, and 194 smaller vessels.

During the American War tremendous tactical advantage had been obtained by the extensive use of copper sheathing to stop the fouling of ships' bottoms, with a consequential increase in the effective manoeuvring speed of British fleets. A start had also been made in the introduction into the fleet of short, lighter, carronades which could fire a heavy shot to a range comparable to effective battle range for longer guns. By 1793 coppering was standard in all the major fleets, but the British had an advantage in the introduction of carronades. The standard in 1793 was for a first rate such as *Victory* to have four 32pdr carronades and six 18pdr carronades on her upper works, while 74-gun ships had two 12pdrs on their forecastles and four or six on the poop. Not every ship conformed to these standards, but by early 1796 carronades were being mounted in considerable numbers. Nine 50- and 54-gun ships purchased from the East India Company were armed with a tier of 32pdr carronades on the upper gun deck. Smaller carronades were also being issued for mounting on ships' launches for coastal assault and cutting-out expeditions.

Manning was always a problem, but Britain still had the mercantile resources to support the largest population of seamen in Europe, and the ability to recruit them for the navy, albeit by the rough methods of the press gang. In February and March 1793 a general port embargo was ordered so that no ship could sail until the navy was adequately supplied with men. The political divisions between senior officers which had played an important part in the defeats of the American War were at an end, quieted by the common cause against the Revolution, although in 1795 Middleton was to resign from the Board of Admiralty rather than comply with the First Lord's instruction

to appoint the comparatively junior Rear-Admiral Christian to command in the West Indies. The sympathy which existed between officers and seamen, however, was under stress due to the Revolution, and was to worsen as the fleet expanded to an unprecedented size. The numbers of landsmen in ships' companies increased, amongst whom many were Irishmen whose resentment at the life they found themselves in was strengthened by feelings of nationalism. The unsettling events in France provided an example which led to mutiny in the Mediterranean squadron in November 1794 when the crew of the 98-gun *Windsor Castle* demanded the removal of all their senior officers, including Rear-Admiral Linzee and the boatswain. Vice-Admiral Hotham complied in part, and pardoned the mutineers. In December 1794 the crew of *Culloden* of 74 guns was to mutiny, and barricade itself below decks. After a week of negotiations it surrendered, and five of the ringleaders were court martialled and hanged. Worse was to follow in the spring of 1797 when there was to be a general mutiny of the fleet in home waters.

Because of the numbers of ships in both fleets which were not really fit for sea, and because of the larger size of individual French warships, the discrepancy of force between the British and French battle-lines was not great. William James reckoned that the British line of 115 ships mounting 8718 guns could throw a

total broadside weight of 88,957lbs. Against that the French could in theory bring seventy-six ships with 6002 guns capable of throwing a total broadside weight of 73,957lbs.[1] The reality, however, was that deficiencies in French dockyards and in French discipline prevented the *Marine de la Republic Française* from bringing anything like that force into action.

When war was declared, Lord Chatham was at the Admiralty as First Lord. It was his task, and that of his Board, to put the navy into its war stations. As it had been when the French entered the American Revolutionary War, the first strategic requirements attended to were the convoy of trade, the reinforcement of the small squadron in the West Indies with seven ships of the line under Rear-Admiral Alan Gardner, and the maintenance in the Channel of a fleet able to prevent the enemy at Brest from acting offensively, and ready to send detachments to match any French deployment. To watch the Toulon fleet, a substantial British squadron sailed in four groups in the spring of 1793 to co-operate with the Spanish Admiral Don Juan de Langara based at Minorca. At the outbreak of war, Spain had a total of seventy-six ships of the line of which fifty-six were in commission, and 128 smaller vessels. Command of the British Mediterranean Squadron was given to Vice-Admiral Lord Hood who had acquired a strong reputation during the American war

'Blackwall . . . at the Launch of the Bombay Castle a 74 gun ship, Built at the Expence of the Honorable East India Company and presented by them to his Majesty', aquatint and etching by Robert Dodd (1748-1815) after his own original, published by J & J Boydell, London, 25 March 1789. This was one example of the strenuous efforts made by British naval administrators to rebuild the Royal Navy's strength in the years after the American War, in this case with the added bonus of not being paid for from the Navy's budget. This was a public relations exercise by the East India Company, which was being criticised at the time for exacerbating the Navy's timber shortages by building large Indiamen. NMM Neg No 2707

1. William James, *Naval History of Great Britain*, London, 1826, Vol 1 p76.

1

The Nootka Sound crisis 1789-1790

THE GOOD condition of the fleet when war with France broke out in 1793 was partly attributable to a major mobilisation of the Royal Navy, occasioned by dispute between Britain and Spain over the seizure by a Spanish squadron of a British settlement and ships in Nootka Sound, Vancouver Island.

A trading post had been established at Nootka Sound in 1788 by the British East India Company to deal in furs for the China trade. A stockade was built and the British flag raised, and the traders built a 40-ton sloop, the *North-West America* (1), the first European ship built on the northwestern coast of Canada. However, since the Treaty of Tordesillas in 1494, the Spanish Crown had laid exclusive claim to the entire Pacific coast of the American continent, and in May 1789 the Viceroy of

2

3

Mexico sent two warships under a Captain Martinez to enforce this right. Four East India Company ships were seized, their crews complaining of rough treatment (2). Captain Colnett, of the *Argonaut*, claimed that his ship was taken by trickery and that Martinez, as was the standard Spanish practice in these situations, treated his captives little better than privateers.

On 11 February 1790, the Spanish envoy in London presented a demand that Spanish sovereignty in the Pacific be recognised and that the British government punish similar activities by its subjects in the future. This was of course totally unacceptable and on 30 April the Cabinet decided to demand redress for Captain Colnett and the others and assert the right of free trade in the Pacific Northwest. To this end, it was also agreed to fit out a naval squadron immediately to back up the claims. This was a large force, comprising twenty-nine ships of the line, nine frigates, two sloops, four cutters and two fire-ships, under the command of Admiral Lord Howe. This mobilisation was also notable for Howe's first issuing of his new system of numerical signals to his fleet, an important step forward in communications in the Royal Navy.

Although both Spain and France made some warlike noises, neither was in a position to oppose British naval power, and furthermore relations between the two old allies were strained because of the Revolution. On 28 October 1790 an agreement was reached whereby Spain would pay reparations for damages suffered, there would be joint rights of trade and settlement (3), and, most importantly, the Spanish abandoned their claims to exclusive rights to the northwestern coast of America. They even permitted freedom of navigation and fisheries in South American waters, although with a ten-mile exclusion zone off their possessions to maintain their monopoly of trade with them.

This mobilisation (4), together with a second in 1791 owing to a dispute with Russia over Turkey, in which thirty-six ships of the line were fitted out under Vice-Admiral Lord Hood, meant that in 1793 the Royal Navy was in excellent condition and fully prepared to take advantage of the weaknesses of the French Marine.

---

1. 'The Launch of the North West America at Nootka Sound, Being the First vessel that was ever built in that part of the Globe', engraving by R Pollard from an original by C Metz, published by J Walter & Son, London, 16 August 1790.
NMM ref PAD6359

2. 'The Spanish Insult to the British Flag at Nootka Sound' engraved and published by Robert Dodd (1748-1815), London, 21 January 1791.
Beverley R Robinson Collection

3. 'View of Nootka Sound with the Spanish settlement, November 1792', unsigned, attributed to H Humphries.
Peabody Essex Museum, Salem MA neg 24067

4. A royal visit to a three-decker at Portsmouth, about 1790. This is probably part of the fleet mobilised during the Nootka crisis.
NMM ref PAH4084

4

Part I   HOME WATERS 1793–1795

COMMAND OF the British Channel Fleet was given to Admiral Lord Howe who was Britain's most experienced sailor. His interest in signals was but a part of his work on tactics. He sought, through giving his officers a useful degree of independence, to overcome the sterility which was so often the consequence of naval tactics which had become optimised for defensive rather than offensive purposes.

His judgment in operational strategy was more open to question, but was based on solid experience. He did not believe that it was good practice to maintain a close blockade of Brest, especially through the winter, because of the damage which it could be expected that the ships beating off-shore would suffer from the weather. The constant patrol of a close block-ade honed seamanship skills to perfection and ensured that the fleet acquired a thorough knowledge of the enemy's home waters, and was demoralising to the enemy penned into its harbour. On the other hand, no close blockade could ever ensure that the enemy could not sail in the falling winds at the end of a gale dur-ing which it would have been necessary for the blockading fleet to seek sea room. If the British blockading force suffered damage in the gale and was driven into dockyard for repairs, the French, once out, would be free to pursue their operational goals. Howe, like most eighteenth century admirals, preferred to send frigate patrols to watch the enemy roads as closely as they could, while keeping the ships of the line in harbour. He chose to keep them as far up the Channel as Spithead, where they could most easily be supplied, but from that position he had difficulty reacting to the sailing of French squadrons.

At the beginning of 1793 the French Marine had twelve ships ready for sea at Brest and Lorient, three at Rochefort, and six at Toulon, and fifteen others fitting for sea. In March Vice-Admiral Morard de Galles was persuaded, against his judgment, to take a small squadron

of two 74-gun ships and the 110-gun *Le Républicain*, to sea in the Channel, but the crews proved to be both incapable and unwilling to go aloft when he encountered a severe gale. 'The vaunted ardour which is attributed to them,' he reported, 'consists uniquely in the words of "patriot" and "patriotism" which they repeat ceaselessly, and the acclamations of *"Vive la Nation", "Vive la République"* when they are flattered. Nothing can make them attend to their duties.'[1] In May, after the outbreak of war, he nonetheless received orders to assem-ble the fleet in the exposed and dangerous waters south of Brittany to prevent the Royal Navy escorting supply ships to support the rebellion which had broken out in the Vendée. These were desperate times. On 23 August 1793, in response to the threat of invasion, a *levée en masse* was ordered of the entire male population of France between the ages of 18 and 25 capable of bearing arms. A few days later, at the invitation of the municipality of Toulon, the British Mediterranean Squadron occupied that port and landed a garrison. News quickly spread to the Brest fleet, and on 13 September the crews obliged their officers to return to port.

In Paris the period known as 'The Terror' had commenced on 2 June when the Convention was purged and parliamentary democracy was brought to an end by the Jacobins, who believed that only a strong revo-lutionary executive could meet the needs of war. The Committee of Public Safety, domi-nated by the puritanical figure of Maximilien Robespierre, sent *deputies en mission* through the countryside with powers of life and death to demand absolute obedience with the help of the guillotine. The Committee's expert on naval affairs, Jean-Bon Saint-André, was sent to Brest. 'They say we exercise arbitrary power,' he wrote, 'they accuse us of being despots: Despots! Us! hah! doubtless, if it is despotism which is necessary for the triumph of liberty, this despotism is political regeneration.'[2]

Morard de Galles was relieved of his command, which was given to Rear-Admiral Louis-Thomas, Comte de Villaret-Joyeuse, who was of noble birth but had shown his capacity to control his crew and was politically clean. With a firm ruthlessness characteristic of his Calvinist upbringing, Saint-André brought order to the fleet by issuing a new code of naval discipline along conservative lines and backed with the guillotine. The expression of popular sovereignty by the Brest municipality was even more ruthlessly suppressed.

Saint-André was not able to persuade the Committee of Public Safety that small raiding squadrons should be sent to sea as soon as pos-sible to train ships' crews. With little compre-hension of the requirements of naval training and morale, it wanted every ship carefully con-served so that they could be used to support an invasion of the British Isles. Economic collapse in France, however, produced by the revolu-tionary government's resort to unbacked paper money, the rapidly-depreciating *assignats*, and the failure of the 1793 grain harvest, forced the fleet to sea. On Christmas Day 1793, Rear-Admiral Vanstabel sailed from Brest with two sail of the line and three frigates to escort home from Hampton Roads in Virginia a large convoy of grain ships and the West Indies trade. On its outward voyage it was nearly brought to action with the entire Channel Fleet, which was cruising to the westward, but managed to get clear and complete its voyage to Virginia. It departed again from America on 11 April, and on the same date Rear-Admiral Nielly sailed from Brest with five ships of the line to meet it, and as it happened also to capture most of the British Newfoundland convoy. Finally, Rear-Admiral Villaret-Joyeuse sailed the Brest fleet to bring the convoy safely in. Deputy Saint-André accompanied the fleet to ensure by his

---

1. Quoted in William S Cormack, *Revolution and Political Conflict in the French Navy*, Cambridge, 1995, p219.

2. I bid, p258.

14

presence, and by the threat that any captain who failed to carry out his orders would be guillotined, that neither disaffection nor incompetence should imperil the convoy.

The Channel Fleet sailed to try and intercept the convoy, but late on 28 May it ran into Villaret-Joyeuse to leeward of the convoy which was itself out of sight. The French were to windward of the British, in an irregular and reduplicated line abreast. The British were on the starboard tack in two columns, with a detached squadron of four of the line under Rear-Admiral Sir Thomas Pasley to windward. The French began to form an irregular line on the starboard tack. Howe responded by engaging the French rear with his advanced squadron. One of his tactical innovations had been conceived for the purpose of picking off the last ship in a fleeing enemy line by engaging it with each of his ships as they came up, and then circling away. In the rear of the French line was the one of four three-deckers in the French fleet, *Revolutionnaire* of 110 guns, which took a heavy beating and eventually struck to the British *Audacious* of 74 guns. Possession was not secured, however, and during the night she managed to get clear and get away to Brest. The badly-damaged *Audacious* withdrew to Portsmouth.

During this action Howe's advanced squadron had been able to work its way somewhat to windward of the French line, probably because Villaret-Joyeuse had other priorities. He later said that he had been threatened with the guillotine if the convoy were taken. In the circumstances, he proved remarkably effective. Rather than scramble to keep the windward position which in any case the poor sailing qualities of his fleet might have prevented, he concentrated on leading the British away from the track of the convoy.

The next day at 4am Howe ordered his fleet to form line of battle 'as most convenient' on the starboard tack. Villaret-Joyeuse was also on the starboard tack and to windward of the main British force. Howe decided to waste no time in forcing action and ordered his fleet to tack in succession starting from the van. This could have led it through the rear of the enemy line, and would have been very dangerous for the French, but Villaret-Joyeuse responded promptly by tacking his own van to come to the support of his rear. Considering

the disciplinary and training problems the French Marine were suffering from, this was a remarkably efficient operation.

Howe was not to be deflected from his purpose and he ordered his van to tack again, but his leading ships did not immediately respond and it was his own flagship, *Queen Charlotte*, which with two others cut through the French rear. The rest of the British fleet passed to leeward of the French rear and joined the flag.

By this time Howe had gained the windward position, and both fleets had suffered considerable damage from the heavy, if generally fairly long-range, cannonade. Villaret-Joyeuse wore his fleet to bring it back between the British and three of his disabled ships. During the next two days the fleets kept in touch with each other in a heavy fog, and by incredible good luck Neilly's squadron was able to join the French line.

Through the night of the 31st both squadrons took up a westerly course under a heavy press of canvas and then on the morning of 'The Glorious First of June', Howe dressed his line and bore down on the French in a larboard line of bearing. His tactical plan was to prevent them refusing close action by having all his ships steer to cut through the French line, and, having fired a raking broadside into each as it was passed, to engage them from the leeward. To do so, the fleet would have to make a dangerous approach nearly head-on, which Howe probably only risked because the French crews were known to be demoralised. The British captains were sufficiently uncertain about Howe's intentions that only seven of his ships managed to complete the manoeuvre, but Villaret-Joyeuse was not in fact seeking to avoid action. The melée action which followed was hard fought. The crew of the *Queen Charlotte* particularly distinguished themselves. The decisive factor probably was superior British gunnery. One French ship, *Vengeur*, was so severely damaged that it sank, and six were taken as prizes. Nothing like that scale of success outside of a chasing action had been seen since the battles of Barfleur and La Hogue in 1692.

Villaret-Joyeuse managed to reform his line to leeward to protect his damaged ships, and make off back to Brest. The convoy was got safely into Brest, and Villaret-Joyeuse kept his head.

The opportunity to strike a major blow against the revolutionary government in Paris,

such as it was, had been missed. Given the draconian measures being employed to keep the country at war, however, it is unlikely that hunger of itself would have brought the collapse of the revolution. Because the grain convoy reached port safely, its strategic importance can only be guessed at.

The French Marine had unquestionably suffered a grievous blow. Barère, the orator of the Committee of Public Safety, succeeded in obscuring the fact with lying rhetoric, but the reality could not be disguised from the navy itself. By the law of 22 Prairial (10 June 1794), juries were instructed to convict without hearing evidence or argument, and the rate of executions increased to 354 per month. Saint-André had to leave Brest to less effective men because of the need to reconstruct the Toulon fleet after the reoccupation of the port, and his own position became less secure when in July a coup (9 Thermidor) toppled Robespierre. The reign of terror continued into the autumn, but the nation was sickened by the violence and by October it was evident to the fleet at Brest that the guillotine no longer gave meaning to the code of discipline. For the navy, however, the coup was on the whole a positive thing. The Directory, which had taken the reigns of power, represented a bourgeois reaction to popular sovereignty to stabilise the French economy provided a framework within which the navy could be reconstructed along its traditional lines. Less fortunate was its neglect of the needs of the army, which converted it from a national force into a praetorian guard, was to lead to the caesarism which Robespierre had feared.

The dangers of sending ships of the line, especially First Rates, to sea in the middle of winter was confirmed late in December 1794, when the Brest fleet made a sortie intended to cover the departure of squadrons under Rear-Admiral Renaudin to the Mediterranean, another commanded by Rear-Admiral Kerguelen of six sail of the line and eight smaller warships with transports for 6000 soldiers to reinforce the French force at Isle de France (Mauritius), and a third intended to restore the authority of the French government in Saint-Domingue. The poverty of the Brest dockyard had made it impossible to fit the ships properly for sea, and most of them were only provisioned with two weeks' rations. These were contributing factors to the loss of five ships of the line in a severe storm. The incompetence of most of the officers was no less important. In the saner conditions after the overthrow of Robespierre, Villaret-Joyeuse felt able to express his criticisms freely.

The British Channel fleet itself had a close call in February 1795 when a south-eastern storm drove into its anchorage in Torbay. Nine ships of the line parted their cables, but were fortunate enough to bring to with another anchor before driving ashore or into other ships.

Howe, who was sixty-nine at the time of the Glorious First of June, had been so utterly exhausted by the five days of manoeuvre and battle that he collapsed at the end of the action. The victory had been less complete than it might have been because he was unable to keep the deck while Villaret-Joyeuse made off with five ships in tow. Howe spent part of the winter ashore, and soon after the Channel operations of February 1795 relinquished active command of the fleet, although remaining nominal commander-in-chief until 1797. He was succeeded by Admiral Lord Bridport, who himself was sixty-eight. At the Admiralty Lord Spencer had been appointed First Lord in December 1794. These new men continued the policy of distant blockade, and continued to favour Spithead for their fleet station despite the fact that it was too far to leeward.

One of the first tasks undertaken by the Royal Navy in home waters had been the support of the expeditionary force under the Duke of York, which was sent as part of an army under the Prince of Saxe-Coburg to assist the Dutch in resisting the advance of the French army. Against all odds, the French had prevailed, and in January 1795 they had entered Amsterdam. The Dutch fleet, frozen in at the Texel, was captured by cavalry galloping across the ice. When in May the new Batavian Republic declared war on Britain, fifteen ships of the line and thirty smaller ships were added to the forces controlled by the government in Paris.

With its base on the North Sea, the Dutch fleet presented a new strategic challenge to the Royal Navy. Vice-Admiral Duncan was given command of the station, and he used his small force operationally to maintain a close blockade of the Texel, while convoying the Baltic

trade. Pitt obtained the support of a Russian squadron under Vice-Admiral Peter Hanikoff, but it proved to be more of a liability than an asset.

The humiliation of Villaret-Joyeuse's winter sortie was not the end of the grim history of the Brest Fleet. In June 1795 Rear-Admiral Vence was sent with three ships of the line to provide protection for the traffic along the southern coast of Brittany. He fell in with Vice-Admiral the Honourable William Cornwallis with five ships, who gave chase. Vence abandoned his convoy, and ran for the shelter of Belle-Isle. He sent a message overland for support, and Villaret-Joyeuse was ordered to sea with nine of the line. Having collected Vence's squadron, on 16 June Villaret-Joyeuse met Cornwallis who had little choice but to flee. *Bellerophon* and *Brunswick* were sailing badly and by the next morning were in danger of capture. Cornwallis formed his squadron into loose line, which was sometimes reported to be a 'V' formation, with his flagship in the leading position. *Mars*, the last ship in the British line, came under heavy attack, but was saved when Cornwallis brought *Royal Sovereign* and *Triumph* around to engage the leading French ships with such a heavy fire that they sheered off. The frigate *Phaeton* played its part in the action from a position ahead of the British squadron by sending imaginary signals, which gave the impression that it was communicating with the main Channel Fleet just over the horizon. Villaret-Joyeuse felt impelled to abandon the action.

In his official report, Cornwallis remarked that

> it was the greatest pleasure I ever received to see the spirit manifested by the men, who, instead of being cast down at seeing 30 sail of the enemy's ships attacking our little squadron, were in the highest spirits imaginable. I do not mean the *Royal Sovereign* alone: the same spirit was shown in all the ships as they came near me; and although, circumstanced as we were, we had no great reason to complain of the conduct of the enemy, yet our men could not help repeatedly expressing their contempt of them.

A week later it was the British who enjoyed a numerical advantage, which was compounded

by the superior seamanship of the British fleet. Bridport with fourteen ships of the line, of which eight were three-deckers, was providing distant cover for a royalist landing on the Quiberon peninsula when he ran into Villaret-Joyeuse with a squadron of nine ships. In accordance with the current instructions, Villaret-Joyeuse shifted his flag to a frigate, and then set course for Isle de Groix off Lorient. His flight was hampered by the slow sailing of *Alexander*, which had been the reason for her capture from the British the previous year. She and *Redoutable* were put under tow, and he ordered his squadron to form line abreast on them, but his captains ignored the order. The next day when the British were coming into range he ordered the squadron to form line of bearing on *Alexander*, but only *Formidable* and *Tigre* obeyed. Those three ships became heavily engaged and were eventually taken. Doubting whether the remaining ships would put up any sort of fight, Villaret-Joyeuse took them into Lorient.

Bridport did not attempt to blockade them. Because of shortage of supplies, Villaret-Joyeuse sent most of the crews to Brest by land. When the coast was clear, the ships were sailed back to Brest three at a time with the ferry crew returning by road for the next lot, an indication of the shortage of skilled seamen in the French Marine. He made no effort to interfere with the Royalist invasion, but it defeated itself by its divided leadership, and by units of the army of the Republic commanded by the brilliant young General Lazare Hoche.

This was the nadir of the fortunes of the French Marine. Villaret-Joyeuse, complaining about the incompetence of his captains who had lobbied for their positions, and of many of his men, warned that 'patriotism alone cannot handle a ship'. The National Convention responded effectively. A new corps of gunners was established, and the entire officer corps was abolished. Many had to be reappointed, but the most incompetent were weeded out. When in October 1795 the Convention was dissolved, and the Directory assumed executive authority, an admiral of the old navy, Admiral Truguet, was appointed Minister of Marine. The task of rebuilding the French Marine forced it to avoid major encounters in 1796, and the wonder is that it was able to undertake serious operations at the end of the year.

First shots of the naval war

A S THE tension between revolutionary France and Britain increased, at the very end of 1792 the brig *Childers* was sent to reconnoitre Brest, the home of the main French Atlantic fleet. Although war was not declared by France until a month later, on 2 January 1793 the batteries of the Brest forts opened fire on the unwelcome intruder (1). If not seriously damaged, the brig was hit and brought home one of the cannonballs to present to the Admiralty as a sign of aggressive French intent. As such it is often regarded as the first shot in the long naval war that, with one short breathing space, lasted until 1815.

The Royal Navy's small ships were soon embarked on an almost unbroken run of single-ship victories. The first prize was the suitably named privateer *Sans Culotte* (celebrating the revolutionary mob who eschewed the garb of the gentry), taken on 13 March by the brig *Scourge* after a fierce three-hour struggle (2). However, the first frigate action was less satisfactory in its conclusion, since the *Venus* had to abandon her combat with the *Sémillante* (both 12pdr-armed and reasonably well-matched) at the point of victory when another French ship hove into view (3).

Success finally came on 18 June, when the ship which had rescued the *Sémillante*, the 12pdr frigate *Cléopâtre*, was brought to action by *Nymphe*, herself a French prize captured in the previous war and now commanded by

3

4

5

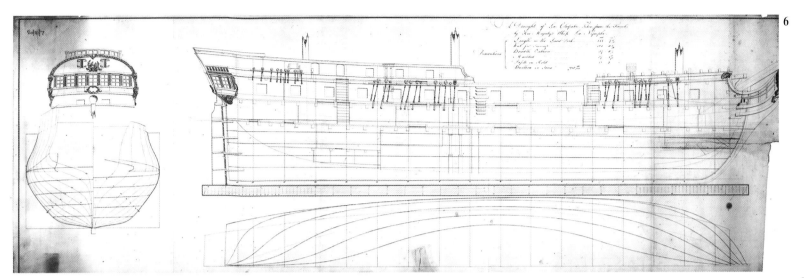

6

7

Edward Pellew (4), who was to become one of the greatest frigate captains of the war. The battle began with a curious exchange of old-world courtesies between the captains, cheering from both ships, and the nailing of a cap of liberty to the main truck of the French ship (just visible in (5)), before the serious business began. Close-range gunnery, a failed French attempt to board, followed by a British counter-attack, carried the *Cléopâtre* in 50 minutes. Because of her carronades, the British ship had slightly greater firepower, but more than offset by a French crew one-third larger. Casualties were high on both sides: 23 killed and 27 British wounded, compared with a total of 63 for the French. The prize was not badly damaged and was bought into British service as the *Oiseau* (6), since the Navy already had a *Cleopatra*.

As the first major naval victor of the war, Pellew could expect to be well rewarded, and indeed he received a knighthood after he was presented to the king. It rapidly became a popular subject for published prints, but they rarely let truth spoil a good story—Pellew did not lead the boarding action, and the hat-raising incident shown in (7) occurred before the ships opened fire; by this stage of the battle Captain Mullon was mortally wounded.

The value of enemy ships taken at sea was divided, on a sliding scale, between officers and crew, and prize money became a major incentive to keep a ship alert and efficient. They were also paid 'gun-and-head money' based on the size of crews of warships captured or destroyed, and in this illustrated scorecard (8) of *Phaeton*'s captures during 1793, the merchantmen are accorded values, but the warships and privateer are listed only by numbers of guns and men. *Phaeton*, commanded by Sir Andrew Snape Douglas, was a big 38-gun frigate and one of the crack Channel cruiser squadrons; she was already ten years old in 1793, but fought right through the war and was not sold until 1827.

8

---

1. 'The Batteries of Brest Harbour firing upon HM Brig Childers 1793', watercolour by Nicholas Pocock (1740-1821).
NMM ref PAH9032

2. 'HMS Scourge capturing the Sansculotte, 13 March 1793', oil painting by Lieutenant Thomas Yates (c1760-1796). The *Scourge* carried sixteen 6pdrs and 70 men to the privateer's eight 8pdrs, one 12pdr carronade, and 81 men.
NMM ref BHC0462

3. 'Action between HMS Venus and the Semillante, 27 May 1793', oil painting by Thomas Elliott (fl1790-1800). The 722-ton *Venus* fired a broadside of 222lb and carried 192 men, to her 940-ton opponent's 279lbs and 300 men.
NMM ref BHC0463

4. 'Sir Edward Pellew', stipple engraving by J Chapman, published London, 1 December 1801.
NMM ref PAD3458

5. 'To the Officers and Seamen of His Majesty's Frigate La Nymphe . . . taking Possession of the French Frigate La Cleopatre', coloured aquatint by Robert Dodd (1748-1815), published by the artist and Woodfall & Freeman, London,

undated. It shows the final stage of the action, after the mizzen was shot away and *Cléopâtre* had swung around.
NMM ref PAH7852

6. Sheer draught of *Cléopâtre*, as taken off after capture, 1793. Admiralty Collection.
NMM neg 6074

7. 'An exact Representation of the Boarding and taking the Cleopatre French Frigate by the La Nymphe Capt Sir Edward Pellew', engraving by J Pass from an original by Robert Dodd (1748-1815).
NMM ref PAD5436

8. 'HM 38 gun frigate Phaeton Captain Sir Andrew Snape Douglas. One year's captures. La Prompte 28 gun frigate—180 men. La Blanche corvette 22 guns. Le General Doumourier 22 guns 196 men 2,400,000 dollars: privateer Domen 16 guns 60 men: merchantman St Jago cargo worth £300,000', watercolour by Irwin Bevan; the painting is undated but the events relate to 1793.
NMM ref PAD9479

1

The Low Countries 1793

FOLLOWING THEIR declaration of war against the United Provinces on 1 February 1793, the French army under Dumouriez had advanced from Antwerp on the 16th, taking Breda on the 26th and reaching the Hollands Diep, besieging the fort of Willemstadt, which was situated on a small island some thirty miles from Hellevoetsluys, preliminary to making a crossing. This threat to Holland caused the British government to agree to the Stadtholder's previous request for military assistance, and on 1 March an initial force of

2

1. Dutch gunboats guarding the approaches to Dordrecht, 20 March 1793. Coloured etching by K F Bendorp from an original by M Schouman, published by W Holtrop. *NMM ref PAF4675*

2. 'This Print representing the Relief of Williamstadt, in Holland by the British Forces under the command of His RH the Duke of York when besieg'd by the French Army . . . Feb 1793', coloured aquatint by Lewis from an original by J Chessell, published 4 October 1802. *NMM ref*

3. 'Dumourier's Army driven from the Siege of Williamstadt by the Dutch Garrison, the English Gunboats and the Syren British frigate commanded by Captain Manley', etching by J Pass from an original by E Godefrey. *NMM ref PAD5428*

4. 'Representation of taking and Seizing the French Stores and Garrison of Ostend by a Detachment from Admiral Macbride, March 30th 1793', engraving by J Pass from an original by Jean Baptiste Le Paon. *NMM ref PAD5429*

5. 'Troops embarking near Greenwich', oil painting by William Anderson (1757-1837). *NMM ref BHC1805*

2000 troops under the command of the Duke of York landed at Hellevoetsluys. Furthermore, Royal Navy crews were sent to man Dutch gunboats, of the type shown in (1), some of which flew British colours, and three of these vessels were instrumental in the first British success of the campaign, the relief of Willemstadt.

On the night of 15 March 1793, a detachment of the crew of HMS *Syren*, 32, lead by Lieutenant John Western, manned three gunboats for an attack on the French batteries besieging Willemstadt (2). Fog and calm conditions enabled the three boats to approach the positions unseen, and brought such an effective fire to bear that the French were forced to abandon their guns. The garrison of the fort took possession of these guns the following morning. Illustration (3) shows a rather dramatised version of the relief, with the *Syren* and gunboats in the background. Unfortunately, Lieutenant Western

was killed a week later whilst attacking another French position, the first British officer casualty of the war.

On 18 March the French army was defeated at Neerwinden by the Austrians under Prince Frederick of Saxe-Coburg, forcing them to abandon the Low Countries. Twelve days later, a squadron from Rear-Admiral John Macbride's command, comprising two frigates, a sloop and the floating battery *Redoubt*, which was armed with twenty large-calibre carronades, successfully co-operated with troops under General Sir Charles Grey in driving the French out of the ports of Ostend and Nieuport, capturing significant quantities of material (4). Ostend became the main port used by the British throughout the Flanders campaign, receiving troops shipped from England (5), until its evacuation in June 1794. Nieuport fell to the French on 16 July 1794, and its garrison, made up largely of French royalists, was massacred by the Republican army.

5

1

Ships of the Royal Navy: the First Rate

FIRST RATES, three-deckers carrying 100 guns or more, were the largest, most powerful and most costly ships to build, maintain and operate, and were probably the most complex industrial constructs of their day. Because they represented such substantial investments, First Rates were built with the greatest care and attention, always in the Royal Dockyards, and using the finest materials. Concern for longevity led to prolonged building times to achieve the most profound seasoning – ten years on the stocks was not unusual.

First Rates were rarely commissioned except in times of war and crisis, so their hulls were not subjected to the continuous stresses of long sea service. They were also maintained carefully while in Ordinary (reserve), and when necessary were treated to extensive repairs, amounting in some cases to major rebuilding. The aggregate effect of this was to endow First Rates with very long lives: as is well known, *Victory* had been afloat for forty years when she fought at Trafalgar, and *Britannia* was three years older. However, *Victory* had been in Dockyard hands for periods of around six months on four occasions between 1771 and 1788 and was substantially reconstructed between February 1800 and April 1803.

There were never many First Rates available, and because of lengthy building times, the substantial pro-grammes of the 1790s were just bearing fruit when the war came to an end.

Year	No in Sea Service	No in Ordinary or Repairing*
1793	1	4
1796	6	0
1799	4	2
1801	4	2
1805	6	1
1808	4	2
1811	5	2
1814	7	0
1815	0	8

*All warships converted to other uses or in harbour service have been excluded; it lists only ships in active service or available for it.

At first sight it is surprising that the world's largest navy did not have the greatest numbers of First Rates, but in 1793 France could boast five of 110 guns and three even larger 118-gun ships; Spain in 1796 was even better off with ten 112-gun ships and the mighty *Santisíma Trinidad*, a nominal four-decker of 136 guns and often regarded as the largest ship afloat, although displacing less than the French giants. These ships were not only larger – the

Commerce de Marseilles measured nearly 2750 tons—but the French ships in particular were more powerfully armed with lower deck 36pdrs (about 40lbs English).

By contrast, the newest ship in the British fleet in 1793 was the *Queen Charlotte* of 2286 tons, carrying thirty 32pdrs on the lower deck, thirty 24pdrs on the middle deck, thirty 12pdrs on the upper deck, plus four 12pdrs and fourteen 32pdr carronades on the forecastle and quarterdeck, and six 18pdr carronades on the poop (1). During the American War the cumbersome 42pdrs had been gradually replaced by the more practical 32s—only the old *Britannia* retained them by the 1790s, earning her the nickname 'Old Ironsides' long before it was applied to USS *Constitution*. The next major step forward was the introduction of the 110-gun class with the *Ville de Paris* (2), ordered in 1788, with thirty ports on each of the lowest two gundecks and thirty-two on the upper (where the calibre was also increased from 12s to 18pdrs); *Hibernia* of 1790 contrived two extra ports per gundeck, and reached 2500 tons. The *Caledonia* of 1794 was the first British 120-gun ship, which mounted thirty-two 32pdrs, thirty-four 24s, thirty-four 18s, and twenty 12s on the quarterdeck and forecastle. The last design of the war was the similar-sized *Nelson* class of identical armament (3, 4, 5). Smaller 100-gun ships came into service in the second half of the war, but there was a tendency to down-rate them to 98-gun Second Rates, the small three-decker being a British speciality with large numbers in the fleet.

In battle the First Rate formed a strongpoint in the line, and since they were almost always flagships inevitably attracted more than their fair share of enemy attention. If possible, three-deckers were opposed to their equivalents, so before the First of June action, for instance, Howe reorganised his line to take account of the French First Rates. French and Spanish admirals sometimes transferred to frigates, arguing that being outside the line gave them a better appreciation of the tactical development of the battle; but British admirals were expected to lead by example, metaphorically at least, although at Trafalgar *Victory* and *Royal Sovereign* led in a very literal sense. As with Howe's *Queen Charlotte* at the Glorious First of June, First Rates were usually in the thick of the action, and could mete out tremendous punishment, not just because of the weight of metal thrown but because of the concentrated firepower of three complete gundecks, which was regarded as a very real tactical and psychological advantage.

The First Rate could also survive very heavy damage—in the opening stages of Trafalgar *Royal Sovereign* was engaged single-handed with the enemy line for fifteen minutes before assistance arrived—and no British ship of this rate was lost to enemy action throughout the eigh-

2

teenth century. Equally, very few were taken from the enemy (although significantly more were destroyed in battle); the first was de Grasse's *Ville de Paris*, captured at the Saintes in 1782 and lost in a gale in the same year. In 1793 the British carried off the huge *Commerce de Marseilles* from Toulon, but she proved so weakly built that she never cruised. Similarly, of the two Spanish three-deckers taken at St Vincent only *San Josef* enjoyed an active career in the Royal Navy—the only prize First Rate to do so.

In terms of deployment, First Rates were almost exclusively reserved for the two main fleets, in the

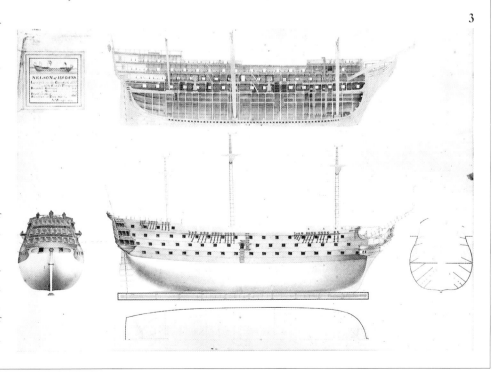

3

4

1. 'Review at Spithead, 1790, showing
Howe's Queen Charlotte', oil painting
by William Anderson (1757-1837).
NMM ref BHC2260

2. 'The Ship Ville de Paris under full
sail', oil painting by Thomas
Buttersworth (1768-1842).
NMM ref BHC2271

3. Pictorial plan of *Nelson*, 120 guns,
line and wash drawing signed 'Jas.
Pringle, 1811'.
NMM neg X22

4. Representation of the Launching of
the Nelson of 120 guns from His
Majesty's Royal Dock Yard Woolwich
the 4th July 1814 . . . to Charles
Cunningham Esqr, Commissioner of
His Majesty's Yards Deptford and
Woolwich', black and watercolour
pen and ink by James Pringle.
NMM ref PAH5250

5. 'The Howe of 120 Guns, Launched
in the Reign of Geo. III during the
Regency', anonymous engraving
from John Fincham's *A History of Naval
Architecture*, published London, 1851.
NMM ref PAD6112

Channel and Mediterranean, priority depending on the
strategic situation. These ships were important assets
that were jealously guarded: First Rates were unwieldy
to handle, drew anything up to 27ft, and needed a major
dockyard close at hand in case of anything but minor
damage. During the war attitudes changed – under Lord
Howe's regime they were not risked off the French
coasts except in the summer months, whereas St
Vincent took a more robust attitude to the blockade.
However, it is worth pointing out the superior characteristics of the newer ships that supported this policy.
Queen Charlotte's lower ports had only 4½ft of freeboard
and after the skirmish of 29 May 1794 her lower gundeck
was full of water; *Caledonia*, in contrast, managed one
foot more, and much of St Vincent's efforts as First Lord
of the Admiralty were directed towards greater gunport
freeboard for line-of-battle ships.

As an example of changing priorities, when Admiral
Bruix's fleet escaped into the Mediterranean from Brest
in 1799 three of the four First Rates in commission were
sent south, leaving only the *Royal George* in the Channel.
Conversely, in 1801 with the threat of imminent invasion from across the Channel, all four First Rates,
including the newly commissioned *San Josef*, were at
home – in fact, including the Second Rates, Cornwallis
could call on fifteen three-deckers! Additions to the fleet
thereafter were few: *Hibernia* in 1805 and *Caledonia* in 1809,
and a couple of First Rates towards the end of the fighting in Europe. After Trafalgar, First Rates continued in
commission in the main fleets, since Napoleon's powers
of organisation made the threat of a revival in French
naval power seem realistic to many in Britain, but the
era of large-scale fleet engagements was over.

5

The Glorious First of June: preliminary skirmishes

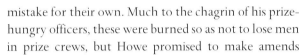

FROM THE beginning of the war the Channel Fleet was under the command of Lord Howe (1), Britain's most distinguished admiral and an officer of advanced tactical ideas. Strategically, however, he was no advocate of the close blockade, used so productively in the Seven Years War and again by his successors later in this conflict, believing that it placed undue strains on officers and ships alike.

In the spring of 1794 his fleet put to sea in pursuit of an important French grain convoy from North America and finding the French fleet still in Brest on 5 May it stood out into the Atlantic to interpose itself between the convoy and what would become its covering force. Apart from the convoy's immediate escort, there was also a supporting squadron under Rear-Admiral Neilly, which had itself captured much of a British New-foundland convoy and its sole escort, the frigate *Castor*. Howe's fleet retook some of these on the 21st which gave him information on the progress of his quarry, and a few days later he was assured of the proximity of the enemy when two French corvettes blundered into his fleet in mistake for their own. Much to the chagrin of his prize-hungry officers, these were burned so as not to lose men in prize crews, but Howe promised to make amends

shortly. On 28 May his frigates spotted the enemy fleet, and he was given the chance to honour his promise.

The French fleet was commanded by Admiral Villaret-Joyeuse (2), a man who had been an ageing lieutenant shortly before the Revolution and his rapid elevation to rear-admiral, but he was a solid seaman who had learned his tactical trade under the great Suffren. He later claimed he was under orders to protect the convoy at all costs, on pain of the guillotine, and to keep him on the political straight and narrow the Convention sent him a 'political commissar' in the shape of Jean-Bon Saint-André—a man who seemed to have believed that revolutionary zeal was a substitute for seamanship and gunnery, which translated into an advocacy of boarding actions.

On 28 May the French fleet had the weather gage—it was up-wind of the British so it was difficult for them to get into action, and only Rear-Admiral Pasley's flying squadron of the fastest-sailing two-deckers could reach the rear of the French line. On his own initiative, Captain Vandongen of the huge three-decked *Révolutionnaire*, 110 guns—which as *Le Bretagne* had been d'Orvilliers flagship at another battle off Ushant sixteen years earlier—fell back and was set upon in succession by the 74s *Russell*, *Bellerophon*, *Leviathan*, *Thunderer* and *Audacious*. The French ship was badly damaged, and is supposed to have struck her colours, but a misunderstanding in the twilight between the equally crippled *Audacious* and the *Thunderer* allowed her to escape to Brest, escorted by the 74 *L'Audacieux*. The British *Audacious* was also sent home.

Battle was renewed on the 29th, with Howe attempting to break through the French line from his leeward position. The misbehaviour of his van ship, the 80-gun *Caesar*, spoiled his original plan, but he was able to get his flagship, the 100-gun *Queen Charlotte* (3), and *Bellerophon* and *Leviathan* through the rear of the line, cutting off

5

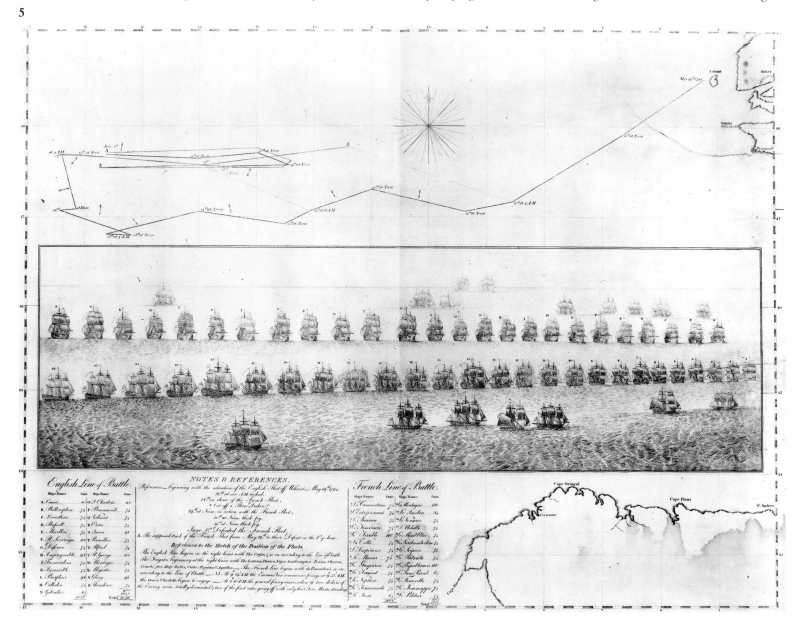

6

three ships. Villaret-Joyeuse put his fleet about, and came down to the rescue of his damaged ships, but at the expense of losing the weather gage (4). About a dozen British ships were seriously engaged, but although some were damaged, none needed dockyard attention; this was not the case in the French fleet, but those detached were replaced by the five ships of Neilly's squadron which were fortunate to find their main force on the following day (5).

As a footnote to the opening moves of the campaign, the *Castor*, 32, which had been captured by *Le Patriote* of Neilly's squadron, was retaken by the frigate *Carysfort*, 28 on the 29th in the Atlantic (6). Some of her original crew were prisoners on board; the remainder, including her captain, Thomas Troubridge, were to be unwilling witnesses of the ensuing fleet battle from on board the French *Sans Pareil*—although Troubridge was to have the satisfaction of striking her colours when she surrendered.

1. Admiral Lord Howe (1726-1799) on the deck of the *Queen Charlotte* during the battle of the Glorious First of June, detail from an oil painting by Mather Brown (1761-1831).
NMM ref BHC2740

2. Admiral Villaret-Joyeuse, French engraving by Forestier after an original by Ambroise Tardieu.
Chatham Collection

3. *Queen Charlotte* in 1800, detail from a coloured aquatint by John Chessell, published 20 April 1803.
NMM neg B256

4. 'To Admiral Earl Howe . . . This View of their gaining the wind of the Enemy's Fleet on the Evening of the 29th of May 1794 which led to their Splendid Victory on the 1st of June following', aquatint from an original by Robert Dodd (1748-1815), published by B B Evans, London, 25 January 1795.
NMM ref PAH7862

5. 'Mercator's chart shewing the Track of Earl Howe's Fleet in pursuit of the French National Fleet from the 19th of May . . . reached within random shot on the 1st of June 1794', brown etching from an original by James Bowen, published by Richard Livesay, Portsmouth, 1794.
NMM ref PAH7861

6. 'Capture of the Castor May 29th 1794', coloured aquatint engraved by Thomas Sutherland from an original by Thomas Whitcombe, published London, 1 June 1816.
NMM ref PAD5476

1

3

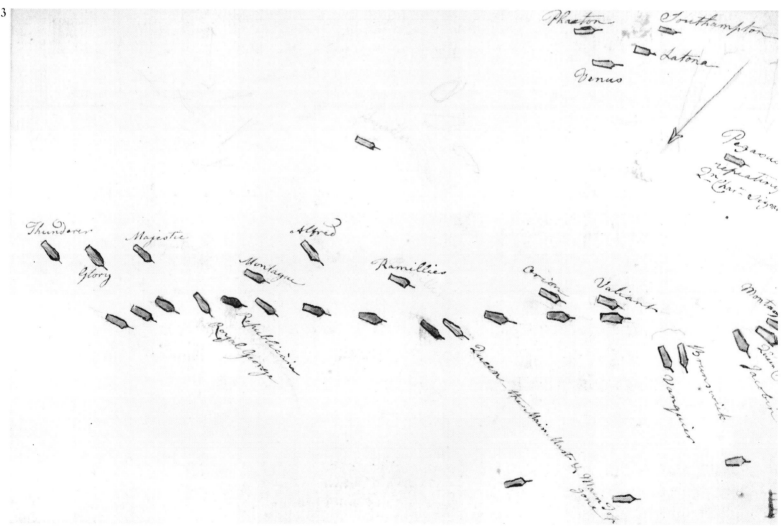

The Glorious First of June: the battle

THE SKIRMISHES of 28-29 May left the British fleet with the initiative. Holding the weather gage, Howe could attack whenever he thought best and the French would have to fight or run the risk of losing stragglers in a chase and, ultimately, the whole convoy. The next days were very foggy, but Howe kept in touch, while Villaret-Joyeuse slowly retired, giving his damaged vessels the opportunity to get away safely, leaving him twenty-six of the line or one more than Howe's fleet. The fog lifted in the middle of the 31st, but Howe held his hand. Captain Troubridge, prisoner aboard the *Sans Pareil*, suffered the mortification of hearing British nerve criticised, but Howe's decision to delay actually revealed his confidence—he was going to win a crushing victory, but needed a whole day to ensure it was complete.

After breakfast on 1 June, the line was carefully formed and signal No 34 was hoisted: '. . . having the wind of the enemy, the Admiral means to pass between the ships in the line for engaging them to leeward.' The fleet approached in a slanting line, called a line of bearing, intending each ship to break through the line and engage from the leeward side, bringing on a melee and preventing any damaged ships escaping. It was risky, since it meant a nearly end-on approach when the British would not be able to return effective fire, but Howe had seen the quality of French gunnery and discipline, and thought it a chance worth taking (1). Unfortunately, not all his captains either understood or

between the French ship's stern and the *Jacobin*, which was to leeward and slightly overlapping. According to Codrington, who was a midshipman commanding a division of lower deck guns, the senior officers were so absorbed by this tricky manoeuvre that they forgot to order the batteries to open fire, which Codrington did on his own initiative, blasting both ships as the *Queen Charlotte* squeezed through. On board the frigate *Pegasus* was the marine artist Nicholas Pocock, a practical seaman in earlier life and one of the most meticulously accurate of his new profession. The frigate was detailed to repeat the flagship's signals, so Pocock was accorded the rare privilege of a grandstand view of the engagement, but from quite close in. His sketchbooks contain numerous details, including the ships identifying pendants (2), and a plan of positions at the height of the fighting (3).

Although the flagship received much of the attention in subsequent illustrations, the first ship through the French line was actually the *Defence*, which went into action under topgallants, to the admiration of the whole fleet. She was heavily engaged and totally dismasted, before the huge *Royal Sovereign* came to her rescue. *Defence*'s captain, James Gambier—nicknamed 'Dismal Jimmy' by the lower deck—was a leading evangelical, and his sombre manner made him the butt of jokes, even among his friends. Seeing the shattered state of *Defence* (4) as he sailed past, Captain Packenham of the *Invincible*

5

agreed, and in the event only *Queen Charlotte*, *Defence*, *Marlborough*, *Royal George*, *Queen* and *Brunswick* obeyed the signal as intended. Nevertheless, the French stood firm and Howe got the full-scale battle he sought.

As was fitting, *Queen Charlotte* made for the opposing flagship, the 120-gun *Montagne*, and forced her way

6

7

1. 'This View of the Action on the Morning of the 1st of June 1794 at the Time of Breaking the French Line, which ended in . . . Victory to the British Fleet', aquatint from an original by Robert Dodd (1748-1815), published by B B Evans, London, 25 January 1795. NMM neg A813

2. 'Table of flags worn by English ships on 1st June 1794', watercolour by Nicholas Pocock (1740-1821). NMM ref PAD8871

3. 'Battle plan of 1st June 1794', pen and ink drawing by Nicholas Pocock. NMM ref PAD8870

4. 'Situation of His Majesty's Ship Defence . . . at the Close of the Action between the British and French Fleets on the 1st of June 1794', aquatint engraved by Robert Dodd (1748-1815), from an original by Lieutenant A Becher, published by B B Evans and T Matthews, London, 1 January 1796. NMM neg 1837

5. 'HMS Brunswick and the Vengeur at the battle of the First of June, 1794', oil painting by Nicholas Pocock, 1796. NMM ref BHC0471

6. 'Combat du Vengeur', engraved and published by Y Le Gouaz from an original by Nicolas Ozanne (1728-1811). NMM ref PAG8928

7. 'To the Memory of the Brave Capt. John Harvey . . . of His Majesty's Ship the Brunswick . . . after breaking the Enemy's Line . . . on the 1st of June 1794 Grappled to and engaging Le Vengeur with her Starboard Guns, and totally dismasting L'Achille', aquatint engraved by Robert Pollard from an original by Nicholas Pocock (1740-1821), 1 January 1796. NMM neg A2656

8. A watercolour sketch of end of action by Nicholas Pocock (1740-1821). NMM ref PAD 8703

hailed: 'Jemmy, whom the Lord loveth He chasteneth!'

Much of the battle dissolved into almost single-ship engagements, none of which was fiercer fought or more widely celebrated than the duel of the *Brunswick* and *Vengeur* (5). Locked together by their anchors so closely that the *Brunswick* had to blast off her own gunport lids, the two ships pounded one another for about four hours —with the occasional intervention of other vessels— until the *Vengeur* struck her colours just after 2pm. She had been very badly hit between wind and water, and when the time came to secure the prizes she was found to be sinking. Boat crews from *Culloden* and *Alfred* approached to take off survivors, but the ship heeled over and went down rapidly.

The defence of the ship became a famous vehicle of republican propaganda, in which the ship was presented as sinking in action, *tricoleur* still flying, and the crew to a man refusing rescue, going down with the cry '*Vive la République*' on their lips. Many prints were produced supporting this fiction, even by reputable artist like Ozanne, (6) but in fact the captain, his son, and 150 of the crew were picked up. Wooden warship very rarely sank in action, and in truth *Vengeur* had put up a very fine resistance.

Her opponent, *Brunswick* (7), suffered the most severe casualties in the British fleet with 44 dead, including her captain, but by the end of the battle damage was widespread (8).

8

1

2

A ship of the line in action

ALTHOUGH A gun could be run out and fired in a moment, preparing a ship of the line for a fleet action was a more considered and time-consuming process. The area below decks was cluttered with all the paraphernalia of living, because a warship was a floating castle, equipped to support its garrison as well as for attack and defence. This was particularly true aft, where the officers enjoyed the privacy of cabins made up of canvas-covered timber frames enclosing their own furniture and a few personal effects. All this had to be carefully stowed out of the way—usually in the hold, but sometimes in the ship's boats, which might be streamed astern to lessen the risk of their being shot to splinters in battle.

As a safety measure, the galley fire was extinguished and no hot food would be available for the crew, however long the combat, so Howe's careful scheduling of breakfast before the First of June battle was a considerate gesture—one of many actions that built him the reputation of 'the seaman's friend'. A contemporary watercolour (1) shows the lower gundeck of the *Bellerophon* with guns run out, but the effect of 250 men crowding around the guns is completely lost. The guns, like the vast majority of the British fleet's main armament, were 32pdrs—guns firing solid shot of 32 pounds nominal weight—which were 9ft 6in long and weighing a little less than 3 tons, plus the heavy wooden carriages. They required a crew of ten or twelve, but on the assumption that only one broadside would be in action at once, the ship's complement only allowed the full number to half the guns; if both sides were engaged, then the gun crews were divided, each also manning the gun opposite. A trained crew in the Royal Navy was reckoned to fire three rounds every five minutes, but this could not be maintained for long. The usual tactic of the British, once battle was joined, was to pound the hull of the enemy ship, to dismount guns and disable their crews, and this would usually induce surrender before the ship was ready to sink—indeed the loss of a ship like the *Vengeur* was a very rare event, since they were very strongly built and not liable to much damage below the waterline.

Behind their wooden walls, the lower gundecks were relatively protected—especially as the French were renowned for firing high to disable rigging—but in battle they were still hell on earth. Midshipman Dillon commanded part of the *Defence*'s main battery at First of June, and points out some of the dangers:

The lower deck was at times so completely filled with smoke that we could scarcely distinguish each other,

3

and the guns were so heated that, when fired, they nearly kicked the upper deck beams. The metal became so hot that fearing some accident, we reduced the quantity of powder, allowing also more time to elapse between the loading and firing of them.

At his quarter he had fourteen killed or wounded, but he was lucky not to be stationed on the upper or quarterdeck—which he described as 'dreadfully shattered'—where additional hazards were small-arms fire (on which the French placed heavy emphasis), and spars, blocks and other top-hamper falling from aloft. Officers were expected to stand in exposed positions with the greatest *sang froid* encouraging the men by example (2).

An additional hazard was the prospect of boarding, another tactic in favour with the French. They generally carried larger crews, often took infantry to sea, and were encouraged to believe themselves superior in this regard. Before First of June Saint-André exhorted the French fleet to 'disdain skilful evolution' and 'try those boarding actions in which the Frenchman was always a conqueror, and thus astonish Europe with new prodigies of valour'. A boarding action was a desperate hand-to-hand affair, in which firearms were less use than a long boarding pike, a cutlass or even a hatchet (much used to cut through rigging as well as the opposition). The discipline under fire of marines or soldiers made them very valuable in these circumstances (3), and the captain of the *Audacious* singled out the men of the 69th

Regiment (serving in lieu of Royal Marines) for special praise for repelling two boarding attempts during the First of June.

Although gunfire was not shared between officers and men in the same proportion as prize money (as the old sailors' prayer would have it), yet there was often a heavy toll among the officers. Two admirals had legs shot off and another was seriously wounded, while the captains of the *Brunswick*, *Queen* and *Montagu* were killed or mortally wounded at the First of June. They had their official commemoration in the hall of fame (4), but more junior officers were often ignored. However, there is an anonymous sketchbook, apparently by a naval officer, that contains a number of portraits of officers engaged at the First of June. They are unsophisticated but apparently from life and some of the titling—'The great Frederick L: *Queen*', for example (5)—suggest familiarity. The *Queen*, with 23 killed and over 50 wounded, was one of the most severely handled during Howe's actions, and fittingly the portfolio contains portraits of some of these otherwise unsung heroes: Mitchell, the master, killed on 29 May (6), and Dawes, the second lieutenant, who died of wounds received on the 1st (7). As well as commissioned officers, the collection also includes Marine officers, a chaplain, and the purser of the *Queen Charlotte*, a Mr Marsh (8).

For those wounded in action, the horrors of the cockpit awaited them (9). Ashore, surgery was crude, with few instruments and minimal anaesthetic and antiseptics, the province of barber-surgeons rather than trained physicians (the reason why surgeons are still called 'Mr' rather than 'Dr'); at sea, it was the same, with the added

complication of makeshift arrangements, a pitching and rolling 'surgery', and some hideous wounds for which there were no civilian equivalents. The surgeons and their assistants—called 'loblolly boys'—often worked for days after major battles, Dillon, for example, crediting *Defence*'s assistant surgeon with working twenty-two hours out of twenty-four; but even their best was inadequate. One problem was the insistence on treating patients on a first-come, first-served basis—even Nelson waited his turn—rather than prioritising attention, as is modern surgical practice. As a result, many saveable casualties died from bleeding while hopeless cases took up the surgeon's time.

In medical terms, the Channel Fleet was fortunate in the presence of a hospital ship—another example of Howe's concern for the welfare of his men, although the ship was singularly inauspicious in her name, *Charon* (in Greek mythology the boatman who carried the souls of the dead into the underworld). In attendance was Dr Thomas Trotter (10), the Physician of the Fleet and an expert on seamen's diseases, in particular, scurvy. However, the ship was neither a surgery nor a recovery ward for serious wounds, but was used to isolate cases of infectious diseases which shipboard life was prone to. After the battle, a number of sick prisoners were sent to the ship, the French fleet having more than its fair share of diseases like typhus, and even smallpox, on board, attributed by the scandalised British to the dirty and damp conditions between decks. Hospital ships accompanying fleets were not entirely new, but, possibly due to Howe's influence, they were to become more common during the war.

10

9

1. 'Gundeck of HMS Bellerophon', watercolour by H Hodgson, no date. *NMM ref PAD6115*

2. 'Shipboard scene of men firing cannons', *anonymous graphite drawing, c1820.* *NMM ref PAD8487*

3. 'Shipboard scene of fighting on deck', *anonymous graphite drawing, c1820.* *NMM ref PAD8485*

4. 'Commemoration of the Victory of June 1st MDCCXCIV (with 34 cameo portraits of admirals and captains)', *engraving and etching by F Bartolozzi, John Landseer, Thomas Ryder and James Stowe, from an original by Sir Robert Smirke, published by R Bowyer, London. NMM ref PAH5661*

5. 'Sketched Portrait of the Great Frederick L of the Queen', *anonymous black and watercolour pen and ink. This may be Lawrie, the 6th Lieutenant who was wounded in the engagement, but his christian name was not Frederick, so 'the Great Frederick' may be a nickname. NMM ref PAH4941*

6. 'Sketched portrait of Mitchell, master of the Queen killed in the battle of the 1st June [sic]', *anonymous watercolour. Actually killed 29 May. NMM ref PAH4927*

7. 'Sketched portrait of Dawes of the Queen killed in the battle of the 1st June', *anonymous watercolour. NMM ref PAH4926*

8. 'Sketched portrait of Marsh, Purser of the Queen Charlotte ca. 1794', *anonymous blue and grey wash. NMM ref PAH4888*

9. 'Scene below decks showing man having leg amputated', *anonymous graphite drawing, c1820. NMM ref PAD8484*

10. 'Thos. Trotter M.D. Physician to the Grand Fleet', *stipple engraving by Daniel Orme Jnr from an original by Daniel Orme, published 1 May 1796. NMM ref PAD3448*

1

The Glorious First of June: aftermath

ALL THE British line had suffered casualties—the official total was 287 killed and 811 wounded, counting the 28-29 May actions—but the French may have suffered as many as 3500 in total, with much the same number made prisoner. Damage to British ships, however, was more localised. Among the most heavily engaged was the *Queen*, 98, which had also suffered on the 29th. She was partially dismasted on the 'Glorious First', and having drifted to leeward at one point found herself facing eleven of the enemy, who were forced to give her rapid and accurate gunfire a wide berth (1). Her casualties were higher than any British ship except the *Brunswick*, but she reached home without external assistance. Another badly damaged three-decker was the 100-gun *Royal George*, which needed assistance after the battle from the frigate *Southampton* (2). She sent

2

over some spare spars which were used to set up a jury foremast.

As the battle drifted to an end during the afternoon, the sea was covered with disabled if not dismasted ships. William Dillon, a midshipman in the *Defence*, counted eighteen British ships with topgallants still across (*ie* not significantly damaged aloft), but there were twelve dismasted French ships in sight, the only British vessels in the same state being *Defence* herself and the *Marlborough*. Despite the fact that French frigates were actively employed recovering some of their dismasted battleships, no order to renew the battle was given; Howe was exhausted and retired to bed, leaving the clearing up to Sir Roger Curtis, the Captain of the Fleet. In the end six prizes were secured, and a seventh sank.

Any disquiet among more active officers was lost in the triumphant return of the victorious fleet to Portsmouth. No matter that the French grain convoy—the principal strategic target—had reached port safely, a morale-boosting victory had been won. Six prizes formed the largest haul of any eighteenth-century sea battle to date, and the King himself came to Portsmouth to greet the victors—an honour never before bestowed (nor ever again). On the quarterdeck of the *Queen Charlotte* the King presented Howe with a magnificent diamond-hilted sword (3), and there followed days of celebration (4). Already an earl, Howe refused any elevation in the peerage, but there were honours for the divisional admirals and a gold medal was struck and presented to officers who were considered to have distinguished themselves. There was some grumbling from those omitted—notably Collingwood, who later refused

3

his St Vincent medal until he received one for First of June—but the only really sour note was the whispering campaign against Molloy of the *Caesar*, who on both 29 May and 1 June had not done his utmost to follow orders. He eventually requested a court-martial a year later, which sentenced him to be dismissed his ship—but too late to dim the public glory of the battle.

4

1. 'Queen 1st June 1794 at noon', grey wash drawing by Robert Cleveley (1747-1809), dated 1794.
NMM ref PAH3968

2. 'The Situation of His Majesty's Ships Royal George . . . and the Marlborough . . . on the Close of the Action of the 1st of June 1794', aquatint published by Thomas Whitewood, 1 July 1796.
NMM neg A7129

3. 'George III presenting a sword to Earl Howe (1726-1799) on board HMS Queen Charlotte, 26 June 1794', oil painting by Henry Perronet Briggs (1792-1844).
NMM ref BHC0476

4. 'George III's Jubilee Review, 25 Oct 1809', watercolour by William Farrington. Although the occasion is different, this gives a colourful representation of how the celebrations during the royal visit would have appeared.
NMM ref PAD5926

1

The Glorious First of June: the prizes

THE SHIPS captured on 1 June made a fine sight (1) as they were brought into Spithead under their jury rigs, and once they were laid up in Portsmouth harbour they became the object of considerable attention from the public in general and artists in particular—see, for example, de Loutherbourg's sketch-

2

es recently published in Nicholas Tracy's *Nelson's Battles*— and there were a number of prints published.

The ships were:

Sans Pareil, 80 guns, 2342 tons, launched at Brest in 1793 (2)

Le Juste, 80 guns, 2143 tons, launched at Brest in 1784 (3)

L'América, 74 guns, 1884 tons, launched at Brest in 1788 (3)

L'Achille, 74 guns, 1818 tons, launched at Brest in 1778

Le Northumberland, 1827 tons, launched at Brest in 1779 (4)

L'Impétueux, 74 guns, 1879 tons, launched in 1787 probably at Brest (4)

As was common practice in the Royal Navy, they were carefully surveyed—the above figures are calculated tonnages by the British method—and plans taken off. Apart from their trophy value, they were of very mixed utility to their captors. In later years, as a prisoner of the British, Villaret-Joyeuse dismissed the prizes as 'half a dozen rotten old hulks', but he was not entirely fair. *L'Achille* and *Le Northumberland* (named after a British ship captured in 1744) were judged not worthy of repair— there was a strong belief in the royal dockyards that French ships were too lightly built to withstand the higher proportion of sea-time required of them in

British service, which meant that they could expect only short active lives (incidentally, it was also believed that Toulon-built ships, where there was access to excellent Adriatic oak, had far greater longevity than those built on the Atlantic coast). Nor was service possible in the case of *L'Impétueux*, which accidentally caught fire on 24 August and burned to the waterline.

The others, however, gave some return to their new masters. *L'América*, according to William Dillon, was surprisingly valuable, having topsides studded with silver dollars, which had been fired into her during the battle by the *Leviathan*, a ship which had acquired some mysterious tins during Hood's occupation of Toulon; they were thought to be canister shot, but actually represented a nobleman's fortune, deposited in the dockyard for safe-keeping! On a more serious note, *L'América*, renamed *Impétueux* to replace the ship lost by fire, was not broken up until 1813; *Le Juste* was employed until 1802; and *Sans Pareil*, the most serviceable acquisition, was a popular command for some fifteen years before being reduced to a sheer hulk. However, the ships also had a further use, as models for the hull lines of new ships. Rate for rate, French ships were usually larger than their British equivalents, which gave them the potential advantages of carrying their guns higher and, with a greater water-line length, making them faster. Copying the lines of prizes was a method of circumventing resistance to growth in ship-size within the Navy's administration

3

and dockyards, and was much used in the 1790s. *L'Impétueux*'s lines formed the basis of a class of two ships ordered in 1795 (confusingly named the *Northumberland* class after another First of June prize), while the *Sans Pareil* performed the same function for a new ship as late as 1840. The ships were built to British construction standards and were not crude copies as is so often claimed.

4

1. 'To the Right Honorable John Pitt, Earl of Chatham . . . This representation of the British Fleet . . . Bringing into Spithead the Six French Ships captured on the First of June 1794', aquatint engraved by Birnie and Robert Pollard from an original by Thomas Luny (1759-1837), published by John Jefferys, London.
NMM neg C647

2. 'French Ship Sans Pareil 3rd Rate, 80 Guns captured at First of June', watercolour attributed to Dominic Serres (c1761-1804), c1800.
NMM ref C837

3. 'Le Juste and Le America [sic] both captured and added 1 June 1794', aquatint engraved by J Wells after an original by R Livesay, published by R Livesay and J Norman, no date.
NMM neg no 1353

4. 'Impetueux and Northumberland', coloured aquatint engraved by J Wells after an original by R Livesay, published by R Livesay.
NMM ref PAD8700

1

'Dangers of the sea': fire

DURING THE whole of the period 1793-1815 the Royal Navy's losses of ships from accidental and natural causes exceeded the figure for enemy action in a ratio of ten to one. In the Naval Prayer these are defined as 'the dangers of the sea' and the 'violence of the enemy', and of the former probably the most feared –although not statistically the most likely–was fire, and the concomitant possibility of explosion. One of the First of June prizes, *L'Impétueux,* accidentally caught fire and was lost before seeing British service.

Wooden ships, crammed with combustible materials like rope, canvas, tar, not to mention gunpowder, were bonfires waiting to be lit–and since ships were illuminated by tallow candles and oil lamps, and food cooked on open galley ranges, potential sources of ignition were all around them. In action, red-hot shot was greatly feared because it might lodge in inaccessible timbers and the fire take hold before it could be located; in practice, however, the difficulties of heating and loading hot shot at sea, although it was tried by the Revolutionary French navy, tended to confine it to coastal batteries. The answer, whether in action or not, lay with prevention rather than cure, and tight discipline surrounded anything to do with naked flame.

The numbers of British warships so lost was not great – eight ships of the line and two smaller between 1793 and 1815–but it afflicted large and important ships out of all proportion, possibly because the bigger the ship the more dark recesses where fire might take hold. The most significant loss during the period covered by this book was the Second Rate *Boyne* of 98 guns, at the time the flagship of that great disciplinarian Sir John Jervis, which caught fire while laying at anchor at Spithead on 1 May 1795. The rest of the fleet sent boats very quickly and all but eleven of her large crew were saved (1), before the ship's loaded guns began to go off, causing casualties and damage all around. Finally the magazine exploded (2), witnessed and graphically described by Captain Brenton:

> The afternoon was perfectly calm and the sky clear: the flames which darted from her in a perpendicular column of great height were terminated by an opaque cloud like a round cap, while the air was filled with fragments of the wreck in every direction, and the stump of the foremast was seen far above the smoke descending into the water.

The cause of the fire was never determined, but one exotic theory was that smouldering cartridges from Marines exercising with muskets on the poop were blown into the admiral's cabin which set alight to his papers.

Sudden explosion was less common than one induced by a fire at large, but it did happen. On 22 September 1796, while completing repairs in Plymouth dockyard, the frigate *Amphion* simply blew up (3). She was due to sail the following day and was filled with relatives as well as the crew: some 300 of the 312 on board did not survive, but the captain, Israel Pellew, had a miraculous escape when he was blown through the stern cabin windows, while a visiting captain he was entertaining was killed.

1. 'View of His Majesty's Ship Boyne of 98 Guns, on Fire by Accident at Spithead, May 1795', aquatint engraved by J W Edy from an original by Captain T M Waller, published by T Whitwood Jnr, London, 1 July 1797. *NMM ref PAH0753*

2. 'Explosion from His Majesty's Ship Boyne after having burnt to the Water's Edge, and grounded on the Horse Shoal near South Sea Castle', aquatint engraved by J W Edy from an original by Captain T M Waller, published by T Whitwood Jnr, London, 1 July 1797. *NMM ref PAH0752*

3. 'Dreadful Explosion of the Amphion Frigate' anonymous coloured aquatint. *NMM ref PAD5505*

1

The Channel Fleet 1794-1795

THE POLICY of distant blockade—which earned Howe the nickname of 'Lord Torbay' after the fleet's habitual anchorage—allowed small French squadrons to evade or brush aside the watching frigates, and so exposed convoys to attack by forces far stronger than their escorts were ever intended to fend off. One

such squadron of five 74s, three frigates and a brig, under the energetic Rear-Admiral Neilly, on the lookout for homeward-bound convoys in November 1794, encountered the British 74s *Canada* and *Alexander* on the 6th returning from convoying the Mediterranean trade to a safe latitude.

The British ships separated and the former escaped, but *Alexander* was a sluggish sailer and was soon overhauled. For two hours she fought off attacks by three of the 74s in succession, until damage to her rigging made escape impossible, and Captain Richard Bligh struck his colours to save further loss of life beyond the 40 killed and wounded already sustained (1). The harsh treatment of the captured crew was the first indication to the British that the era of eighteenth-century civilities was over, and a grim foretaste of the ideological hatreds to come. The capture of a British 74 was a rare event during these wars—only five were lost, four of which were recaptured, compared with eighty-seven French ships of the same rate taken or destroyed by the British. However, the one-sided appearance of the conflict was not apparent in 1794, and what has been called the Royal Navy's 'habit of victory' was not yet established.

Despite the victory of First of June, the Channel Fleet at this time was neither as efficient nor as well motivated as it was to become. The crew of the *Culloden* (2), a ship whose First of June performance was far from glorious, mutinied in December, claiming the ship was unfit for

2

3

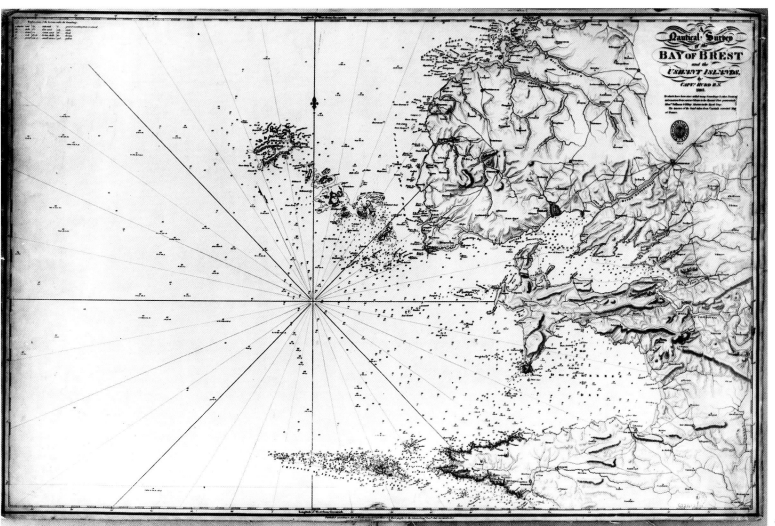

4

6

sea. Admirals Bridport, Cornwallis and Colpoys could not persuade the men to return to duty, but Thomas Pakenham, a popular captain and Irishman like many of the mutineers, did the trick. However, when they surrendered, ten were tried and eight hanged, which the men regarded as a breach of promise, and apparently never forgot. This incident had sinister portents for the future: notes from the mutineers were signed 'a delegate', a word which alarmed the authorities with its overtones of revolutionary committees and one which would surface again with greater menace in 1797. During the Great Mutiny, 'Remember the *Culloden*' became a rallying cry against all those who favoured negotiation.

Despite these travails, the main task of monitoring the activities of the Brest fleet went on. One of the arguments against the close blockade was the constant risk attending a rock-strewn bay that was a lee shore in prevailing winds; it placed almost unbearable stress on ships and men alike (3). The port itself was too far inland to allow observation from the sea, but ships riding in the inner roads could be seen through the narrow channel known as *Le Goulet*, and fleets ready for sea often lay at anchor in Bertheaume Bay to the north or Camaret to the south (4). To make worthwhile reconnaissance required a ship to get in very close, and one of the most audacious was Sir Sidney Smith's incursion in the frigate *Diamond* on 3 January 1795. He possessed a fluent command of French and under the *tricoleur* took his ship right up to the entrance to *Le Goulet* and even spoke to a number of French ships without arousing their suspicions.

This achievement simply underlined the difficulty of blockading Brest. When on station, the British fleet usually cruised off Ushant to give them a safe amount of sea-room, but they needed frigates inside the bay to spot emerging French ships. The frigates could be easily driven off by adverse weather or superior force, whereupon there were a number of exit routes open to a seagoing squadron—the *Passage du Four* to the northwest and the *Passage du Raz* to the southwest being the main ones. In short, it was never possible to prevent the escape of small squadrons in all circumstances, and British detachments were at risk when this happened. One of the most famous of such incidents was the fighting retreat forced on Vice-Admiral Cornwallis's squadron when it encountered a large part of the French fleet on 16 June 1795. His flagship, the 100-gun *Royal Sovereign*, was forced to go to the assistance of one of his four 74s, the *Mars*, which was heavily pressed by advanced units of a fleet comprising one 120-gun ship, eleven 74s, and eleven frigates. After a long chase the French were mislead by one of Cornwallis's frigates, the *Phaeton*, making signals to an imaginary fleet, which when coupled with Cornwallis's confident counter-attack persuaded them that help was at hand. They broke off an action in which all five British ships should have been taken, and 'Cornwallis's Retreat' became as famous as many of the Royal Navy's real victories (5). Cornwallis (6) was well-practiced in the art of withdrawal under fire, having carried out almost a dress-rehearsal against de Ternay in the West Indies in June 1780.

1. 'This Representation of His Majesty's Ship *Alexander* . . . ten minutes before she struck her colours to a French Squadron . . . on the 6th of November 1794', coloured aquatint engraved by J Wells after an original by T Guest, published by T Guest, 20 June 1800.
NMM neg A5137

2. '*Culloden* man of war', grey pen & ink & wash by Dominic Serres, no date.
NMM ref PAF5783

3. HM Ships (left to right) *Galatea*, *Valiant*, *Tremendous*, *Thunderer* and *Queen* in heavy weather, a watercolour attributed to Joseph Gear (1768-1853). Although undated, it probably represents a squadron of the Channel Fleet about 1795; the conditions are typical of those to which the blockading ships were exposed off Ushant.
Peabody Essex Museum, Salem MA neg 15299

4. 'A Nautical survey of the Bay of Brest and the Ushant Islands by Captn Hurd RN, 1807'.
NMM neg B8780

5. 'Admiral Cornwallis's Retreat from the French Squadron, Belle Isle 17 June 1795', aquatint engraved by Wells from an original by William Anderson, published by Bunny and Gold, 1 March 1802.
NMM ref PAD5491

6. 'Hon. William Cornwallis, Admiral of the Blue Squadron, Rear-Admiral of England', engraving by Charles Turner from an original by Thomas Unwins, published by J Stratford, 22 June 1805.
NMM ref PAD3292

5

Bridport's action, 23 June 1795

3

FOLLOWING ITS failure to capture Cornwallis's squadron, the French fleet under Villaret-Joyeuse found the roles reversed a week later when it ran into the Channel Fleet of two 100-gun First Rates, six 98s, six two-deckers and some frigates. Commanded by Lord Bridport while Howe was recuperating ashore, it was providing cover for the landing of an *emigré* French royalist army in Quiberon Bay escorted by a small squadron under Commodore Warren.

Outnumbered, the French retired, and Bridport sent a flying squadron of *Sans Pareil* (the 80-gun ship captured at First of June), and the 74s *Orion, Colossus, Irresistible, Valiant* and *Russell* in pursuit, but soon ordered the whole fleet in general chase. A day-long hunt developed, but it was

4

5

not until the early hours of the following day, 23 June, that the rear of the French line was seriously engaged (2). Rearmost was the *Alexandre*, no better a sailer now than when captured from the British as the *Alexander* the previous year; she was recaptured along with the *Formidable* and *Tigre*, two new 74s that were added to the Royal Navy, the former as the *Belleisle* (supposedly under the impression that the battle had been fought off that island rather than Isle de Groix).

Much of the damage had been wrought by the flying squadron's *Sans Pareil* and *Irresistible*, plus the surprisingly fleet-footed *Queen Charlotte* (3), although owing her prominence to skilful handling rather than sheer speed. When Bridport's flagship, the *Royal George*, came up about 8am (4), she surprisingly signalled the leading ships to discontinue the action when at least a further handful of French ships were within the fleet's grasp (5). It was a victory, but of a partial kind that would be unsatisfactory within a few years: Jervis and, above all, Nelson would not settle for anything less than annihilating the enemy.

1. 'View of Lord Bridport's action off L'Orient 1795', aquatint published by Bunny & Co, London, 1 April 1799.
NMM ref PAG7059

2. 'Lord Bridport's Action off Port L'Orient June 23rd 1795', coloured aquatint engraved by J Bailey from an original by Thomas Whitcombe (c1752-1824), published 1 May 1816.
NMM ref PAD5492

3. 'An Exact Representation of the Capture of Three Ships of the Line, and Total defeat of the French Fleet, by a Squadron under Command of Admiral Lord Bridport, on the 23 of June 1795', engraving by J Pass from an original by F Godefroy, published 1 October 1795.
NMM ref PAD5494

4. 'Lord Bridport's Action off L'Orient at the Close of the Action in the Centre is seen the Royal George Continuing the Chase the Tigre having Struck her Colours & Bore up appears to the Left on the Right is Formidable & Alexander . . . The Isle de Groix with Port Louis & L'Orient in Distance on the Right', watercolour of the eighteenth century British school.
NMM ref PAD8507

5. 'View of the Close of the Action between the British and French Fleets, off Port L'Orient on the 23rd of June 1795', aquatint engraved by Robert Dodd (1748-1815) from an original by Captain Alexander Becher RN, published by the engraver 12 June 1812.
NMM neg 867

1

2

3

The Channel frigate squadrons

IRRESPECTIVE OF whether the French Brest fleet was subject to close or distant blockade, there was always the possibility of frigates and smaller craft putting to sea from lesser ports, not to mention the usual swarm of privateers. The normal level of convoy escort could cope with the smaller ships, but for the Admiralty, the perceived danger was of squadrons of powerful frigates cruising against trade, and indeed in the early years of the war the French dispatched several raiding groups of this nature.

The British response was to form what were in effect hunting squadrons, composed of the most powerful

4

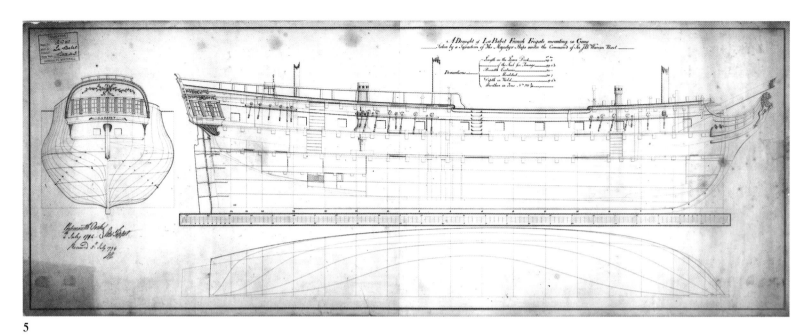

5

frigates and the most competent captains. As a stream of new 18pdr-armed ships came into service in the 1790s, they were assigned to these squadrons, which at one time or another included many of the officers who were to become the Royal Navy's best-known frigate captains –Sir John Borlase Warren of the *Flora*, 36; Sir Edward Pellew of the *Arethusa*, 38; Sidney Smith of *Diamond*, 38; Sir Edmund Nagle of the *Artois*, 38; Sir Andrew Snape Douglas of the *Phaeton*, 38; Sir Richard Strachan of the *Concorde*, 36; and Richard Goodwin Keats of the *Galatea*, 32, to name but a few. In 1796 the Channel cruisers comprised three 24pdr, seventeen 18pdr and only five 12pdr

ships, the cream of the British frigate force. The number of prizes, both privateers and national cruisers, taken by these squadrons in the early war years is a tribute to their effectiveness.

One of the first to make a name for himself was Sir James Saumarez, knighted for capture of the *Réunion* by the *Crescent* on 20 October 1793. This, one of the first victories of the war, was hard-fought, and became a popular subject for the print industry, among the most detailed being those by Robert Dodd (1, 2). Saumarez, a Guernseyman by birth, was given command of a small squadron operating off the Channel Islands, and in a

6

7

smart little defensive action in June 1794 demonstrated his tactical skill against a far superior French force. He was in company with the *Druid*, 32 and the *Eurydice*, one of the notoriously slow-sailing small post ships of 24 guns (3). Being reluctant to sacrifice her, Saumarez's two ships fought off two big cut-down 74s (called *rasées* by the French), two 36-gun frigates and a brig, plus some small craft. Once the *Eurydice* was safely away, the two British ships made for Guernsey, but so closely pursued that Saumarez had to change course and run down the line of the French squadron to further distract their attention (4). He then took his ship into Guernsey Road through a rock-strewn channel never previously used by a large warship.

The French *rasées* constituted a particular worry, and the British responded by cutting down three fast-sailing 64s, the *Indefatigable*, *Anson* and *Magnanime*, all of which had 24pdr main batteries, but the French also built limited numbers of very large frigates with 24pdrs. In theory there was nothing in the Royal Navy to match them, but the practical answer seemed to be the frigate squadron. The most successful of these in the first years

8

9

of war was that commanded by Sir John Borlase Warren, and he was destined to take the first French 24pdr ship to fall into British hands, in a well-handled squadron action on 23 April 1794. With the 18pdr frigates *Flora*, *Arethusa* and *Melampus*, and the 12pdr-armed *Concorde* and *Nymphe*, he fought and captured the *Pomone* (with a main battery of twenty-six 24pdrs), the 12pdr *Engageante* and the 20-gun *Babet* (5); only the *Résolue*, 36 escaped (6). Along with other prizes taken on Warren's cruise, the squadron made a fine sight as it came into Falmouth harbour (7). At nearly 160ft length on the gundeck and 1239 tons the *Pomone* was a particularly valuable prize, and the British laid down a ship on her lines called the *Endymion* whose excellent sailing qualities made her a favourite for over thirty years.

The 24pdr ships were few in number, but France also experimented with very large 18pdr-armed frigates. These rarely had the opportunity to prove themselves, so close was the British control of the Channel and its approaches. The brand-new *Révolutionnaire* of 1148 tons, for example, was barely a week out of Le Havre when on

21 October she ran into a squadron comprising *Arethusa*, *Artois*, *Diamond* and *Galatea*; *Artois* was the best sailer and got into action first, but the French ship only surrendered as the other frigates came up. She was another very large frigate, and caused considerable interest in the Royal Navy. Besides the lines being taken off in the time-honoured fashion, a fine model survives (one of the very few models of a named French prize in the official Admiralty style, (8) and there is also a naïve watercolour of the ship as captured (9). Years later in 1802 a frigate was ordered to her lines, but the keel was moved from one yard to another and the *Forte*, as she was named, was not launched until 1814, by which time her size was not unusual.

Warren's squadron operated close in to the French coast, so that even small warships were denied freedom of movement. One example was the pursuit of a small detachment of a frigate and two corvettes in August 1794, the latter being chased ashore and boarded right under the defending batteries in Audierne Bay, just outside Brest, by the *Flora* and *Arethusa* (10).

10

Ships of the Royal Navy: the 18pdr frigate

1

THE FRIGATE as understood at this period was defined as a ship with a single gundeck, quarter-deck and forecastle, but with a complete, unarmed lower deck (appropriately termed the 'berth deck' in the US Navy, since it accommodated the crew). This lower deck was important because it gave frigates much greater freeboard for their single main battery—often 7ft or more in British ships—which meant that they could use their guns in all weathers, unlike two-deckers which might have to close the lower deck ports in stormy conditions. The most famous scenario of this kind was the *Indefatigable*'s harrying to destruction the French 74 *Droits de l'Homme* during a January gale in 1797.

To use a modern analogy, the heavy cruiser of the 1790s was a frigate of between 32 and 40 guns armed with 18pdrs on the main deck. They had been introduced by the British in 1778, at a time during the American War when the Royal Navy's traditional numerical superiority was under threat, in an attempt to counter larger numbers with more individual firepower. The resulting *Minerva* class 38s, with main batteries of twenty-eight guns, and the 36s of the *Flora* and *Perseverance* classes, with

1. A stern view of a frigate, showing rigging, including studding sails. Anonymous grey pen and ink and wash drawing. Although the ship is unidentified, it may be said to represent the general appearance of the main run of frigates of the 1790s. *NMM ref PAF5789*

2. 'Frégate Anglaise en panne', Plate 29 from *Collection des Toutes les Especes de Batiments* drawn and engraved by J J Baugean, 3rd edition, Paris, 1826. Although unidentified, the ship's disposition of gunports marks her out as a 36, and most probably one of the numerous *Apollo* class. *NMM ref PAD7405*

3. 'The *Pomone*, Captain Robert Barrie RN', coloured lithograph by T G Dutton (c1819-1891) after an original by G F St John, published by Day & Sons, London, no date. The ship was the second of the standard *Leda* class and an exact sister of Philip Broke's famous *Shannon*, having been built in the same yard in the previous year, 1805. *NMM neg 5666*

4. A pictorial plan of *Lively* at ⅛th of an inch to the foot scale; one of a pair with the 120-gun *Nelson*. The drawing depicts the latest and largest standard class of 38 by the closing years of the Napoleonic War. *NMM neg X1976*

5. '*Bacchante* off Deptford 1811', an anonymous watercolour. One of the last of the *Lively* class, the ship was only launched in November 1811, so must depict the ship fitting out. *NMM ref PAH0785*

2

3

4

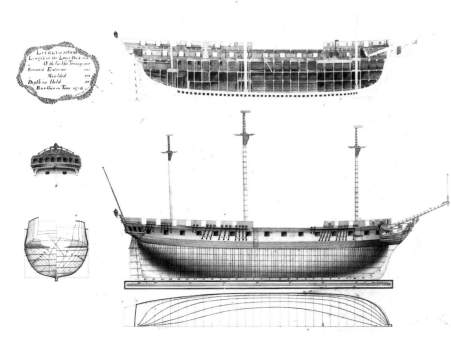

two less, were very powerful cruisers and for some years they had no equivalent in the navies of the main naval powers, a superiority enhanced by the addition of carronades to the 9pdr long guns on their upperworks. However, like so many British ships, they were found to be too small for their batteries, and as a result when new classes of 36s and 38s were ordered in the 1790s (1) there was a move towards increasing the space between the guns. At the time there was also a wider concern that French ships seemed faster under sail, and this was considered to be a result of the relatively short hull favoured by British designers for strength and manoeuvrability. Therefore, the ships tended to get proportionately longer, but Lord Spencer's administration promoted significantly larger ships (as it was simultaneously doing with ships of the line).

For frigates the new policy manifested itself in a rapid increase in absolute size, frequent design changes, with many 'one-off' and experimental hull forms, and a shift in proportions towards longer and shallower hulls. French designs became the focus of concerted attention for the first time since the 1760s, and a number of prizes were 'copied'—although their structure and layout followed British practice, which required far more robust and better-appointed ships suitable for very long range cruising. Armament was considerably augmented at the same time by the gradual adoption of 32pdr carronades for the upperworks, leaving only two or four 9pdr chase guns, giving a total of forty-six to a nominal 38-gun frigate. As part of the drive towards bigger frigates, two vessels (*Acasta* and *Lavinia*) were ordered with thirty 18pdrs and rated as 40-gun ships, but later designs preferred the greater space allowed by twenty-eight gunports and a pair of bridle ports for occasional use with chase guns.

The new heavy frigates were a high priority in the 1790s and their numbers increased rapidly from both new construction and numerous prizes:

Year	No in Sea Service	No in Ordinary or Repairing
1793	11	6
1795	36	0
1797	45	2
1799	46	4
1801	68	1
1804	57	7
1808	76	15
1812	98	9
1814	103	11

Such was the speed of change under Spencer that no standard 38 or 36 had emerged by the time St Vincent

took over as First Lord in February 1801. The new administration, believing the Peace of Amiens would last, dedicated itself to retrenchment and dockyard reform. What few orders were placed followed St Vincent's stated belief that ships had become unnecessarily large, and reverted to older and smaller designs, including a return to the original 36-gun 18pdr of 1778.

Although the 1790s had established the 36 and 38 as the current norm for frigates, there were a few smaller 18pdr ships rated as 32s. The early 800-ton ships were an attempt to build a minimal 18pdr ship and the rapid leap to 900 tons pointed to their inadequacy. The main difference from 36s was the quarterdeck and forecastle armament of 6pdrs and 24pdr carronades, giving the nominal 32 a total of 40 guns.

The nature of the conflict changed after Trafalgar, particularly once the introduction of the Continental System and the economic blockade made it a war of attrition. Numbers became even more important, while after a decade or more of almost uninterrupted success against all comers technical improvement in ship design seemed less of an issue. As a result, frigate building was confined to large numbers of standard designs—as with the 'Surveyors' class' 74s or the *Cruizer* class brigs. However, for frigates the designs were well-proven and all dated from the 1790s: the chosen 36 was the *Apollo* (2), the medium 150ft 38 the *Leda* (3), and the large 154ft 38 the *Lively* (4, 5). The *Leda* was based on the French *Hébé*, captured as far back as 1782, but still employed as a hull form by the French Navy so not outclassed; the other two were designs by Sir William Rule and were fine all-round ships. These were the only frigates ordered between 1806 and the outbreak of the War of 1812. Even then, although larger 24pdr ships were designed, the existing classes continued to be built. In fact, a fir-built 'austerity' variant of the *Apollo* called the *Scamander* class and a fir-built of version the *Leda* formed the backbone of the war emergency programme.

Part II   WAR ON TRADE

VILLARET-JOYEUSE'S gallant defence of the grain convoy at the battle of 'The Glorious First of June' put an end to the British attempt to starve France into submission. Experience in earlier wars had made it apparent that the difficulties involved in stopping the flow of supplies to France were generally too great to be overcome. Only where it was possible to focus blockade effort on a cargo such as the heavy timbers, tar and hemp from the Baltic, which were used in shipbuilding and maintenance, and which had to be carried by sea to a few clearly identified destinations, was a tight blockade operationally practicable. The typical commercial blockade of the eighteenth century was a relatively open *guerre de course* intended as much to enrich the captors as to undermine the credit of the French government. These operations obtained their results through their cumulative effects. Most effective were those directed at reducing the flow of trade goods from the West Indies which, when re-exported to European markets, accounted in 1787 for 34.7 per cent of French export trade.

The total contribution of West Indian commerce to the French economy was probably 20 per cent, and it was at least as important that it employed 25 per cent of French mercantile tonnage, and 20 per cent of seamen registered for the *Inscription Maritime*. These proportions made the French West Indian trade a major consideration in the competition for naval power. In reply to a question put by a Commons committee in 1790, Admiral Lord Rodney said he was 'fully convinced that had it not been for the French West Indian commerce, that nation could not have been in a condition to dispute with Great Britain the empire of the ocean in the last war.'[1] The Chairman of the Committee on Colonies in the French National Assembly, Barnave, declared much the same thing that same year, that 'almost all our navigation at this time is the direct or indirect result of the possession of our colonies. From that I conclude that if we abandoned them we would lose

the means to form and occupy during peace the number of seamen necessary to sustain our naval forces in war.'[2]

The possibility of disrupting the French war effort by injuring French trade, however, was less important than was the profit which might be made by British interests, and which could help pay the expense of Britain's war effort. Britain's West Indian commerce contributed 10 per cent of her larger trading economy, and British investment in the West Indies generated 7 per cent to 10 per cent of Britain's annual income. Capture of Saint-Domingue, for instance, could more than compensate Britain for the loss of the American colonies.

In the mid-eighteenth century, advanced economic theorists in Britain had began to call in question the entire mercantilist system. In 1776 Adam Smith published *The Wealth of Nations* which attacked the idea that states should seek to monopolise wealth. Only wealthy states, he argued, had the capacity to be good markets. The growing awareness of the value of free trade, however, did not immediately lead to an end of the great mercantilist trade war. In 1786

William Eden negotiated a lower level of tariffs with France which encouraged trade, but French manufacturers objected that freer trade benefited the more advanced British industry, and the Eden tariffs became one of the grievances in the French Revolution. The wars of the French Revolution and Empire were fought with unswerving mercantilist purpose, and with mercantilist means. French strategy was as much mercantilist as was that of Britain, although the French had more reason to hope that Britain could be driven out of the war through attacks on its trade.

Hope that Britain could be driven to seek peace by undermining her mercantile prosperity had been fed by grave doubts felt in the most respectable banking quarters about the stability of the British economy. To a Frenchman, that economy seemed to be fundamentally unsound because it lacked the strong agricultural base which France enjoyed. The British national debt, which in 1775 had been £124 million, was £230 million in 1793. At the time of the Peace of Amiens in 1802 it was to be no less than £507 million, which was only £80

'Shipping Sugar, Antigua', coloured lithograph engraved by Thomas Goldsworth Dutton from an original by W S Andrews, printed by Day & Sons. Sugar was one of the crops that made the West Indies central to the economies of the European powers and ensured that it became a major theatre of fighting in any war. NMM ref PAH2989

million less than it was to be in 1914. It appeared to be inevitable that a campaign against British trade would lead to the failure of Britain's international credit. No less an authority than Adam Smith had drawn attention to the vulnerability of Britain through trade war by demonstrating that it had been exports of manufactured goods, not of bullion, which paid for the Seven Years War.

In contrast to France and Britain, Spain was a relatively easy target for naval action against trade. Spanish credit depended upon the flow of silver from the mines of Peru, and the annual Spanish treasure convoys were always an important object of war. However, the fact that the naval officers who succeeded in capturing a Spanish treasure ship could become immensely wealthy may have been more important than any other strategic rationale in ensuring that naval resources were devoted to that purpose.

Squadron action against French convoys from the Indies, privateer attacks on individual merchant ships, and combined operations to seize control of the islands where the sugar crops were grown, were all part of the navy's action against French trade. The French islands at the outbreak of war were in a state of turmoil because of the revolution, with its promise of *liberté* and *égalité*, which with differing interpretations were demanded by the poor whites, mulattos and black slaves. The need to arrest the spread of these dangerous doctrines in order to preserve intact the economies of the British islands, as well as the hope to acquire valuable new colonies, had made operations in the West Indies a priority at the outbreak of war. Vice-Admiral Laforey, who commanded the small British squadron at Barbados, carried a force of soldiers under Major-General Cuyler to recapture the island of Tobago which had been lost to the French in the American War. The fort at Scarborough was carried by storm, and the island capitulated. Rear-Admiral Gardner, who had been hurried out to the West Indies with seven of the line and two regiments of foot under Major Bruce, was less successful in an effort to bring Martinique to declare for the royalists. They were forced to evacuate the royalist insurgents who would certainly have been put to death. The commander of the Jamaica station, Commodore John Ford, was luckier when he

responded to the requests from French colonists in Saint-Domingue for protection from the republicans. The mulattos had revolted, and commissioners from the National Assembly, hoping to strengthen their hand against the forces of colonial independence, had proclaimed the emancipation of the black slaves at the end of August 1793. Dreadful cruelties were committed by the warring factions, and the *Grandes Blancs*, the leading white planters, welcomed the British as protectors. One of the best harbours in the islands, St Nicholas Mole, protected from the sea by a strongly-sited battery, was thus closed to enemy privateers. In Newfoundland waters, the French fishery island of St Pierre was captured by a small force out of Halifax.

The British did not reinforce their establishment in the West Indies until the spring of 1794 when Vice-Admiral Sir John Jervis and Lieutenant-General Sir Charles Grey were sent to capture Martinique, St Lucia, and Guadeloupe. Martinique was taken in March 1794 after a successful combined operation in which sailors moved heavy guns up prodigious heights to bring fire on enemy positions. St Lucia resisted briefly but its defences were taken by storm and the island capitulated on 4 April. On 12 April the post at Fleur d'Epée on Guadeloupe was stormed by soldiers and seamen who had to climb a steep hill under fire and charge the walls with pike and bayonet. The other posts on Guadaloupe capitulated without further resistance.

The decision was then made to send the soldiers not required for garrisoning the captured islands, reinforced by four regiments from Ireland which had arrived at the end of the season, to secure the position on Saint-Domingue which had begun to deteriorate after the initial, but incomplete, success. This proved less fortunate, perhaps because Grey and Jervis were so interested in plunder that they directed operations against Port-au-Prince, where merchant shipping had taken refuge, rather than the militarily more important post of Cap Françoise on the north coast or the republican strongholds at Les Cayes and Jacmel on the south coast. The plundering throughout the captured islands was so comprehensive that the French colonists began to reconsider their hostility to the French republic.

The absence of a large part of the British

force in Saint-Domingue had disastrous consequences when a small force of two frigates and transports, which had been able to get out of Brest because of Howe's decision to keep the Channel Fleet at Spithead, arrived at Guadaloupe. By the time Jervis and Grey learned of the development, the French had recovered Point-à-Pitre and moved their ships into harbour behind the guns of the batteries. They were able to depend on local support, of which Commissioner Victor Hugues made certain by carrying the Reign of Terror to the colony. The decimation of the British army by yellow fever eventually forced it to evacuate the island on 10 December 1794. When Hugues had secured his reconquest, Paris sent out reinforcements with which he recaptured St Lucia, and stirred up revolt throughout the other British-held islands.

British cruisers attacked French commerce, and employed 'the Rule of War of 1756' to justify the seizure and condemnation of neutral American ships carrying cargoes for the French, which French navigation regulations would not have permitted them to carry in peacetime. It was legally impossible, however, to stop Americans carrying French cargoes to American ports and then reloading them into American ships bound for neutral European harbours, or to intercept Americans trading between neutral ports, but Jervis's captains transgressed on these distinctions to such an extent that the United States embargoed the shipment of provisions to the British islands, and Grey had to deploy troops to meet an expected American act of war. When the Admiralty courts in the islands refused to condemn half of the captures, Grey and Jervis established new, more compliant, but unauthorised courts.

Unlike all earlier wars in the eighteenth century, with the exception of the end of the War of the Austrian Succession, the British government forbade the provision of insurance by the British market to enemy ship owners. The Traitorous Correspondence Act was

---

1. Great Britain, House of Commons, *Sessional Papers*, 'Reports and Papers 1790. Slave Trade,' 177, 183. See: Michael Duffy, *Soldiers, Sugar, and Seapower, The British Expeditions to the West Indies and the War against Revolutionary France*, Oxford: Clarendon Press, 1987, pp5-33.

2. *Procès-verbal de l'Assemblé National*, xiv (Paris, 1790) no. 223, 9-11.

far from being an obvious measure, because traditionally British mercantilist objectives had been furthered by forcing the enemy to pay exorbitant war risk premiums, but generally it was obeyed. The revolution had changed the nature of the public attitude to war, vastly increasing the stakes.

French efforts to protect their trade had begun soon after the outbreak of war, when a small French squadron of three ships of the line had sailed under Rear-Admiral Sercey to the West Indies, where it joined another ship which had sailed out previously. Because of the threat to the French islands, the usual convoy to France was diverted to Virginia, where in the spring of 1794 it joined the grain convoy to Brest. Sercey's squadron had returned to Brest late in 1793.

In strategic terms, the injury which was done to French re-export business by the cruisers, and by the island campaigns, was cancelled out by the French Treasury which exacted levies on the countries conquered by French armies. The retention by their commanding generals of the specie they seized, and its use to relieve the suffering of the soldiers, helped to turn the national army into an instrument which the generals could use to establish their political power. Edmund Burke's prediction was to prove correct, that the war would be 'long and dangerous,…the most dangerous we were ever engaged in.'

In the East Indies fighting had commenced as early as November 1791. Cornwallis, then a commodore, used force to stop and search a French frigate believed to be carrying supplies to Tipu Sahib. Tipu, the Sultan of Mysore, was carrying on the policy of his father, Hyder Ali, in violent opposition to the British East India Company. News of the declaration of war in 1793 reached the British at Calcutta promptly because Mr Baldwin, consul at Alexandria, sent a message overland. French posts in India were immediately occupied. That at Pondicherry, which was the only real fortress in French India, was subjected to a heavy bombardment at the end of July, and capitulated.

A small squadron under Commodore Peter Rainier sailed from home waters for Madras to protect British trade. To ensure that the French were not able to use the leverage provided by Dutch colonial assets in Africa and Asia, Pitt decided to send squadrons under Sir George Elphinstone, Lord Keith, and Commodore Blankett to land troops under General James Craig at Cape Town. The settlement was occupied in June 1795 with little resistance, and was used as a base for blockade of the French post at Isle de France (Mauritius), but Rainier did not have enough force to contain the aggressive efforts of the French. In August 1795, however, he was able to seize the Dutch post at Trincomalee, which was the only safe harbour in the Bay of Bengal. The same month another force under Captain Newcome captured Malacca on the southwest coast of the Malayan peninsula, and in early 1796 Rainier occupied Amboyna in the Moluccas, and Banda, from the Dutch. These conquests ensured that Britain would retain control of the trade from Asia, although they could not prevent privateers out of Isle de France raiding British shipping. A strong squadron was stationed at Cape Town to prevent any French effort at reconquest.

In response to the French recapture of Guadeloupe, in late 1795 a force of eight ships of the line under Rear-Admiral Christian, with 137 transports and support vessels carrying 16,000 soldiers under General Abercrombie, was ordered to sail from Portsmouth to the West Indies. In total, 30,818 soldiers, virtually half of the active British army, was sent out to the West Indies between December 1795 and March 1796. Christian's convoy encountered a severe Channel storm and was forced to return to Portsmouth. A second attempt to sail in December was similarly prevented, and it was not until April and May 1796 that the force was to reach the islands. It was thereby condemned to go on service in the rainy season.

The wastage of British manpower in the islands due to disease was so great that 40,000 died and a like number were left unfit for service. No provision had been made to move the soldiers to a healthier climate during the sickly season, and planter opposition to copying the French use of black soldiers held back that development until 1797, when the government was reduced to purchasing the cargoes of slave ships in order to fill the ranks. As an offensive measure, the island campaign was hardly cost-effective.

General Abercrombie and Rear-Admiral Christian overcame stiff resistance to recapture St Lucia, and the revolts in St Vincent and Grenada were suppressed. The Dutch colonies were also occupied without resistance. When it became possible for them to turn their attention to Saint-Domingue however, their forces were so reduced that it was impossible to achieve anything. In any event, the revolution and war had so profoundly affected the plantation economy that possession of Saint-Domingue could have done little to improve Britain's financial position. The ceding of Santo Domingo by Spain to France in June 1795, as part of the peace settlement by which Spain left the First Coalition, widened the scope of the island conflict but added nothing to Britain's advantage. Although St Nicholas Mole was held until 1798, its hinterland was difficult to defend. The enfranchised blacks and mulattos found a leader in Toussaint l'Ouverture who proved himself a military genius.

The warfare in the Windward and Leeward islands did serve to prevent any serious attempt by the French to act offensively against Jamaica, although a revolt amongst the Maroons had to be suppressed at great expense.

Guadeloupe remained a threat to British commerce in the islands, but the entry of Spain into the war on the side of France in 1796 diverted attention to the easier prospect of seizing her possessions. Spanish privateers were no less of a threat than were those of France, so the capture of Spanish islands served a defensive as well as a mercantilist purpose. In February 1797 General Abercrombie received the surrender of Trinidad with little resistance, and three Spanish ships of the line were destroyed by their own crews in the harbour. They mustered little more than half of their proper complement, and had been quite unable to force their way out of harbour. An attempt on Puerto Rico, on the other hand, showed that that island was too strongly held to be similarly taken.

French squadron attacks on British shipping had only got under way when the difficulties of equipping the battlefleet needed to guard against invasion had been met. Political attention was focused on the question of Britain's vulnerability to blockade of food supplies in 1795, when there was a poor harvest that reduced yields by 20-25 per cent. However, Britain weathered that crisis. French resources were not well suited for an attempt to deny Britain access to supplies, and in fact that was never the focus of French strategy. In October

1795 Rear-Admiral Joseph de Richery, with three ships of the line and six frigates, which had with great difficulty been fitted out at Toulon, attacked a Smyrna convoy. *Censeur* of 74 guns, which had been captured from the French in the Mediterranean in March, was retaken, and thirty of the sixty-three merchantmen were captured. Rather than continuing across the Atlantic as planned, he retired into Cadiz with his prizes and spent the rest of the winter finding buyers for them. Eighteen ships were taken out of the Jamaica convoy by a squadron of French frigates, forty prizes were taken off the Madeiras, and during the summer of 1796 Richery at last proceeded on his mission. He repeated Neilly's 1794 success, and destroyed over 100 fishing vessels from the Newfoundland fleet, and burned fishing stations along the Newfoundland coast.

The weakness of the French battlefleet encouraged a return to Marshal Vauban's early eighteenth century operational strategy of exploiting the predatory instincts and skills of the French maritime community to conduct a *guerre de course* against British shipping. The commerce raiding of the French Marine was seconded by the efforts of French privateers. Their number never reached that which had been seen in the wars of the early eighteenth century, however, and in the early years of the Revolutionary War the *guerre de course* was motivated primarily by the need to obtain badly needed trade goods for the domestic market, especially cargoes of food. From the British perspective, the depredations of the small luggers in the Channel working out of Boulogne, Calais, Dunkirk and ports in the Netherlands were especially dangerous.

The abolition of the *assignats* in 1796, which enabled merchants to return to an undepreciated metallic currency, restored enough confidence that there was an increase in the number of privateers fitted out. The French islands in the West Indies, and from 1796 the Spanish islands, became nests of privateers. In Guadeloupe, Commissioner Hughes all but abandoned his efforts to recover French colonies because his attentions were diverted to the profits he could make as a privateer. Indian Ocean trade came under attack from privateers based on Isle de France (Mauritius). The most successful was Robert Surcouf who early in 1796 took up a position off the Hooghli river

'*View of Bridgetown and part of Carlisle Bay in the Island of Barbadoes*', watercolour by Edward Pelham Brenton. This illustration by a serving naval officer—who also became a historian of the war—shows the main assembly point for the rich convoys whose protection was such an important function of the naval forces in the region.   NMM ref PAF8416

and even used a captured pilot brig to tempt his prey within range. In 1797 British commerce was to suffer its worst losses.

The Royal Navy convoyed overseas trade, and trade to the Baltic. In 1792 there had been 1495 clearances from British ports on the long-distance trades, all of which required convoy except for a relatively few fast ships which sailed as independents: 878 clearances were issued for voyages to southern Europe, and 3101 to northern European ports. There were at the outbreak of war about 5500 British ships in foreign trade, and these made on average about one and a half return voyages to southern European ports each year, two to Baltic and Scandinavian ports, and three or four a year to the Netherlands. To protect ships sailing independently on coastal voyages, cruisers were deployed to attack French privateers. It was notoriously difficult to find the privateersmen, however, who were more familiar with the British coast than were the sort of unenterprising junior officers who tended to be put in command of small craft. The fact that the Channel Fleet did not maintain a close blockade of Brest during the early years of the war reduced the difficulty for French privateersmen in getting their prizes safely home. Some recaptures were made, however, by British privateersmen earning 'prize salvage' from shipowners.

Abercrombie's failure to secure Saint-Domingue had put an end to the ability of Pitt's administration to finance the war on credit. Government stocks were being offered for sale at 48 per cent of par. Lord Malmsbury was twice sent to negotiate peace with France, but the Directory sent him away because Britain's position appeared to be so desperate that France

need make no concessions for peace. The writing appeared to be on the wall when in 1797 the Bank Restricting Act released the Bank of England from its obligation to redeem paper currency. The mutinies in the Channel and North Sea appeared to be the final blow, although the Channel Fleet mutineers made it clear that they would sail if it was necessary to do so to escort home a convoy. To Frenchmen, the evils of paper currency were all too obvious. Precarious credit, and blockade of a narrow range of manufactures, were expected to put many of Britain's 'over-specialised' labour out of work, and thus lead to revolution.

In fact, Pitt was able to weather the storm by the introduction of income tax which raised national revenue adequate to pay for the war, provided liabilities in the West Indies were abandoned. Lieutenant-General John Simcoe conduced a brilliant campaign in Saint-Domingue in early 1797, but the government had already decided that the island should be evacuated. Carefully playing off the hostile factions against each other, the island was handed over to Toussaint and his army of former slaves. The privateer war had diverted some naval resources to trade protection, and there was dislocation of commercial patterns. British shipowners and insurers, however, retained their capacity to make compensations for marine war risk. The losses of ships to privateers throughout the war probably did not exceed 2½ per cent of the volume of trade. The British Treasury strengthened as the war progressed and was able to subsidise the military efforts of each successive coalition formed by Pitt, and later by Addington, to confront first the Revolution, and then Napoleon's Empire.

The West Indies 1793-1794

THE WAR in the West Indies began with the recapture of the island of Tobago from the French in April 1793. The commander of the Barbados station, Vice-Admiral Sir John Laforey, sailed from Bridgetown on 12 April with his flagship *Trusty*, 50, the 18-gun sloop *Nautilus*, the armed schooner *Hind* and the merchant ship *Hero*, carrying 470 troops under the command of Major-General Cuyler, arriving in Great Courland Bay, Tobago on the 14th. The troops were landed that night and the fort at Scarborough, held by Lieutenant-Colonel Monteil, the commandant of the island, and approximately 200 men, was ordered to sur-

render. This being refused, the British troops stormed the fort at 1am on 15 April, with minimal casualties to themselves (1). As was common in assaults on fortifications, particularly at night, the soldiers of the 9th and 60th regiments attacked with the bayonet alone, to prevent the assault breaking down as men stopped to return the defenders' fire.

A later attempt by Laforey's successor at Barbados, Rear-Admiral Gardner, to take Martinique was a failure. The decision of the French Assembly in 1791 to grant citizenship to the slaves on the French West Indian islands had provoked a state of virtual civil war on many of them, with French colonists declaring for the royalist cause and seeking British help and protection. Gardner arrived with his squadron at Martinique on 14 June 1793, accompanied by a French 74, the *Calypso* and the frigate *Ferme* which had declared for the royalists, and landed 1100 British troops and some 800 royalists, intending to march overland and attack the French forts at St Pierre on the 18th. However, the royalist contingent accidentally fired upon one another during the approach, and fell back to the landing site, forcing the British troops to

do likewise, as they now believed themselves outnumbered by the Republican defenders. By the 21st the whole force had re-embarked, and as many of the Royalist inhabitants of the island as possible were evacuated to spare them from reprisals.

In September, Commodore John Ford's Jamaica squadron, which comprised only his flagship *Europa*, 50, a few 12pdr frigates and some smaller vessels, achieved far greater success at Saint-Domingue. Having been approached by a representative of royalist sympathisers at Jérémie offering terms for the town's capitulation to the British, Ford's squadron arrived on 19 September and was warmly welcomed by the inhabitants of the town. Hearing that the republicans intended to take the fine harbour of St Nicholas Mole (2), Ford proceeded there on the 21st to forestall this. The town, with its strong defences, agreed to the same terms as Jérémie, its inhabitants fearful of the reprisals the republicans and the liberated slaves would take. By the end of the year, other areas of the island had likewise surrendered to the British.

The arrival of Vice-Admiral Sir John Jervis on the

4

Barbados station at the end of January 1794 ushered in a highly active campaign against French possessions in the West Indies. On 2 February 1794, a squadron consisting of Jervis's flagship *Boyne*, 98, two 74s, two 64s, eight frigates, four sloops and the bomb vessel *Vesuvius*, sailed from Bridgetown carrying 7000 soldiers under Lieutenant-General Sir Charles Grey for an attack upon Martinique, arriving off the island three days later.

Landing were made in three locations, to prevent the defenders concentrating their forces, and by 16 March the whole island except for Forts Bourbon and Royal had fallen to the British. Throughout this campaign, sailors from the squadron were highly active on shore, principally in the establishment and manning of batteries of guns and mortars for the attack on the French fortifications, where their ability to get guns into positions thought inaccessible both by the enemy and their military colleagues caused great astonishment. They also took part in the assaults on the various French positions on the island, storming them with boarding pikes and pistols (3).

On 17 March the batteries established by the navy opened fire on the French forts defending the town of Fort Royal, and an attempt was made by the boats of the squadron to cut out the French frigate *Bienvenue*, moored in the harbour. The ship was taken, despite heavy fire from the shore, but could not be sailed out of the harbour and had to be abandoned. However, the success of this attack decided the British to make an immediate attack upon Fort Royal (4), combining a seaborne assault against the town and its principal fortification, Fort Louis, with a land attack against Fort Bourbon. This plan was put into action on 20 March. Illustration (5) shows the boats of the squadron carrying troops with scaling ladders against the town itself. In the lead boats are men from the three battalions of grenadiers in Grey's force. Nearly half of Grey's army was made up of grenadier and light infantry companies taken from their regiments and formed into elite battalions, giving the British a considerable qualitative advantage on land. The landing is being directly supported by fire from the warships, including high-angle mortar fire either from the bomb vessel *Vesuvius* or the batteries established ashore. Meanwhile, Fort Louis was taken by the bold action of Captain Faulknor of the sloop *Zebra*, 14, who brought his small ship right up alongside the fort and then led his ship's company over the side and took it by storm (6, 7). The capture of the fort caused the French governor in Fort Bourbon, General Rochambeau, to ask for terms, and on 22 March the fort capitulated. The capture of Martinique was followed by a similarly-conducted assault on the island of St Lucia, by a detachment of the forces which had taken Fort Royal, which lasted only four days, the French garrison surrendering on 4 April 1794, with no fatalities on the British side.

The next objective was Guadeloupe, where the squadron arrived on 11 April, making landings immediately. The strong fortified position of Fleur d'Epée was

6. 'N. E. View of Fort Louis in the Island of Martinique, 5 Feb–22 Mar 1794', coloured aquatint engraved by Samuel Alken, published by the Reverend C Willyams after his own original, 1 August 1796. *NMM ref PAG8922*

7. 'S.W. View of Forts Bourbon and Louis in the Island of Martinique, 5 Feb–22 Mar 1794', coloured aquatint engraved by Samuel Alken, published by the Reverend C Willyams after his own original, 1 August 1796. *NMM ref PAG8924*

8. 'View of the Bay and Town of St Pierre (Martinique)', coloured aquatint engraved by Samuel Alken, published by the Reverend C Willyams after his own original, 1 August 1796. *NMM ref PAH3023*

9. 'View and Plan of French occupied Guadeloupe', anonymous black and watercolour pen and ink. *NMM ref PAH5035*

5

6

stormed the next day by a mixed force of soldiers and seamen, the naval contingent under the command of Captain Faulknor of the *Zebra*. The rest of the island, including the nearby islands of the Saintes and all other dependencies of Guadeloupe, were surrendered to the British on 20 April 1794. However, on 3 June a French squadron of nine ships arrived and landed troops commanded by Victor Hugues, taking the British very much by surprise. Although many French settlers had initially welcomed British rule, they had been alienated by the eagerness with which the British commanders pursued prize money, threatening to confiscate all property on those islands which had offered resistance and laying claim to all the French shipping in the harbours they had captured. The inhabitants of St Lucia paid an estimated £150,000 in lieu of confiscation of their property, and it was rumoured that the British were to demand £250,000 from Martinique (8). The republican army was able to recapture Fleur d'Epée and the other posts on the island (9).

Jervis had returned to the island in force once the arrival of the French became known, landing a relief force on 22 June. Fighting was indecisive, with the British army badly weakened by sickness, and following a costly failed attack on the town of Pointe á Pitre, British forces were evacuated from Grande Terre on 3 July. Basse-Terre likewise fell to the French in October, although many of the British troops were successfully evacuated. The garrison of St Lucia had also been taken off in the armed storeship *Experiment* on 19 June, having suffered greatly both from disease and the enemy.

Following the surrender of St Nicholas Mole on the southern side of Saint-Domingue in 1793, Commodore Ford of the Jamaica station had offered terms to the French garrison of Port au Prince in February 1794, which were refused. A campaign was launched against the fortifications around the town on 31 May, and on 2 June the important position of Fort Brissoton was taken by assault, and two days later Port au Prince surrendered, leaving the British in control of several principal strongpoints on the island, although many areas were still under French control.

7

8

9

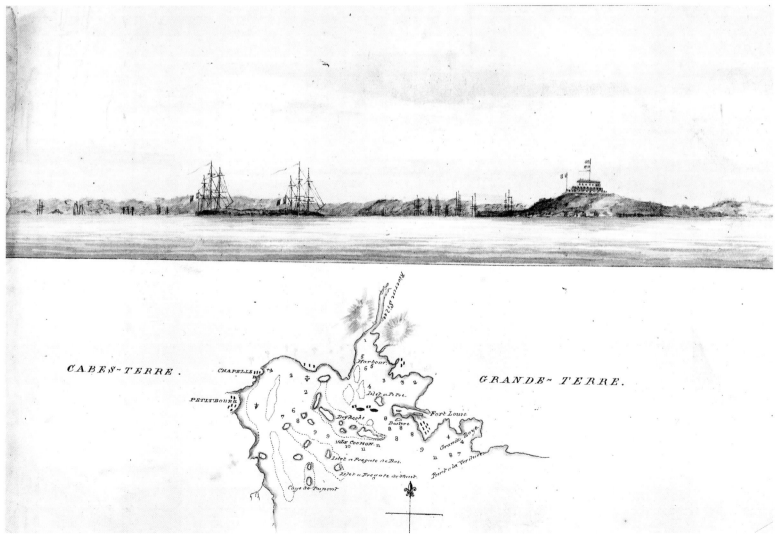

CABES-TERRE.   CHAPELLE   GRANDE-TERRE.

Commerce warfare in the West Indies

THE WEALTH of the West Indies made it a favoured hunting ground for French privateers, which were helped by the maze of tiny islands and narrow passages where large warships could penetrate only at great risk to themselves. The average size of West Indian privateers was quite small and the Royal Navy was always hard put to provide enough small cruisers to combat them. The West Indies merchants were also well organised politically and could lobby for additional protection if they felt especially threatened.

However, this powerful caucus was also a potential source of patronage to indigent artists and printsellers. One such partnership, between William Elmes and John Fairburn, seems to have specialised in West Indian actions, although not to the exclusion of other waters. Elmes employed a crude but vigorous style that made him highly distinctive. His forte seems to have been very small scale actions, some of which—like the packet *Antelope*'s repulse of the privateer *Atalante* (1)—would not merit a mention in most modern histories, but was doubtless of importance to local commerce. It was, in fact, a very gallant action, and was celebrated by better artists than Elmes.

Since his principal concern was drama rather than accuracy, he was quite happy to exaggerate the relative sizes of combatants. The August 1796 encounter between the *Raison* and the *Vengeance* is a case in point (2). Admittedly, the British Sixth Rate measured only 472 tons to her opponent's 1180, but their relative lengths were about 110ft to 160ft, rather than the 2:1 the artist

presents. However, a ship with 9pdrs fighting off one of the largest 18pdr frigates in the French navy was indeed a David-and-Goliath contest, so doubtless the artist felt justified.

Much of the Navy's commerce protection force was made up of brigs, both the larger 16- to 18-gun vessels rated as sloops (entrusted to a Commander), and the smaller gunbrigs (commanded by Lieutenants). During the course of the war they were to become the most numerous type on the Navy List, and although some were involved in notable actions, for the majority life was a mundane round of patrols, with the occasional excitement of a chase (3).

Because warship development, in the eighteenth century as in the twentieth, involved growth, the smallest ships of each rate tended to be the oldest. Small frigates like the 28s, effectively obsolescent by the 1790s, were often sent to the West Indies where they might be useful against French corvettes and the larger privateers. One of Elmes's better compositions is inspired by one of these, the *Lapwing*, 28, which captured the *Décius*, 20, and drove the *Vaillante*, 10, ashore in November 1796 (4).

3

4

1

Capture of the Cape 1795

2

THE FRENCH victory in the Netherlands and the formation of the Batavian Republic as a satellite state of France made it vital for the British to secure the Dutch colony of the Cape of Good Hope (1), so as to safeguard communications with the East Indies. Consequently, an expedition was sent from England, under the command of Vice-Admiral Sir George Keith Elphinstone (2), comprising *Monarch, Victorious* and *Arrogant*, all 74s, the 64-gun ships *America* and *Stately*, and the sloops *Echo* and *Rattlesnake*, both of 16 guns. A detachment of troops from the 78th Regiment of Foot, commanded by Major-General Craig, was also embarked.

The squadron arrived in Simon's Bay, Cape of Good Hope, in early July, and the Dutch governor, General Sluysken, was requested to place the colony under British protection. This was refused, and Sluysken evacuated the population of Simonstown, intending to burn the town, but a mixed force of soldiers and marines landed and took possession of the place before this could be done. The Dutch had taken up positions on heights blocking the way to Capetown, and on 7 August the British advanced against them. Elphinstone had landed a detachment of 1000 sailors, bringing the land forces up to some 1800 men, and had improvised a gunboat and

armed the squadron's boats with carronades to give support to the attack. The Dutch positions were brought under fire from the sea by *America, Stately* and the two sloops, driving the defenders out well before the troops under Craig reached the place, which was finally occupied that afternoon. A Dutch counter-attack on the following day was beaten off, the seamen on shore playing the major part and being praised by Major-General Craig, who likened their performance to that of regular infantry.

On 3 September 1795, the Dutch were about to make a general attack on the British camp, when the arrival of fourteen East Indiamen bringing reinforcements to Craig caused them to call off their offensive. With these new forces, the British decided to move immediately on Capetown, the troops beginning their march on the 14th, whilst the *America*, the two sloops and an East Indiaman sailed to Table Bay (3) as a diversion. At this, the Dutch commander asked for terms, and the colony surrendered on 15 September 1795. Two Dutch East India Company vessels, the *Castor* and the armed brig *Star*, fell into British hands at Capetown, the latter being commissioned into the Royal Navy as the *Hope*.

In February 1796 a small Dutch squadron (4) under

3

Rear-Admiral Englebertus Lucas slipped through the British blockade of the Texel with the intention of recapturing the Cape, and arrived in Saldanha Bay, fifty miles north of Simon's Bay on 3 August. Elphinstone's squadron, now numbering two 74s, five 64s, a 50, two frigates and four sloops, sailed to intercept them. Outnumbered and outgunned, having two 66-gun ships, a 54, four frigates and a sloop, all with under-strength crews, Lucas surrendered without a shot being fired. The Cape remained in British hands until it was returned to the Dutch under the Treaty of Amiens in 1802.

1. 'The Cape of Good Hope. La Cap de bonne Esperance', engraving from an original by Jan Van Ryne, published by Robert Sayer, London, 1754.
NMM ref PAD1919

2. 'Admiral Lord George Keith Elphinstone (1746-1823), 1st Viscount Keith', oil painting by William Owen.
NMM ref BHC2815

3. 'View from the anchorage in Table Bay, Cape of Good Hope. A squadron of ships beating into the bay', watercolour by Lieutenant William Innes Pocock (1783-1836).
NMM ref PAF0076

4. A Dutch Frigate from two angles, shown flying the flag of the Batavian Republic, anonymous watercolour.
NMM ref PAD5485

4

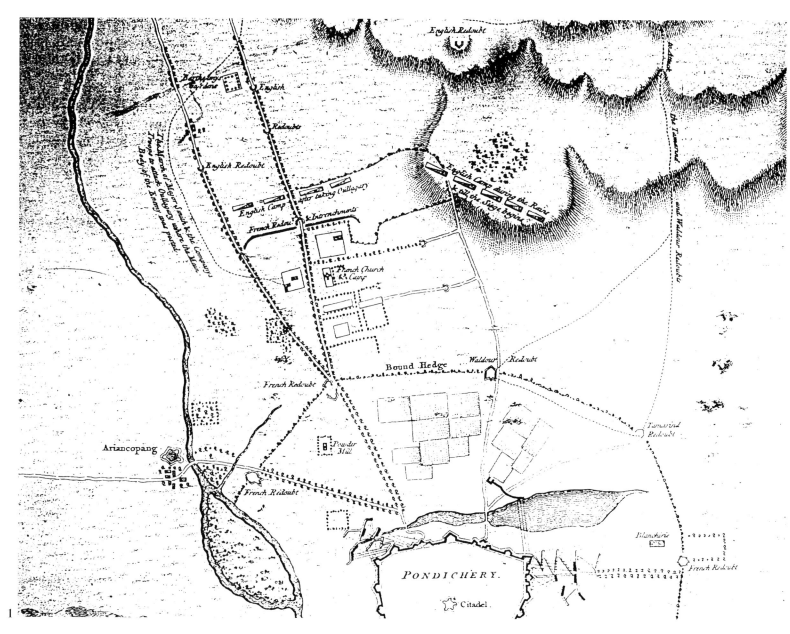

1. 'Pondicherry 15 Jan 1761',
anonymous etching, 1761.
NMM ref PAD5291

2. 'Marine Francais. La Prudente et La
Cybelle (de 36 et de 40) . . . Contre le
Diomede et la Centurion . . . 22
Decembre 1794', coloured lithograph
engraved by Jean Baptiste and Henri
Durand-Breger after their own
original, published by Jeannin and the
Anaglyphic Company, 15 August
1844.
NMM ref PAG8932

3. 'View of the waterfront of
Colombo', anonymous graphite
drawing.
NMM ref PAH2698

4. 'Distant View of Trincomale
Ceylon', coloured aquatint published
by Samuel Daniell after his own
original, 1 March 1807.
NMM ref PAI0224

3

East Indies 1793-1796

ALERTED TO the outbreak of war with France by the British consul in Alexandria in June 1793, British forces in India immediately moved against the French possessions there. The naval commander at Madras was Commodore The Hon William Cornwallis, with the *Crown* of 64 guns and a few frigates and sloops based at or near Calcutta. The majority of the French factories in India fell without resistance, except for the major fortress of Pondicherry (1). The illustration shows the previous siege in 1761, but the defences were reported to be in as good a condition in 1793 as they had been in the Seven Years War, and a formal siege was begun on 1 August, lasting until the 23rd of that month, during which time Cornwallis in the *Minerva*, 38, drove off a small French squadron attempting to get supplies into the town. By the end of 1793, almost all the French possessions in the Indian Ocean had fallen, save for the important exception of Isle de France (Mauritius), where French ships continued to pose a threat to British trade. On 22 October 1794, the British *Centurion*, 50, and *Diomede*, 44, engaged a French squadron off Mauritius, comprising the *Cybèle* of 40 guns, the *Prudente* of 36 guns, *Jean Bart*, 20, and *Courier*, 14 which had sailed to engage the British squadron (2). *Centurion* was badly damaged thanks to the inactivity of the *Diomede*, whose commander, Captain Matthew Smith, was consequently court-martialled and dismissed from the service. The French ships all returned to Mauritius, which remained in French hands until 1810.

In May 1794 a convoy under Commodore Peter Rainier sailed from England with reinforcements for the Madras station, arriving in November after a non-stop voyage, without losing a ship. In June 1795, having been promoted to Rear-Admiral, he began operations against the Dutch possessions in the Indian Ocean. By the end of July all the posts in Ceylon (3) had surrendered, Trincomalee, the major fort (4), having done so on the 26th. A separate squadron had secured Malacca at the same time.

Although the campaign in the East Indies was minor from the point of view of actual fighting, the economic value of the French and Dutch possessions was more important, not least to those responsible for their capture. When Rainier's squadron took the Moluccan islands from the Dutch in February 1796, the five captains present were reported to have each received £15,000 in prize money, an astronomical sum in those days. By 1796 the British were in overall control of the Indian Ocean.

4

1

London—commercial capital of the world

LONDON WAS both capital city and principal port of Great Britain and her empire. It had developed at the lowest convenient bridging point of the River Thames over fifty miles from the sea, and in 1775 its population was growing at a rate that matched that of Britain as a whole. In 1700 it had housed about 575,000 people. By 1750 this figure had risen to 675,000 and by 1801, the year of the first national census, its inhabitants had increased to 900,000. At the beginning of the eighteenth century, the old city walls enclosed about a third of this population; a hundred years later they enclosed less than one-sixth. Urbanisation on the south bank was limited before 1750 by the existence of only one bridge, London Bridge; but that year Westminster Bridge was built, and Blackfriars Bridge in 1769.

The new suburbs were occupied not just by immi-

2

grants from rural southern England, shedding population with economies and innovations in agriculture, but by Scots, Welsh, Irish, Germans, Dutchmen, Frenchmen (especially Huguenots), and Jews, especially from eastern Europe. There was also an increasing number of negroes and Indian lascar seamen, respectively brought back through the slave trade with east Africa and by the East India Company which was always shorthanded on the return voyage from the east. The main thrust of expansion was east along the banks of the Thames to absorb the riverside villages of Wapping and Shadwell on the north bank and Rotherhithe on the south (1). Here the new inhabitants mainly served the river. The only wet docks along these banks were the Brunswick Dock at Blackwall used by the East India Company, and the Greenland Dock at Rotherhithe, dug between 1696 and 1700, and used by the South Sea Company's whalers. Otherwise shipping had to unload their cargoes at twenty Legal Quays, where imports were assessed for customs duty, and twenty-one Suffrance Wharfs, mainly on the southern bank of the river. These wharves were mainly below London Bridge, which blocked upward passage of ships ascending the Thames, so that ships moored predominately in that reach of the river just below the bridge and called the Pool of London (2).

Here ships moored raft-fashion from either bank, with a narrow channel in the middle, their masts forming what seemed a solid forest. Here, after the American War, a survey of the shipping claimed that between May and October each year there were over 400 West Indiamen of 200-500 tons, mainly importing sugar; nearly the same number of timber ships from the Baltic, many discharging their cargoes directly into the river and taking up twelve times their own mooring space; over 300 colliers, discharging coal into barges; and about 50 East Indiamen, most moored below Deptford. In addition there were smaller coasters, and over 3000 barges, lighters, hoys and punts.

Population, shipping and trade brought industry and commerce. Many trades met the luxury consumption demands of the wealthy as well as the basic needs of the middle and lower orders, but the greatest proportion—employing perhaps a quarter of the population—depended on the port. These trades included ship-, boat- and barge-building; and in the 1720s Daniel Defoe noted thirty-three yards for refitting, repairing and building merchant ships. Subsidiary industries like cooperages, breweries, distilleries, sugar-refining also flourished. Many others manufactured for export, especially to the North American colonies, but also to northern, nearby and southern Europe (3). By 1700 London handled no less than 80 per cent of England's imports, 69 per cent of her exports, and 86 per cent of her re-exports; and to convey this trade London owners possessed more than the combined shipping tonnage of the rest of the nation: about 140,000 tons, as opposed to 103,000 tons owned in other ports.

Moreover, London's trade and shipping grew during the eighteenth century. In 1700 its foreign imports were worth £4.8 million; £5.5 million in 1750; and £12.3 million by 1790. London's exports over the same period rose from £5.4 million to £10.7 million. London-owned ship-

3

1. 'The Cities of London and Westminster accurately copied from the table of the Camera Obscura in the Royal Observatory at Greenwich', etching by Tomlinson from an original by Pugh, published by Sherwood, Neely and Jones, 1 March 1809.
NMM ref PAH2187

2. 'The South East Prospect of London From the Tower to London Bridge 1746', coloured engraving and etching by John Bowles from an original by Maurer, published by J Bowles & Son, London, 25 March 1746.
NMM ref PAH2186

3. 'A view of Blackwall and Dock Yard, looking towards Greenwich', etching published by Carington Bowles, London, 2 March 1773.
NMM ref PAD1393

4. 'The Custom House', anonymous etching.
NMM ref PAD1405

ping engaged in foreign trade rose from 157,000 tons in 1705, to 235,000 in 1751, and to 620,000 tons in 1794.

Managing this trade and shipping were the great sixteenth and seventeenth century merchant companies: the East India, South Sea, Africa, Russia, Levant and Hudson Bay companies. During the eighteenth century these great companies were being gradually outgrown by the vast number of independent merchants like those trading to the West Indies, who formed their own looser organisations. All benefited from the existence of trading centres like the Royal Exchange, founded in 1566, and by the development of London's financial market.

Insurance was originally undertaken by merchants meeting brokers and underwriters on the floor of the Royal Exchange or at nearby coffee houses. Insurance companies like the London Assurance, the Westminster, the Hand-in-Hand, and the Sun Fire Office, had all came into existence by 1720; numerous others by 1791, included the Phoenix, Union, Equitable and Amicable. The need for shipping information to calculate risks prompted the owner of Lloyd's coffee house to produce a specialist news sheet. This in 1734 became the still-extant *Lloyd's List*. A record of the opinions of surveyors who examined the hulls and assessed the seaworthiness of ships was also established in 1764 and was known as *Lloyd's Register*. Lloyd's insurance company subsequently came to dominate all others in the field of marine insurance.

London's goldsmith bankers had been the mainstay of the government in the mid-seventeenth century.

However small private banking companies like Child's, Stone's, Hoare's, and Martin's were all in existence by the end of the century, above thirty-five separate private banking concerns by 1760, with fifty-six by 1789. By then these banks were extending their services outside London, acting as agents both for individual clients and for country banks, of which there were 150 by 1776 and 280 by 1790. Operations became more fluid after the foundation of a central clearing house in Lombard Street in 1775.

These private banks were already under the central influence of the Bank of England, founded by a group of London merchants in 1694. This bank's main functions were to issue notes and to discount Exchequer and Navy bills issued by the government's Treasury. It also acted as the guardian of the Consolidated Fund and other balances deposited by the government; and of the reserves accumulated by the London and country bankers. These deposits permitted the Bank of England to lend at interest, and to discount commercial bills on behalf of British and overseas merchants.

Such was the capital accumulated by the Bank of England in the late eighteenth century, and such was the strength and stability of the London financial market, that investors in government stocks and bonds were attracted from other European countries, including France, Holland and Switzerland. Loans too were made on an international scale, some indeed to foreign nationals with whom Britain went to war. For London by 1793 had become the financial capital of Europe.

4

The West Indies 1795-1797

THROUGHOUT 1795 and 1796 fighting continued between British forces on West Indian islands and the French and their supporters among the local populations. In early January 1795 the British frigate *Blanche* of 32 guns, commanded by Captain Robert Faulknor, was operating off Guadeloupe, which had been retaken by the French the previous year. Faulknor found the 36-gun French frigate *Pique* in the harbour of Point à Pitre, and after a few days of indecisive manoeuvring, succeeded in luring the French ship out from under the cover of the shore batteries by taking a captured American schooner in tow and setting sail for Dominica on the evening of 4 January. When the *Pique* was seen to be pursuing, the *Blanche* cut the schooner free and turned to attack her.

The ships were closely engaged, broadside to broadside, for two and a half hours until, at 2.30am on the 5th, the *Blanche* surged ahead of the *Pique* in an attempt to turn and rake her bows. But at that moment her main and mizzen masts fell and the *Pique* collided with her (1). Whilst trying to lash the two ships together, Captain Faulknor was killed by a sharpshooter (2). A second attempt was successful, and the *Blanche* effectively took the *Pique* in tow. But fire from French sharpshooters and the ship's deck guns continued, to which the *Blanche* could make little effective reply, as she lacked any stern gunports. These were, however, rapidly improvised by

3

4

5

simply firing two 12pdrs through the stern-frame. Fire from these guns brought down the *Pique*'s main mast (3) and at 5.15am the ship surrendered, having lost all her masts. Out of a crew of 279 men, the *Pique* had lost 76 killed and 110 wounded. The *Blanche*, on the other hand, lost only 8 killed and 21 wounded. This wide disparity in casualties was to increasingly become the norm in such engagements as the war continued. The *Pique* was towed to the Saintes, and later commissioned into the Royal Navy.

The French made numerous attempts to reinforce their islands, and on 10 October 1795 the British frigate *Mermaid* of 32 guns captured the French *Brutus* of 10 guns (4), and four days later the 18-gun *Républicaine*, intercepting troops on their way to Grenada.

On 9 December 1795 a large convoy of transports, accompanied by seven warships commanded by Rear-Admiral Sir Hugh Cloberry Christian, had set sail for the West Indies to recapture the islands lost the previous year, but bad weather drove the fleet back to Spithead (5), where it was forced to remain until 20 March 1796, not arriving at Barbados until 21 April. The first task undertaken was the recapture of St Lucia, an attack which proceeded along standard lines, and French forces capitulated on 24 May. The expedition then moved on to take St Vincent, which fell on 11 June, and Grenada which surrendered a few days later.

Campaigning on Saint-Domingue continued with an attack on the French positions at Léogane (6), a combined operation between ships from the Jamaica station and troops marching overland from Port au Prince under the command of Major-General Forbes. A landing was made on 21 March 1796, but the place proved stronger than expected and following heavy damage to the masts and rigging of *Leviathan*, 74, and *Africa*, 64, by the guns on shore, the attack was abandoned. Despite the strength of British forces in the West Indies, and the blockade of the French ports in European waters, the French were still able to send two squadrons in early 1796 with reinforcements for their garrisons on Saint-Domingue, both of which delivered their cargoes and returned safely to France.

An attempt by the French to land troops on the island of Anguilla in November 1796 was frustrated by the frigate *Lapwing*, 28, commanded by Captain Richard Bowen (7). His arrival on 26 November caused the immediate re-embarkation of the French forces aboard the *Décius*, 20, and *Vaillante*, 10. *Décius* was captured by *Lapwing* after an hour's fighting, and *Vaillante* was destroyed by the frigate's guns after running ashore.

In February 1797, a squadron under the command of Rear-Admiral Henry Harvey, carrying troops under Lieutenant-General Sir Ralph Abercromby, sailed from Martinique to attack the Spanish island of Trinidad, where on 16 February they discovered four Spanish ships of the line, the *San Vincente* of 80 guns, the three 74s

1. 'Action between HMS Blanche and the Pique, 5 January 1795', oil painting by John Thomas Baines, February 1830.
NMM ref BHC0478

2. 'The Death of Captain Faulknor', engraving by J Rogers, from an original by Thomas Stothard, published by the London Printing and Publishing Company.
NMM ref PAD5485

3. 'La Blanch towing La Pique, a French prize, 1795', watercolour by Robert Dodd.
NMM ref PAF5856

4. 'His Majesty's Ship Mermaid on the 10th of Octr 1795, at Requin ... Grenada, run aground in Chase of the French Corvette Brutus ... to prevent the landing of ammunition', aquatint and etching by Robert Pollard from an original by Nicholas Pocock, printed and published by William Faden, 12 February 1798.
NMM ref PAH7889

5. 'Admiral Christian and Convoy on their Voyage to the West Indies ... from Portsmouth on the 9th of December 1795 ... tossed about the Channel for near Six Weeks were driven back by ... Stormy Weather', mezzotint published by Robert Pollard, 21 April 1796.
NMM ref PAH7891

6. 'Vue de La Rade de Leogane, Isle St Dominique' engraving and etching by Nicolas Ponce from an original by N Ozanne, 1795.
NMM ref PAH3000

7. 'Capture of Le Desius Novr 25th 1796. Captured French Decius (20) and drove the Vaillante (20) ashore at Anguilla. Next Day Lapwing was chased and Barton was Compelled to Burn Her', coloured aquatint engraved by Thomas Sutherland from an original by Thomas Whitcombe, published for J Jenkin's *Naval Achievements*, 1 September 1816.
NMM ref PAD5513

8. 'The capture of Trinidad, 17 February 1797', oil painting by Nicholas Pocock, 1800.
NMM ref BHC0494

9. Sheer draught of *San Damaso* as captured, dated Portsmouth Dockyard 29 March 1798. Admiralty Collection.
NMM neg 928

6

7

8

Gallardo, Arrogante and *San Damaso,* and the 34-gun frigate *Santa Cecilia,* in Shaggaramus Bay, defended by a battery mounting twenty guns and two mortars. Given the apparent strength of the enemy, Hervey sent his transports to find a berth some distance away, and anchored his four ships of the line in gun range of the Spanish ships and batteries, preparing to attack them the next day. But on the night of the 16th the Spanish set fire to their ships (8), only the *San Damaso* surviving to be taken by the British (9), since they had less than half the number of men available needed to man them. Troops took possession of the battery, and on the 17th a landing was made near Port of Spain, which surrendered peacefully and the next day the whole island capitulated. The squadron then moved on to attack Puerto Rico, arriving there on 17 April, but San Juan was found to be well-fortified and actively defended by gunboats, and the attempt was abandoned on 30 April.

9

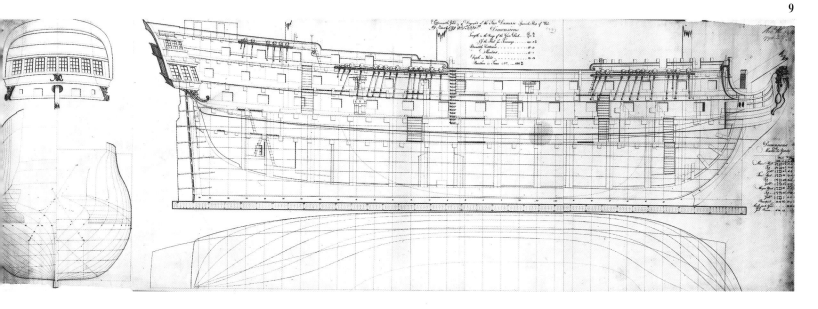

The cruise of a frigate

AMONG THE many sketchbooks at Greenwich which appear to be the work of serving officers is one by a Lieutenant Edward Bamfylde Eagles of the Royal Marines. Although he seems to have served after the Napoleonic Wars, his sketchbook depicts scenes of warfare against the French which can only refer to that period. Whether or not he had personal experience of these events, they amount to a lively representation of the kind of everyday incidents that are rarely the subject of more formal art. The books themselves have no sense of sequence, but it is possible to arrange the drawings to form a fictional, but in many ways typical, cruise of a frigate in wartime.

The story begins with the ship lying at anchor, boat streamed astern, in light airs—perfect weather to loose the 'small sails' (staysails and other fore-and-aft canvas) to dry. If this were truly a postwar ship, one would expect gaff-headed spencers between the masts, rather than staysails, which tended to be replaced after 1815 (1). With the wind getting up, the frigate decides to shift her berth, setting fore and mizzen topsails; the boat is probably carrying out a kedge anchor (2).

Having received orders to sail, the ship flies the Blue Peter from the fore truck, and with topsails backing and filling, weighs anchor; the cable is 'up and down' and the crew preparing to fish and cat the anchor are visible on the forecastle (3). In this case, the harbour was Portsmouth and the frigate leaves in fine style, under all plain sail to skysails (4). First duty on patrol is to check the identity of all vessels encountered, and having been challenged by the frigate, this British merchant brig responds with her number, a two-flag signal from the foremast (5); even today, some people describe intro-

4

ducing themselves as 'making my number'. Many of a frigate's duties are similarly humdrum, but none is so frustrating as convoy escorting. Seen here bringing a convoy out of St John, Newfoundland (6), the officers of the frigate will have been driven mad by their wayward charges long before they reach the other side of the Atlantic. Relations between the merchant service and the Royal Navy have always been ambiguous, and many a merchant skipper chafed under the discipline of convoy—the logs of ships on escort duty are replete with references to firing shots across the bows of their charges to bring them into line, literally as well as figuratively.

However, the appeal of a frigate to both officers and men was the chance for independent action and the consequent prospect of prize money. It is surprising how often during the course of the Napoleonic War that frigates of comparable force met in single combat, but as the war went on the British were increasingly compelled to force action on a reluctant enemy: here (7) it involves a chase in heavy weather carrying all plain sail, which is only resolved by the French frigate losing her main topmast. Having struck her colours in token of surrender the chase heaves to (8); a small prize crew will then be put on board to sail the ship to a friendly port, so the victor removes part of the complement of the defeated ship to reduce the chance of the prisoners rising and retaking the ship (9) .

For the victorious frigate, her greatest moment of glory comes as she leads her prize into harbour, with the Union flag over the French tricolour (10). Similar scenes were enacted hundreds of times during the war, but for those involved it never lost its savour.

5

6

7

8

9

1-10. Black pen and ink drawings from a sketchbook by Lieutenant Edward Bamfylde Eagles, dated to *c*1840 but clearly depicting events, real or imaginary, of the Napoleonic War.

1. 'Light airs and clear. Small sails loos'd to dry'.
NMM ref PAF2618

2. 'Moderate Breezes, Frigate shifting her Berth'.
NMM ref PAF2604

3. 'Blue Peter up, getting under weigh'.
NMM ref PAF2665

4. 'Frigate leaving Portsmouth Harbour'.
NMM ref PAF2631

5. 'Brig showing her number to the ship under the land'.
NMM ref PAF2634

6. 'Outside view of St John's Newfoundland. Frigate coming out with a Convoy'.
NMM ref PAF2613

7. 'The Enemy's Main Topmast going over the side'.
NMM ref PAF2582

8. 'The Chase just struck'.
NMM ref PAF2598

9. 'Taking the Prisoners out of the Prize'.
NMM ref PAF2668

10. 'Frigate going into Harbour with her Prize under Jury Masts'.
NMM ref PAF2637

10

Part III

MEDITERRANEAN THEATRE

1793–1797

THE ROYAL Navy squadron which had been assembled in the Mediterranean in the spring of 1793 under the command of Vice-Admiral Lord Hood was made up of two First Rates of 100-guns, *Victory* and *Britannia*, three 98s, twelve 74s and four 64s. Facing them at Toulon under the temporary command of Rear-Admiral the Comte de Trogoff were seventeen ships of the line ready for sea, including the 120-gun *Commerce de Marseilles*. Another four were refitting, and nine repairing. Co-operating with the British fleet was a Spanish squadron operating out of Minorca under the command of Admiral Langara. The prospect of an Hispano-British fleet engaging the French Toulon fleet, however, was short-lived.

The Jacobins had obtained control of the Toulon municipality in November 1790, but the excesses throughout France following the execution of the king led to their overthrow in Toulon in July 1793. When the government in Paris sent an army to restore its control in Provence, the Toulonese, out of desperation, invited Hood to occupy the port. He stipulated that they must make a declaration in support of the the Dauphin. The crews of the French fleet were at first determined to resist the British, but in the end large numbers of them deserted so as to avoid a civil war with the people of Toulon.

Hood landed two regiments of British infantry and 200 marines, and a Spanish army was rushed across the frontier to provide its landward defence. Captain Horatio Nelson, in command of *Agamemnon* 64, and Sir William Hamilton the British Minister at the Court of Naples, persuaded King Ferdinand to send another by sea. Small contingents were also sent by the Piedmontese and the Sardinians. Command of the troops was given to the Spanish Rear-Admiral Don Federico Gravina. The French fleet moved into the inner harbour and landed its gunpowder. About 5000 of their crews were put onboard four disarmed and

unserviceable 74s, and sailed under passport to the Atlantic ports before the arrival of the army of the Republic under General Carteau and General Lapoype. On their arrival at Brest and Rochefort, the sailors found that were regarded as deserters for not having defended their ships.

Nelson had acquired a poor opinion of Spanish naval manpower when he visited Cadiz on his way to the Mediterranean, which is not surprising considering that the Spanish mercantile marine was so small that only about 10 per cent of the muster role of Spanish warships could be filled with experienced seamen. More surprisingly, the Spanish army proved to be no more capable. Professional and national jealousies impeded the defence. When Gravina was wounded, a Spanish lieutenant-general, Valdez, asserted his own claim to be placed in command of all the allied troops. To support him, Langara moved his three-decker flagship into a position broadside on to *Victory* with two other three-deckers on her bow and quarter. Hood, however, resisted this attempted intimidation.

After winning a desperate fight for control of the high ground overlooking Toulon harbour, the French army used its artillery, under the command of the young General Napoleon Bonaparte, to overcome the fire from *Princess Royal*, 98, a Spanish 74, and two floating batteries. On 14 December the defences on the landward side were driven in. Toulon was taken, thousands of the leading citizens being guillotined.

Before Toulon was evacuated, British and Spanish incendiary parties commanded by Sir Sidney Smith were sent to destroy the arsenal and the ships in the harbour, but he was unable to burn more than ten of the Toulon fleet. Langara later admitted that he had ensured the Spanish contingent did not play its part, because he did not want Britain to acquire too disproportionate a naval strength. Hood, however, was able to get fifteen French ships out of

Toulon before the fall. This number included the *Commerce de Marseilles* of 120 guns and *Pompée* of 74, both of which were found to be exceptional ships, although the *Commerce* proved to be too structurally weak for service in the British fleet. She was converted into a store ship, but was strained so badly during the storm which forced Rear-Admiral Christian to put back from his relief of the West Indies in November 1795 that her enormous cargo was unloaded and she never put out of harbour again. Hood also took with him an *Ingénieur de Marine*, Jean Louis Barrallier, who was to be appointed Assistant Surveyor of the Navy in 1796. In that office he was able to bring French scientific study of ship design to the service of the Navy Board, but the opinion of British shipwrights was that he was so absorbed in theory that he was inefficient.

Soon after the Mediterranean Squadron was driven from Toulon, Captain Samuel Hood returned from a cruise in the frigate *Juno* late at night and brought her right into the inner harbour, where she took the ground. A kedge anchor was put out, and succeeded in hauling her clear, but when the port authorities came out to the ship it gradually dawned on the ship's company that they were prisoners of war. The wind just made possible a course for the harbour entrance, however, so the French officials were disarmed and hustled below. Through a cross-fire from the batteries around the outer harbour, *Juno* was taken back out to sea.

A less happy conclusion occurred when *Ardent*, 64, was on a patrol. She did not return and a large piece of her quarterdeck was discovered floating in the sea, making all too clear that she had blown up, killing all hands.

While still in occupation of Toulon, Hood had sent a small squadron made up of three ships and two frigates under Commodore Robert Linzee to attempt to persuade the French garrisons on Corsica to declare for the royalists. He did not have any success in that, but he did succeed in gaining possession for a short time of a round gun tower near Cape Mortella guarding San Fiorenzo Bay. The design was so greatly admired that it became the basis for similar defensive works along the south coast of England, and guarding colonial harbours. Corsica had only been incorporated into France in 1768 in the teeth of strong local opposition led by General Paoli, who again sought British assistance to establish an independent government. When the fleet was forced to leave Toulon, Hood moved to Hyères Bay on the Riviera, but when on 24 January 1794 officers he had sent to communicate with Paoli returned with encouraging reports, it was decided to return to San Fiorenzo Bay.

The tower at Mortella had to be retaken, and its three guns beat off the bombardment made by *Juno* and *Fortitude*, damaging the latter considerably. It was only when guns established ashore employed red-hot shot to set the bass-wood backing for the parapet alight that the garrison asked for terms. A redoubt at Fornelli was then attacked by a battery of 18pdrs hauled by the sailors straight up the side of a cliff. With the anchorage secure, Hood moved on to lay siege to Bastia, using only sailors and marines, and with Paoli's irregulars in support. It capitulated 21 May, and a

Corsican Corte voted to separate from France and accept a British viceroy, Sir Gilbert Elliott. On 10 August Calvi was taken after another difficult siege during which Nelson received the wound which cost him the sight of his right eye.

Control of the Mediterranean was vital to the efforts of the Austrians, Spaniards, and Neapolitans to co-ordinate their military efforts against the French revolutionaries. The remaining ships of the Toulon fleet were as short of supplies as were those at Brest, and as poorly manned, but Jeanbon Saint-Andre energetically set to work restoring order. Rear-Admiral Pierre Martin was put in command with orders to clear the way for a military force to reconquer Corsica, but he felt entirely inadequate to the task: it had been only two years since he had received his commission as lieutenant. When Saint-André returned to Paris, however, Deputy Letourneur was left to stiffen Martin's resolve. Command was divided between them. The opportunity to destroy this incapable force, however, was twice

missed by the Mediterranean squadron.

Hood was succeeded in command of the British squadron in the Mediterranean by Vice-Admiral William Hotham, who proved to be unsuited to the task of command-in-chief. He ran into the Toulon squadron in March 1795 when on both sides together over a thousand men were killed or wounded in a passing action, and again in July. Both times he failed to make the most of his advantage, being glad enough to make no major mistake.

This relative failure was to be an important contributing factor to the defeat of the Austrian army on the Riviera. Nelson had been detached on 4 July with a small squadron consisting of his *Agamemnon*, a small frigate, a sloop and a cutter, to attack French shipping to the westward of Genoa. He had some little success, and was sent back again with more force in August, and was in action in the Gulf of Genoa again the following March, but, with the threat from Toulon unresolved, Hotham could not detach enough of his ships to stop French traffic altogether.

Spanish fleet in Leghorn Roads to receive the Infante 29 April 1794. Engraving by G Bougean, 1797. During the few years in which the Spanish operated alongside the British, their allies formed no great opinion of the level of Spanish training and skill (the French had harboured a similar view during the previous war) and this was to be confirmed at the Battle of Cape St Vincent after the Spanish changed sides. NMM ref PAI0060

The only bright side from the British point of view was the spirited part played by Nelson in attacking an 80-gun ship, *Ça Ira* during the March encounter. He was forced by *Ça Ira*'s effective use of stern chasers to open fire earlier than he wished, but thereafter he kept *Agamemnon* weaving across the stern of his enemy so that he could repeatedly rake her, and suffer no damage himself.

At a quarter before eleven A.M., being within one hundred yards of the *Ça Ira*'s stern, I ordered the helm to be put a-star-board, and the driver and after-sails to be braced up and shivered, and as the Ship fell off, gave her our whole broadside, each gun double-shotted. Scarcely a shot appeared to miss. The instant all were fired, braced up our after-yards, put the helm a-port, and stood after her again. This manoeuvre we practiced till one P.M., never allowing the *Ça Ira* to get a single gun from either side to fire on us.[1]

The poor seamanship, poor gunnery, and generally poor equipment of the French fleet told, and eventually Nelson was on hand to take

possession of the prize. The *Censeur* had also struck, to be retaken in October when Rear-Admiral Richery attacked the Smyrna convoy, but against that had to be set the capture of *Berwick* of 74 guns by the French before the action. She had been dismasted and was struggling under jury rig to rejoin the Mediterranean squadron when she was caught. The losses on both sides became even when the *Illustrious*, 74 guns, ran ashore after breaking her tow following the battle.

In the June encounter, Martin had had no choice but to flee from superior numbers and vastly more capable officers. His last five ships became engaged by the leading British units, and one of them, *Alcide* of 74 guns, was set on fire and blew up. Hotham, however, recalled his fleet just as they were getting in amongst the enemy.

The arrival of Admiral Sir John Jervis to take command in December 1795 produced a dramatic change in the efficiency of the Mediterranean squadron. His standards of discipline and drill, his care for the health of his men, his own obedience to duty, and his honesty, were unparalleled. Toulon was to be closely blockaded for 150 days the following

summer. Nevertheless, he could not arrest the progress of French arms because its own leadership had been transformed.

Napoleon had been arrested when Maximilien Robespierre fell from power, because he had been employed by his brother Augustin as military planner for the Army of Italy, but he was saved from the guillotine by Deputy Saliceti who was a fellow Corsican. Still under a shadow, he was in Paris when in October 1795 he secured his position by turning his guns on the Paris mob which reactionaries were trying to use against the corrupt bourgeois Directory to force a return to constitutional government. Napoleon's 'whiff of grapeshot' put an end to its political power. As a reward, he was appointed in March 1796 to command the Army of Italy, to which he brought a new spirit.

A starving rabble were inspired with confidence in its ability and with the hope for plunder. Nice was captured, the Austrian army was defeated at Millesimo on 13 April 1796, and the Piedmontese at Mondovi on 22 April. Having studied the failure of Maréchal de Maillebois's 1745-46 campaign on the Riviera, when a British squadron cut the supply route along the Corniche road, Napoleon combined the use of coastal batteries to protect the road, and parallel supply routes through the mountains, to ensure that his conquest of northern Italy

Vue de Bastia Isle de Corse', black and gouache pen and ink by Zacherie Felix Doumet, c1794. The short-lived capture of Corsica inspired a number of illustrations of the island itself as well as the events of the campaign.   NMM ref PAH8378

would not be thwarted. King Victor Amadeus was forced to conclude a separate peace with France, Nice and Savoy being ceded to the French Republic. Napoleon then pursued the Austrians and defeated them at Lodi on 10 May. He entered Milan on 15 May 1796 and the King of Naples, the Pope and the Dukes of Parma and Modena paid heavy prices for a truce.

A break from the operations in support of the Austrian army occurred in March 1796 when Vice-Admiral Waldegrave had to be detached from the Mediterranean Squadron and sent with *Barfleur,* 98 guns, and four 74s to Tunis where *Nemesis,* a 28-gun British frigate, had been taken as a French prize. Under the guns of the force, sailors in the ships' launches cut her out, and also took one of her captors, a ship-corvette called the *Sardine.*

In May 1796 Napoleon moved south from Milan, laid siege to Mantua, and forced the Duke of Tuscany to make peace. French soldiers entered the port of Leghorn on 25 June, closing it to the British Mediterranean squadron, and cutting them off from their principal source of supply. Corsica itself was threatened. Jervis maintained a close blockade of Leghorn, based on Porto Ferrajo in Elba which Nelson, whom Jervis had appointed a commodore, occupied in July. He succeeded in keeping Napoleon from passing soldiers to Corsica until mid-October, but the situation was precarious.

In July 1795 Spain had been forced to conclude peace with France, and in August 1796, by the Treaty of San Ildefonso, the imbecile Charles IV was committed to war against Britain and Portugal. This was finally precipitated in October after Pitt sanctioned an ill-conceived attempt to seize the homecoming Spanish treasure ships. The Spanish fleet, although woefully badly manned, was large enough to make the danger of it cooperating with the Toulon fleet a serious threat to Jervis's command. Worse, the Queen of Naples, Maria Carolina, warned that a plan had been developed to use the combined naval strength of France, Spain and the Netherlands to make possible the invasion of the British Isles.

Admiral Langara sailed from Cadiz with nineteen sail of the line and ten frigates, brushing aside Rear-Admiral Man's division which Jervis had posted to watch Cadiz, and passed into the Mediterranean. Langara collected the seven ships at Cartagena and cruised as far as Cape Corso. He did not attack the British lying in San Fiorenzo Bay, but proceeded to Toulon, where the combined Franco-Spanish fleet, totalling thirty-eight ships of the line, heavily outnumbered the Mediterranean squadron which had lost a third of its strength when Man fled precipitantly back to the Channel.

The threat in home waters, and the impossible odds against Jervis in the Mediterranean, necessitated a change of operational focus for the Mediterranean squadron from the Gulf of Lyons to Cadiz. It was also known that francophile Corsicans were preparing to rise against the British. Orders were sent from London to evacuate Corsica, but on 19 October, before they could be carried out, General Casalti managed to get the first part of the French invasion force out of Leghorn. A small division of soldiers were landed, and reached Bastia two days later with a large body of Corsican supporters. As a Briton who was present in Bastia remarked: 'when they found that the English intended to evacuate the island,' the Corsicans 'naturally and necessarily sent to make their peace with the French.'[2] The British garrison and viceroy were withdrawn from Corsica, and taken to Elba.

Jervis sailed to Gibraltar, and there, in a heavy gale, *Courageux* was wrecked and four other ships were damaged. Four others were grounded in the Tagus, where Jervis had gone to provide the Portuguese with moral support, and two others were damaged after he sailed to take up his station at Cape St Vincent. This reduced his force to ten ships of the line, but the Admiralty was able to reinforce him with another five under Rear-Admiral Sir William Parker when winter weather put an end to any immediate threat to Ireland.

Without British naval support, Naples had no choice but to seek peace with France, and in April 1797 Austria came to terms. Napoleon then occupied Venice, which was ceded to Austria as part of the Treaty of Campo Formio in October.

Nelson had been sent back in a frigate from Gibraltar to withdraw the garrison at Elba, and at the end of January 1797 he steered for the rendezvous off Cape St Vincent. West of Gibraltar, in the dark, he sailed right through the Spanish fleet which had sailed from Cartagena to escort home an immensely valuable convoy of four ships laded with mercury for refining silver from the mines of Peru. He reported to Jervis in the morning, rehoisted his flag in *Captain* of 74 guns, and was on hand to take a dramatic and important part in the action which took place on St Valentines's Day.

When the fleet, now commanded by Admiral Don José de Cordova, appeared out of the mist the next morning, it greatly outnumbered the British. It was in poor order, however, and there was a wide gap between the convoy with its close escort and the twenty or twenty-one ships of the main force. Jervis had kept his squadron in close formation during the night, in a double column, but he now ordered it to 'form the line of battle ahead and astern as most convenient' to prevent delays while slower ships tried to reach their proper position in the formal order of battle, and signalled: 'The admiral means to pass through the enemy's line.' His purpose was to give the Spaniards no time to reform their line. Cordova, however, took the chance and, in order to retain the weather gage, ordered his fleet to form line 'as convenient' on the larboard tack. In foggy weather, this movement, which required captains with badly-manned ships to tack while forming up, only completed Spanish disorganisation.

Jervis had once declared, 'Lord Hawke when he ran out of the line [at the Battle of Toulon] and took the *Poder* sickened me of tactics.' His consummate qualities as an admiral, however, included a strong grasp of tactical possibilities. When he had taken over command of the Mediterranean squadron he had issued an additional instruction to the standing Fighting Instructions which indicated that, in the event of the enemy succeeding in gaining the weather gage, the fleet was to decrease sail, form into a strong body, and force through the enemy line from leeward. It was then to tack and engage those enemy ships cut off from their centre and rear, and to prevent their reuniting. Meanwhile, the British centre and rear would engage the enemy centre and rear, doing

1. 'Transactions on Board His Majesty's Ship *Agamemnon,* and of the Fleet, as seen and known by Captain Nelson', Sir Nicholas Harry Nicolas, *Dispatches and Letters of Vice-Admiral Lord Viscount Nelson,* 7 vols, London, 1846, Vol 2 pp10-15.

2. James, Vol 1 p447.

everything possible to prevent them from reuniting with their van. This proved to be a remarkable anticipation of what actually happened off Cape St Vincent. This idea may have owed something to the work of John Clerk of Eldin who had published the first part of his *An Essay on Naval Tactics* in 1790. The full edition was not to be published until 1797, but the manuscript had previously been circulated amongst 'his friends'. Clerk had written that if a large fleet advancing in thick weather in an irregular line abreast with the wind abeam should run into a smaller fleet coming the other way in rough line ahead, the admiral of the latter could hardly do better than proceed on his course to split the larger fleet.

Captain Cuthbert Collingwood, who commanded the *Excellent*, wrote that

> The truth is, we did not proceed on any system of tacticks. In the beginning we were formed very close and pushed at them without knowing, through the thickness of the haze, with what part of the line we could fall in. When they were divided, & the lesser part driven to leeward, the Admiral wisely abandoned them, made the signal to tack, and afterwards stuck to the larger division of the fleet, which was to windward, and could not be joined by their lee division in a short time. After this we had neither order nor signals, for the Admiral was so satisfied with the impetuosity of the attack made by the ships ahead of him that he let us alone.[3]

Collingwood, however, was confusing manoeuvre with tactics. Jervis's intention was to disorganise the Spaniards by the immediacy of the attack, and to make most use of his own fleet's seamanship and gunnery.

The action which followed makes it evident that Jervis's discipline and training had created a highly effective force. Captain Thomas Troubridge in *Culloden* led the line which opened fire in passing the disordered Spanish fleet. Jervis then signalled it to tack so as to come on the same course when overwhelming fire could be brought against the Spanish rear. So familiar was Troubridge with Jervis's intentions that he had his acknowledgment at the masthead, stopped and ready, before the signal was made to tack. He brought his ship around

on the instant, and engaged the Spanish line with his port guns.

Cordova responded by ordering his fleet to tack. There was some danger that the Spanish van would be able to join the convoy escort passing across the British rear. To forestall this, Nelson wore the *Captain* out of line, passed back through it, and attacked the Spanish van. This, placed his ship in extreme danger, confronted by seven Spanish ships, three of which were of 100 guns, and a fourth the only four-decker in the world, the 130-gun *Santisima Trinidad*. Jervis immediately signalled Collingwood, last in the line, to leave his station and tack into Nelson's wake to provide support, and soon Nelson was also supported by the British van coming down along the Spanish line. St Vincent's flag captain, Sir Robert Calder, later remarked that Nelson's breaking the line was unauthorised, to which Jervis responded: 'It certainly was so…and if ever you commit such a breach of your orders, I will forgive you also.'[4] Had the Spanish fleet been as well-trained and manned as was the British, Nelson's action would have been suicidal. But as it was, his prompt response to a tactical requirement was a nicely judged stroke.

Only four Spanish ships were captured, but the evident capacity of Jervis's command, and his victory against such apparent odds, discouraged the Franco-Spanish forces at Brest from seeking action in the Channel. The British public regained its confidence, and the ministry was saved from political defeat. Jervis was elevated to the peerage as Earl St Vincent, as much for the training he had given his command as for his victory. Nelson, whose promotion to Rear-Admiral was already confirmed, was at his request made a Knight of the Bath. Cordova was dismissed from the Spanish navy, and forbidden to appear at court.

The mutinies at Spithead and the Nore in April and May tested St Vincent's capacity as a commander to the limit. The news travelled fast, by letters and by the deployment of ships to join the Mediterranean squadron. His response was to keep up his unremitting attention to the welfare of the men, and to visit any manifestation of insubordination with court-martial and prompt execution. The introduction of lemon juice into the sailors' diet for the first time and despite the expense proved to be of fundamental importance. Scurvy, the curse

of blockading squadrons, was eliminated. British society was spared the horrors of revolution by isolating and outwitting sailors attempting to alter their condition.

St Vincent knew that the boredom of unremitting blockade was too dangerous for him to permit. Nelson was put in command of the inshore squadron watching Cadiz and he distinguished himself in a night boat action. Three times his coxswain saved his life, once interposing his hand to ward off a sword blow aimed at Nelson. His motive for a flag officer risking his life in this way was to support St. Vincent's disciplinary efforts with a demonstrable willingness to share his men's hardships and dangers. Nelson was a man who always led from the front, and his men responded accordingly. On 11 July he wrote home 'Our Mutinies are I hope stopped here, the Admiral having made some severe examples, but they were absolutely necessary.'[5] His own part had also been important.

As a reward, St Vincent gave Nelson command of a detachment sent a few weeks later to capture Spanish merchant shipping in the harbour of Santa Cruz de Tenerife. His determination that all odds must be overcome led him to persevere even when it was discovered that the Spanish garrison and island militia were far more capable than had been anticipated. He later wrote that he 'never expected to return.'[6] He burnt all the letters from his wife before going ashore from *Theseus*. The operation was a disaster. The defenders included thousands of militia, their morale high and their arms effective. Troubridge tried to bluff the Spaniards into surrender by threatening to burn the town, but in the end was only able to negotiate an honourable withdrawal after promising to cease to attack the Canaries. Nelson lost his right arm, and almost lost his life.

3. To Carlyle, 3 June 1797, Edward Hughes, ed, *The Private Correspondence of Admiral Lord Collingwood*, Navy Records Society, Vol 98, London, 1957, 42 p83.

4. J S Tucker, *Memoirs of Admiral the Rt Hon the Earl of St Vincent*, 2 vols, London, 1844, p262n.

5. Nelson to his wife, 11 July 1797, George P B Naish, *Nelson's Letters to His Wife and other Documents 1785-1831*, Navy Records Society, 1958, No 192 p330.

6. 24 July 1794, Anne Fremantle, *The Wynne Diaries 1789-1820*, Oxford: Oxford University Press, 1982, p278; and Nelson to Sir Andrew Hamond, 8 September 1797, Naish, *Nelson's Letters to His Wife*, p280.

The naval officer: duties and privileges

IN THE latter half of the eighteenth century there were three types of naval officer serving at sea in the Royal Navy: commissioned, warrant and petty officers.

The commissioned officers held authority from the Crown and received their commissions from the Board of Admiralty. They included admirals, captains and lieutenants. Admirals were divided into three squadrons, dating from the mid-seventeenth century, which wore either a red, a white or a blue ensign. Within these squadrons, the admirals were divided by seniority into the most senior, full admirals, and their subordinate vice-admirals and rear-admirals. Some captains, termed Commodores, were ordered to hoist a broad pendant as a distinguishing flag and assume command of small squadrons of ships themselves commanded by other captains; they exercised most of the authority of an admiral but held only temporary commissions. In the same way, some senior lieutenants were temporarily commissioned to command particular ships as commanders. They assumed the authority of a captain and, with this experience, were usually appointed to their own ship. Ships bearing commissioned captains were known as post ships; they ranged from Sixth Rates to First Rates; and their commanders were known as post captains.

Warrant officers were so-called because they were appointed by a board warrant rather than a commission. They included the master and surgeon who received their warrants from the Navy Board; the purser, carpenter and boatswain who received theirs from the Board of Admiralty; and the gunner who received his from the Board of Ordnance.

Petty officers also received a warrant but were initially appointed by a ship's captain. They included the surgeon's mates, armourer, cook, master-at-arms, sailmaker, chaplain and schoolmaster.

Distinct from the warrant and petty officers, because they were regarded as potential sea-officers, were midshipmen and master's mates, who might be drawn from the most socially elevated families in the land (1). Like the commissioned officers, they were permitted the all-important distinction from other ranks of being permitted to walk the quarterdeck—the after end of the ship was generally regarded as 'officer country' (2), and remained so in British warships until well into this cen-

1

2

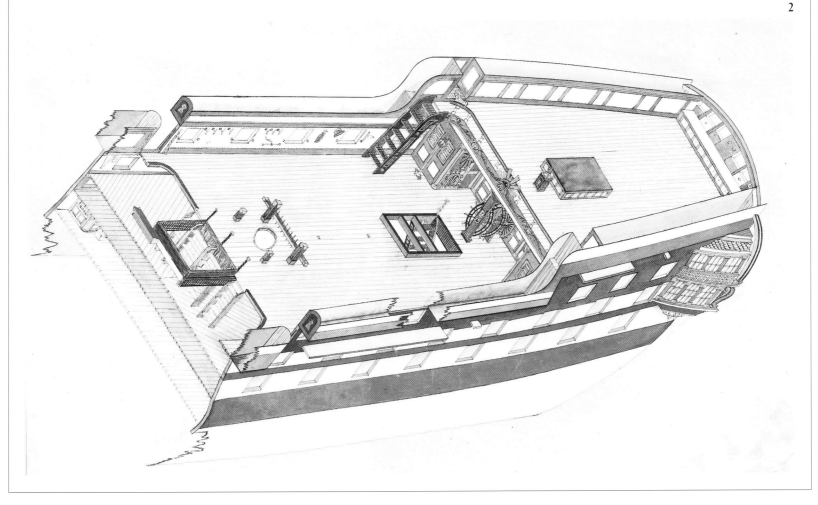

3

tury; there were rigid rules about access and a quarter-deck etiquette reflecting the hierarchy of the officers. Both midshipmen and master's mates were generally appointed by the captain to assist the lieutenants and other officers carry out their duties in managing the ship. The number of Midshipmen varied in proportion to the size of the ship: twenty-four to a First Rate, eighteen to a Second Rate, twelve to a Third Rate and so on. Usually aged thirteen on entry, though they could be younger, their own purpose was to learn the skills and knowledge of a sea officer. After two years, at the age of about fifteen, if sufficiently skilled in navigation and seamanship, they might obtain promotion to the situation of a master's mate, a position in which they were given charge of boats or sailing prizes into port. At the age of nineteen, if they had six years experience at sea, they became eligible to take an examination, upon passing which they could receive a commission as a lieutenant. However, most ships held numerous older midshipmen who had been unable to pass their examination. Master's mates had often passed their examination but had not yet received an Admiralty commission as a lieutenant.

Midshipmen, like admirals, commanders, and lieutenants, received an established uniform in 1748 (3). These, with their side-arms, separated them from the common seamen who frequently wore slops—the standard style of dress issued to a purser for sale (by deduc-

tion from their wages) to seamen—but had no formally designated uniform until the mid-nineteenth century. Admirals and captains often dressed their own boats' crews in distinguishing hats and jackets (4), but this was a point of individual prestige, depending on the wealth and conceit of the officer, rather than standard procedure. The more flamboyant also spent money on the appearance of their ship, and its boats were particular objects of display (5).

A lieutenant was one of several in any rated ship: a First Rate had ten or more. These lieutenants managed a ship on behalf of the captain; indeed, the first, most senior, lieutenant deputised for the captain in his absence, and all had authority to place any subordinate under arrest. Each took their turn in commanding watches, when they were expected always to be on deck, checking the sailing trim and navigation of the ship, keeping account of the men then under their particular command, and sending master's mates or midshipmen around the ship to check the conduct of the seamen off watch and to detect any source of fire or other danger to the welfare of the vessel and her company. In action, each had a particular role as deputised by the captain, some to assist him on the quarterdeck, others to supervise sections of the crew on the gundecks or aloft. A specific part of their duty was to keep a journal or log of their ship's progress and of incidents on board which, with certificates of service, had to be passed at the

4

5

Admiralty before they were permitted their pay. However, from the beginnings of their careers they were taught to observe and note, and even as midshipmen they would usually have kept semi-official journals, which they filled with navigational, astronomical and meterological observations, and information on any of the sciences pertaining to their profession. An important aspect of this was the encouragement to draw, which might manifest itself in practical objects like pilotage sketches (6), but often developed into more artistically sophisticated work, some of which survives and forms an excellent first-hand impression of the Navy of the sailing era.

Captains were given responsibility for larger ships as they obtained experience in smaller ones. Their burden was comprehensive, a captain being answerable for any questionable conduct in action, in navigation, in his ship's equipment, in the management of his subordinates, and, through them, in the behaviour of his crew. From the time of the receipt of his commission, he was expected never to sleep out of his ship until that commission was ended. Being responsible for the appropriate punishment of transgressors of ship regulations, including the Articles of War, he was expected himself to act as a model of moral virtue. He was responsible for the proper surveying and receipt of the designated quota of stores, and for obtaining as nearly as possible his complement of crew. Through his officers, he had to exercise and train this crew to engage enemies in battle, as well as to cope with adverse conditions of weather and navigation. During all such eventualities, he had to provide leadership, and set an example of courage and resolution.

For it was upon his captains that an admiral depended in arranging and fighting his fleet. The latter oversaw everything for which a captain was responsible, temporarily appointing his officers, or arranging and discharging courts martial as they became necessary. But above all he was accountable for the achievement of the purposes for which his fleet was equipped and set out. Military engagement was the most likely possibility and he had to practise his ships in tacking, going about, sailing line abreast, and forming a line of battle composed of ships in the order he had decided was the most balanced and specific for the tactical object in mind. Whether anchoring or sailing, he had to have considered all dangers, and ensured at all times he was equipped with all possible information from scouting frigates of the whereabouts of the enemy. His ability to draw up clear instructions to his captains was vital, as was a capability to impose his will on them, arranging councils of war as necessary, entering into diplomatic negotiations, or offering advice to the King's ministers. It was ultimately upon the capability of the Admiral that the effectiveness of a fleet at sea relied. For a Royal Navy admiral, whose decisions might determine the safety of the country, the responsibility was awesome: not surprisingly, at the end of major battles the stress reduced many commanders to a state of collapse, and is probably the reason why many a partial victory was not followed up.

1. 'William IV 1765-1837 . . . As midshipman on board Prince George 1782', stipple engraving after an original by Benjamin West. *NMM ref PAD3482*

2. 'Diagram and section of the well and poop decks of HMS Canopus', anonymous black and watercolour pen and ink, no date. *NMM ref PAH0758*

3. 'Unknown gentleman wearing officers uniform of 1795-1812. One of four painted at Malta. Shows captain's undress coat, epaulettes, cocked hat, white waistcoat, white pantaloons, black hessian boots, sword, sword belt, white stock and yellow gloves', anonymous watercolour, no date. *NMM ref PAD3111*

4. 'Sketch of Andromeda's barge crew', anonymous grey wash, no date. The particularly splendid headgear may date from the period when the frigate was commanded by Prince William Henry (later King William IV). *NMM ref PAH4899*

5. 'A naval barge with eight oarsmen', grey wash by Nicholas Pocock (1740-1821), no date. *NMM ref PAD8876*

6. 'The Land from Point . . . to the Town of . . . near Belle Isle in the Bay of Biscay Sketched on board HMS Ramilles by R F Hawkins August 1st 1793. *NMM ref PAD8520*

6

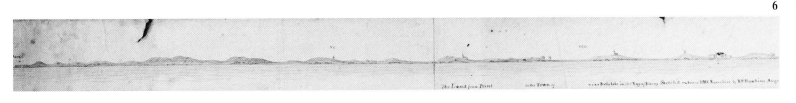

2

Occupation of Toulon

THE MEDITERRANEAN command, traditionally second only to the Channel, was entrusted to Vice-Admiral Viscount Hood, himself second only in distinction to Lord Howe among Britain's active naval officers (1). During the American war, he regarded himself as unfortunate to be so often second-in-command to the second-rate, and was fond of telling others how an action could have been fought better. Given this shortcoming, he was to do remarkably well in a position which required co-operation not only with army officers and politicians, but also with difficult allies and quasi-enemies.

When his fleet of twenty-one ships of the line went out to the Mediterranean it had no clear plan beyond defend-

1

3

ing British trade, and relieving the pressure that French republican armies were putting on the Sardinians, but it was known that there was serious opposition to the extremes of Jacobinism in parts of the south of France, and the possibility of capturing Toulon, Marseilles or Corsica was mooted. Frightened by the merciless advance of local republican forces, the authorities of Toulon opened negotiations with Hood, and the British fleet was invited to enter the port, the political fiction being that it was held in trust for the restored French monarchy, and the white Bourbon flag was raised. The British insisted that the French fleet be disarmed and the forts turned over to their control, and after a few days of internal struggle the royalists emerged victorious. On 28 August, with the newly arrived Spanish fleet of seventeen in attendance, the British entered Toulon. It was an amazing coup: as Nelson said, '…that the strongest place in Europe, and 22 sail-of-the-line should be given up without firing a shot. It is not to be credited.'

It was a very well-equipped arsenal with two large basins within the defences – the Old Port to the east (2) and the New Port alongside it to the west (3). Beyond this was the Inner Road (or *Petit Rade*), but it was shallow and could not provide safe anchorage for much of the fleet, but was protected by two arms that were defended by the Aiguillette and Balaguier forts to the south (4), and the *Grosse Tour* to the north. A fleet ready for sea normally lay in the Outer Road (or *Grand Rade*), but it was not entirely safe from the levanter winds common on that coast. This contemporary view (5) shows its northern shore from Cape Brun to the *Grosse Tour*, with a fleet lying in the Inner Road.

To take Toulon was one thing, but to keep it was another. The principal difficulty was that the town and anchorages were surrounded by high ground (6), and to protect the fleet involved defending a perimeter of fifteen miles. Hood had a few troops employed in lieu of marines, but nothing like the numbers needed, and his appeals to the mutually jealous allies produced few more and often of poor quality. The French royalists were mistrusted, and there were still many Jacobin supporters in the town, and so many in the fleet that in September Hood sent four old disarmed French 74s to the Atlantic ports with the disaffected seamen to avoid the danger of a 'fifth column'. There were great calls on the seamen of the fleet, and they were magnificently led while ashore by Captain Elphinstone (later Lord Keith). Problems abounded, not least the difficulty of mooring the three-deckers in the shallow Inner Road where they could be used for effective counter-battery fire.

Sir Sidney Smith's own map (7) makes the topography clear. The republican attack was concentrated to the west, especially after Bonaparte arrived in September to superintend the artillery, and there were soon batteries on the shore of the Inner Road, but he was thwarted in his attempt to take the heights above the village of La Seyne. The heights to the north of the city were also captured, but instantly retaken in a spectacularly efficient counter-attack, but as republican victories in the surrounding areas freed troops for the siege, Toulon's position became ever more precarious. By November the allies could muster about 12,000 effective troops, made up of a rag-bag of Spanish, Neapolitan, British, Piedmontese (Sardinians) and French royalists, and Hood was so short of seamen that he was forced to hire 1500 from the Grand Master of the Knights of Malta.

4

5

6

1. 'Admiral Samuel Hood (1724-1816)', oil painting after the style of Sir Joshua Reynolds (1723-1792).
NMM ref BHC2775

2. 'Le Port Vieux de Toulon Vu de l'atelier de Peinture Reduit de la Collection des Ports de France dessines pour Le Roi en 1776', engraving by Yves Marie Le Gouaz after an original by Nicolas Marie Ozanne, 1776.
NMM ref PAD1630

3. 'Le Port Neuf de Toulon, de dessus le vieux Mole Reduit de la Collection des Ports de France dessines pour Le Roi en 1776', engraving by Yves Marie Le Gouaz after an original by Nicolas Marie Ozanne, 1776.
NMM ref PAD1633

4. 'View of the South Side of the Inner Road of Toulon with the Forts Balaguer and L'Equillette, Hauteur de Grasse etc, from the anchorage in the Inner Road', coloured aquatint engraved and published by Francis Jukes,

London, after an original by Lieutenant G Raper, 1 January 1796.
NMM ref PAH2315

5. 'Cape Brun to the Gorge of St Andre, Toulon', coloured aquatint engraved by Francis Jukes after an original by Captain Knight, published by W Faden, London, 31 March 1794.
NMM ref PAH2319

6. 'Vue de Toulon. T. 1er Page 328, Album Maritime', etching after an original by Cauvin and Dunaime, printed by Chardon and published by Baillieu, 1838.
NMM ref PAD7322

7. Sir Sidney Smith's map of Toulon. 'From the original formerly in the possession of Sir Sidney Smith.' John Barrow, *Life and Correspondance…*, London, 1848.
Chatham Collection

7

. La Ville de Toulon
. Nouvelle Darse & Arsenal
. Vieille Darse
. Fort de la Malgue
. Grosse Tour
. Fort St Louis
. Poste du Cap brun
. Retranchement de St Anne
. Fort St Catherine
. Fort de l'Artigues
. Fort de Faron
. Cazernes de Faron
. Redoute de la Crête de Faron
. pas de la Masque
. pas des Monger
. poste St Antoine le grand.

17. Poste de St Antoine la Petite Redoute
18. Fort des Pomets
19. Poste de l'André Redoute
20. Poste de Malgrave
21. Redoute de Graffe
22. Red.te Malbousquet
23. Batterie de Missiessi
24. Batterie de Sablettes
25. Lazarette
26. Hopital St Mandrier
27. Croix des Signaux.

Postes de l'Ennemi.

A. Poste de la hauteur des Arens Batterie
B. Batterie de la Gavenne
C. Batterie de Bregaillon
D. la Seine Village
E. Batterie des 4 Moulins
F. 2de Batterie
G. Batterie du Croton
H. Batterie de Faubregas
I. Six fours Village
K. Olliouller Village
L. La Poste des Ameniers
M. Chateau St Marguerite
N. la Valette Village
O. Batterie avancée de St Marguerite.

Sir Sidney Smith's map of Toulon

TOULON,

où Sont marqués les différentes postes de l'attaque
& de la défense de la Ville.

From the original formerly in the possession
of Sir Sidney Smith.

PETITE RADE

GRANDE RADE

Fort l'Equillette

Tour balaguier

ECHELLE.

Toises.

500   1000   2000   3000

2

Political tangles

THE DEFENCE of Toulon was potentially com-
promised by the many other duties that fell to
Hood's fleet—indeed, only the five three-deckers
spent much time in the port. These duties were complicated by the tangled politics of the region: the south of
France itself was riven by factions ranging from one end
of the political spectrum to the other, and these shock-
waves rippled out to the numerous small nominally

1

neutral states of northern Italy. Corsica, which had been
French for no more than a generation, added a further
dimension, when patriots rose against the republican
garrisons and appealed to the British for aid. In
September 1793 Commodore Linzee was sent with a
small squadron to co-operate with the insurgents, but
they never appeared, and after a rapid success over the
soon-to-be-famous tower at Mortella, suffered a more
bruising encounter with the fort at Fornelli in San
Fiorenzo bay (1). The damaged squadron was withdrawn, having achieved nothing.

  Many of the Italian ports on which the British fleet
depended for supplies had pro-revolutionary factions
and most were actively involved in shipping foodstuffs
to the republican armies operating in war-ravaged
southern France. One of the most important was
Genoa, which was regarded as too pro-French in its
stance. The British had complained of the provocative
behaviour of a French frigate and two armed tartans, but
receiving no redress, decided to cut them out. Two 74s

3

and a brig, led by Captain Robert Mann of the *Bedford*, made short work of the opposition, and brought out the *Modeste* and the tartans. Militarily efficient, but politically inept, the incident was made the subject of republican French propaganda about the 'massacre' of the crews (2) —even though casualties were very light—but relations were broken off, and one very damaging long-term consequence was that the 5000 seasoned troops offered by Austria for the defence of Toulon could not embark from Genoa, and in the event never arrived at all. However, another frigate, the *Impérieuse*, was cut out at La Spezia, and Leghorn (as Livorno was known to the British) was more successfully coerced, the Grand Duke of Tuscany stopping supplies to the French.

To Hood's way of thinking, malign French influence stretched to the other side of the Mediterranean, where it was necessary to send an expedition to remind the Bey of Tunis where his best interests lay. Traditionally, Britain had been very tolerant of the Barbary states, since they were a source of water and victuals for the Royal Navy when the European shore might be very hostile, but Hood was intent on stopping the French supply convoys from Tunis, and ordered Linzee's refitted squadron to undertake the task. As a reinforcement, he was sent the 64-gun *Agamemnon*, but with the luck of her captain, Horatio Nelson, she ran into four French frigates returning from convoy duty to Tunis, and in a running battle gave the *Melpomène* a pounding before damage to her own tophamper forced the *Agamemnon* to break off the action (3). *Melpomène* limped into Calvi, where she was captured the following August, after a siege where the ubiquitous Nelson again played a major part (4). The mission to Tunis, dismissed by Nelson as 'a damn palaver', was a complete failure.

1. 'St Fiorenzo in the Island of Corsica, drawn on the spot by Captn Percy Fraser RN 1794', coloured aquatint engraved by Francis Jukes, no date.
NMM ref PAH2313

2. 'Massacre de l'equipage de la Modeste dans le Port de Genes par les Anglais le 5 Octobre 1793, ou 13 Vendemiaire An 2 de la Republique', engraving by Berthault after an original by Nicolas Ozanne, no date.
NMM ref PAD5441

3. 'The Agamemnon engaging four French Frigates', watercolour by Nicholas Pocock (1740-1821), 1810.
NMM ref PAF5873

4. Draught of *Melpomene* as captured. Admiralty Collection.
NMM neg 1649

4

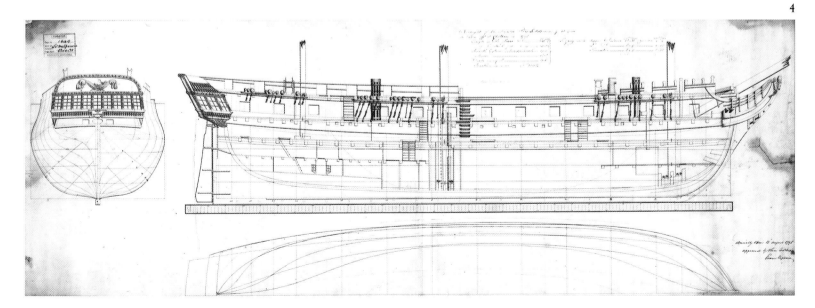

The original Martello tower

MORTELLA TOWER. *Corsica*

A *Middle Story*
B *Second Story*
C *Colouring door*
D *Powder room*
E *Kitchen*
F *Embrasures for Defence*
G *Cistern*
H *Sloped for carrying the water off return*

1

WHEN THE British attacked a simple gun tower on Cape Mortella during their campaign against Corsica in February 1794, they could not have guessed at the impact it would have on defence policy over the next fifteen years. Although its gun crew had fled the previous year when faced with the frigate *Lowestoffe*, this time it was better supplied, and beat off a determined attack by the 74-gun *Fortitude*, causing serious damage from red-hot shot and over 60 casualties. It eventually capitulated to shoreside bombardment, but a garrison of thirty-three men fighting a 6pdr and two 18pdrs had proved itself a serious obstacle. Both the army and the navy were impressed.

A somewhat crude but detailed drawing was made of the tower by an army engineer (1, 2, 3), and Admiral Jervis forwarded a model to the Admiralty, noting, 'I hope to see such works erected…on every part of the Coast likely for an enemy to make a descent on.' Other officers present on Corsica during the campaign included George Elphinstone (later Lord Keith), David Dundas, Abraham D'Aubant, Thomas Nepean and John Moore, all of whom were to have some influence on the development of British coastal gun towers. These were not uncommon in the Mediterranean, and the British themselves built somewhat similar towers on Minorca, when the island was commanded by Sir Charles Stuart (another Corsica veteran), while Lord Keith had some erected to defend the anchorage of Simonstown after he captured the Cape from the Dutch in 1795.

However, the tower entered the national consciousness when the Defence Committee of 1804, faced with the serious threat of French invasion, proposed a line of over a hundred towers along the south and east coasts, based on the tower at Mortella. However, the name became garbled in transit, and they became known as Martello towers. As is so often the case, the danger was

3

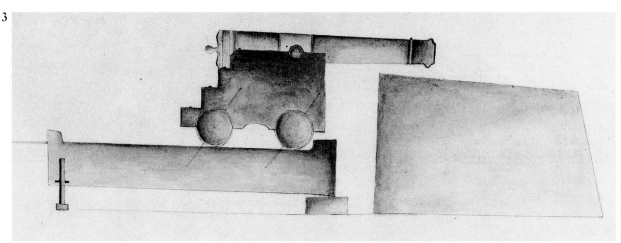

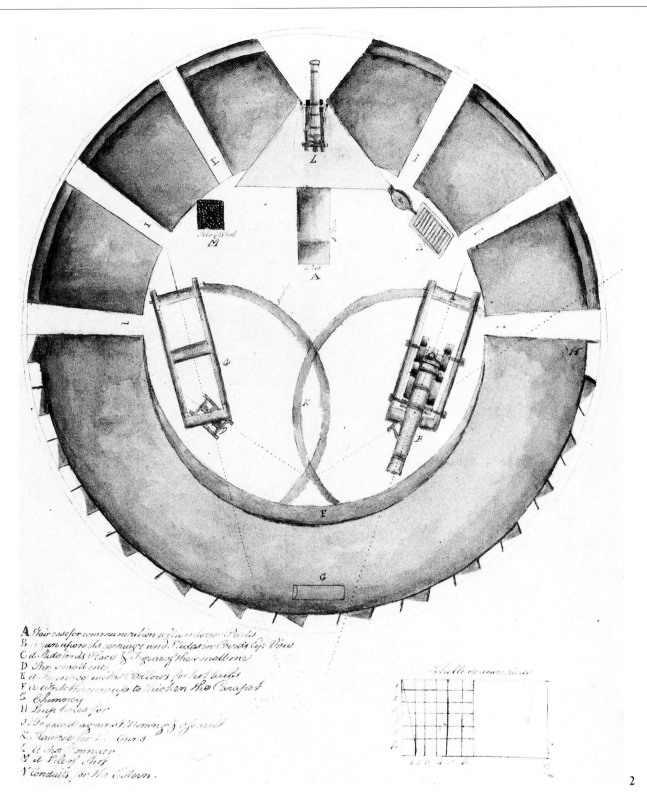

A Stair case for communication with interior Roots
B a gun upon its carriage and Nicholas in Birds Eye View
C d. Plate in its Place & Figure of the small one
D The small one
E a Furnace with Colours for hot balls
F a Work thrown up to thicken the Parapet
G Chimney
H Loop holes for
J to guard against Storming & assault
K Furnace for the Guns
L a Six Pounder
M a Pile of Shot
N Conduits for the Cistern.

2

over by the time the programme was complete, but some saw service in later wars and many still survive. The British design was rather different—aptly decribed as looking like an upturned flower-pot—being more squat and often having an elliptical cross-section that made the walls thicker on the seaward side where the threat was greater, but they seem to have been directly inspired by an incident in an otherwise fruitless campaign.

1. 'Mortella Tower, Corsica (elevation). First illustration in Plan of Mortella Tower, St Fiorenzo Bay, Corsica 1794', watercolour by C F D, 1794. *NMM ref PAD1621*

2. 'Inside view of Mortella Tower (plan). Second illustration in Plan of Mortella Tower, St Fiorenzo Bay, Corsica 1794', watercolour by C F D, 1794. *NMM ref PAD1622*

3. 'A cannon at Mortella Tower. Third illustration in Plan of Mortella Tower, St Fiorenzo Bay, Corsica 1794', watercolour by C F D, 1794. *NMM ref PAD1623*

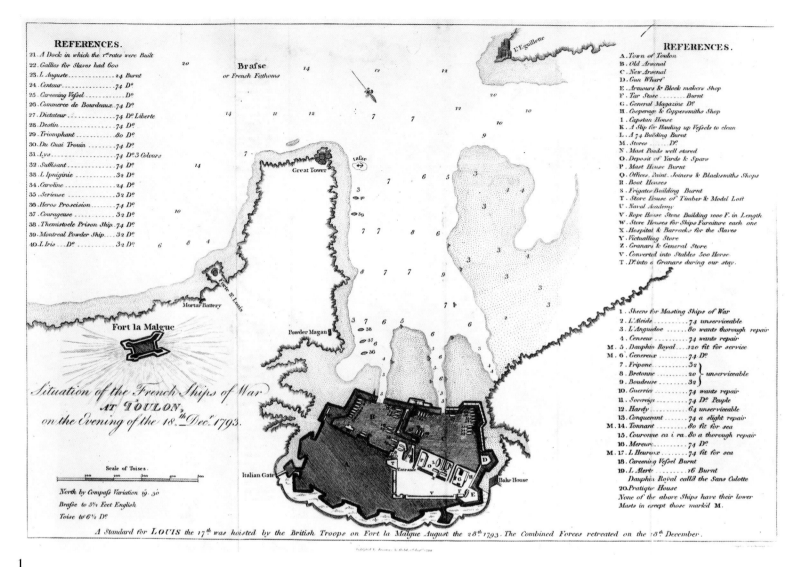

REFERENCES.

21. A Dock in which the 1st rates were Built
22. Gallies for Slaves had 600
23. L. Auguste . . . . 24 Burnt
24. Centaur . . . . 74 Dᵒ
25. Careening Vessel . . . . Dᵒ
26. Commerce de Bourdeaux . 74 Dᵒ
27. Dictateur . . . . 74 Dᵒ Liberte
28. Destin . . . . 74 Dᵒ
29. Triomphant . . . . . . 80 Dᵒ
30. Du Guai Trouin . . . . 74 Dᵒ
31. Lys . . . . 74 Dᵒ 3 Colours
32. Suffisant . . . . 74 Dᵒ
33. L. Iphiginie . . . . . . 32 Dᵒ
34. Caroline . . . . 24 Dᵒ
35. Serieuse . . . . 32 Dᵒ
36. Heros Proseision . . . 74 Dᵒ
37. Courageuse . . . . . . 32 Dᵒ
38. Themistocle Prison Ship 74 Dᵒ
39. Montreal Powder Ship . 32 Dᵒ
40. L. Iris . . . . Dᵒ . . . 32 Dᵒ

Brafse
or French Fathoms

Great Tower

Tour St. Louis

Mortar Battery

Fort la Malgue

Powder Magan

Situation of the French Ships of War
AT TOULON,
on the Evening of the 18th Decr. 1793.

Scale of Toises.

North by Compass Variation 19.30
Brafse to 5½ Feet English
Toise to 6½ Dᵒ

Italian Gate

Bake House

L'Y.guillette

REFERENCES.

A. Town of Toulon
B. Old Arsenal
C. New Arsenal
D. Gun Wharf
E. Armours & Block makers Shop
F. Tar Store . . . . Burnt
G. General Magazine Dᵒ
H. Cooperage & Coppersmiths Shop
I. Capstan House
K. A Slip for Hauling up Vessels to clean
L. A 74 Building Burnt
M. Stores . . . . . . Dᵒ
N. Mast Roads well stored
O. Deposit of Yards & Spars
P. Mast House Burnt
Q. Offices, Paint, Joiners & Blacksmiths Shops
R. Boat Houses
S. Frigates Building Burnt
T. Store House of Timber & Model Loft
U. Naval Academy
V. Rope House Stone Building 1000 F. in Length
W. Store Houses for Ships Furniture each one
X. Hospital & Barracks for the Slaves
Y. Victualling Store
Z. Granars & General Store
V. Converted into Stables 500 Horse
T. Dᵒ into a Granars during our stay.

1. Sheers for Masting Ships of War
2. L'Alcide . . . . 74 unserviceable
3. L'Anguedoe . . . . . 80 wants thorough repair
4. Censeur . . . . 74 wants repair
M. 5. Dauphin Royal . . 120 fit for service
M. 6. Genereux . . . . . 74 Dᵒ
7. Fripone . . . . 32 ⎫
8. Bretonne . . . . . . 20 ⎬ unserviceable
9. Boudeuse . . . . . . 32 ⎭
10. Guerrier . . . . . . 74 wants repair
11. Sovereign . . . . . . 74 Dᵒ Peuple
12. Hardy . . . . 64 unserviceable
13. Conquerant . . . . . 74 a slight repair
M. 14. Tonnant . . . . . 80 fit for sea
15. Couronne ca i ra . . 80 a thorough repair
16. Mercur . . . . 74 Dᵒ
M. 17. L Heuroux . . . . 74 fit for sea
18. Careening Vessel Burnt
19. L. Alerte . . . . . . 16 Burnt
Dauphin Royal call'd the Sans Culotte
20. Pratique House
None of the above Ships have their lower
Masts in except those markd M.

A Standard for LOUIS the 17th was hoisted by the British Troops on Fort la Malgue August the 28th 1793. The Combined Forces retreated on the 18th December.

1

2

Evacuation of Toulon

AS 1793 drew to a close, the position of Toulon's defenders deteriorated rapidly. Ever since the fall of Lyons in October, republican reinforcements had arrived in ever larger numbers, while a misunderstanding of the situation by the British government led them to remove some of Hood's precious few British regulars. The end came on 17 December when Bonaparte finally managed to capture Fort Mulgrave on the heights above La Seyne and a separate force took Mount Faron to the north of the city. A rapidly convened conference among the allies agreed that evacuation was the only course open, and it was decided to burn as much of the dockyard and the demilitarised French fleet as possible. Sir Sidney Smith, who had recently arrived in his own small sloop from the Levant, volunteered to organise the conflagration, in concert with a Spanish party under Don Pedro Cotiella.

This remarkable drawing (1) shows the exact position of all the ships on the night of the evacuation. With a few disreputable exceptions—the Neapolitans are said to have broken and fled without orders—the troops fought an effective rearguard action, and most were taken off by boats from the shoreline near Fort la Malgue, but there were also many royalist refugees to consider, and the chaos must have resembled Dunkirk in 1940. There were only six of Hood's ships in port, and of these the damaged *Courageux* had to be warped out without a rudder.

3

In the meantime Sir Sidney set about the ships and installations in the basins, lashing the properly primed fireship *Vulcan* across a trot of ships. He was under fire, and threatened by 600 galley slaves who provided the dockyard's heavy labour force, but in the end nine ships of the line, three frigates and three corvettes were destroyed; others were damaged but not fatally (2, 3). The buildings were less successfully fired, and since the Spanish are often accused of dereliction of duty, it is worth noting Smith's own report:

4

1. 'Situation of the French Ships of War at Toulon on the Evening of the 18th Decr. 1793', etching published by Bunny & Gold, London, 1 August 1799.
NMM ref PAH7846

2. 'A exact Representation of burning the Arsenal & blowing up the French Ships of War in the Harbour of Toulon 18 Dec 1793', etching by J Pass after an original by Crystal, published 1 July 1794.
NMM ref PAD5444

3. 'Burning the Ships of war at Toulon', anonymous engraving, no date.
NMM ref PAD5445

4. 'To the Rt Honble Lord Hood . . . employ'd in the defence of Toulon . . . the conflagration effected there on the night of the 18th Decr 1793 under orders . . . of Sir Sidney Smith', aquatint and etching by Archibald Robertson after his own original, published 28 April 1794.
NMM ref PAH7847

5

they, as well as ourselves, were in a manner thunderstruck by the explosion of some thousand barrels of powder on board the *Iris* frigate, lying in the inner road without [outside] us, and which had been injudiciously set on fire by the Spanish boats, in going off, instead of being sunk as ordered; the concussion of the air, and the shower of falling timber ignited, were such as nearly to have destroyed the whole of us. Lieutenant Patey of the *Terrible*, with his whole boat's crew, nearly perished; the boat was blown to pieces, but the men picked up alive. The *Union* gun-boat, which was nearest to the *Iris*, suffered considerably, Mr Young being killed, with three men, and the vessel shaken to pieces. . . . I had given it in charge to the Spanish officers, to fire the ships in the basin before the town, but they returned and reported that various obstacles had prevented their entering; we attempted it together, as soon as we had completed the business in the arsenal, but were repulsed in our attempt to cut the boom, by repeated volleys of musketry from the flag-ships and the wall of the *Batterie Royale* . . .

The explosion of the *Iris* is depicted in all its gruesome drama in this illustration (4), with the other powder ship, the *Montreal*, being fired in the distance by a Spanish lateen rigged gunboat. The republicans are firing from L'Aiguillette, and two-decker nearest the Great Tower is the *Themistocle*, a prison ship whose inmates were freed by Sidney Smith before she was burned. Although anonymous, this watercolour (5) and its accompanying key (6)

. . . The guns of the fire-ship going off on both sides, as they heated, in the direction that was given them, towards those quarters from whence we were most apprehensive of the enemy forcing their way in upon us, checked their career; their shouts and republican songs, which we could hear distinctly, continued till

5. 'Evacuation of Toulon 1793 (showing many ships on fire)', anonymous watercolour, no date. *NMM ref PAH3230*

6. Key to above. Anonymous brown pen and ink, no date.
1. Windsor Castle barge. 2. Victory's boat. 3. Spanish barge. 4. Swallow armed Tender. 5. Hero[s] 74.
6. Themistocle. 7. Powder frigate.
8. Frigate that had been exchang'd by the Sardinians for the Alceste. 9. Old Corvette. 10. Arsenal with 8 sail of the line &c on fire afloat as well as several parts on shore. 11. Old Arsenal.
12. Town of Toulon. 13. Part of the Heights of Pharon. 14. Malboquet throwing shells. 15. Grand Tour abandon'd. 16. Fort Balaguier firing.
17. Fort Equilette firing.
18. Neapolitan fortified hill. 19. Spanish fortified hill. 20. Fort Mulgrave on les Hauters de Grasses. *NMM ref PAH3231*

7. 'Commerce de Marseilles', coloured etching published by John Sewell, 21 March 1801. *NMM ref PAD6037*

8. 'His Majesty's Frigate Juno Escaping from the Inner Harbour of Toulon, on the night of the 11th of January 1794', coloured aquatint by Robert Dodd after his own original, published by the artist 1 May 1800. *NMM neg B9410*

6

show a remarkable knowledge of the events, although the timescale is somewhat truncated.

The British brought off fifteen ships, and once a few had been transferred to the allies, they retained three large frigates, *Perle, Arethuse* and *Topaze*, two 74s, *Puissant* (which never cruised) and *Pompée*, and the huge 120-gun *Commerce de Marseilles* (7). This ship was over 20 feet longer, and over 600 tons more burthensome, than the *Victory*, and was regarded as a fine sailing ship. However, in confined waters she was a menace, at full load drawing nearly 30 feet—the same as a Second World War battleship—and was so weakly built that she was converted to a gigantic storeship. With over 1100 men and their equipment, plus 500 crew, the ship attempted to sail with Christian's ill-fated convoy to the West Indies in November 1795; after a short but nightmarish voyage, she was forced back into Spithead and never put to sea again, becoming a prison hulk the following year.

The last act of the black farce of Toulon occurred in January 1794, when on the 11th the frigate *Juno*, with some of Hood's levies from Malta, sailed into a darkened inner harbour. A French boarding party attempted to persuade them to go further up the harbour, but the ship was actually aground, and by the time she had

7

hauled herself off, the tricolour cockades of the boarders had been noticed; they were bundled below, and *Juno* fought her way past the batteries and safely out to sea (8).

8

Ships of the Royal Navy: fireships

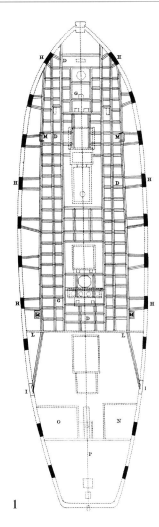

1

A S A TACTIC, the release of a burning vessel to drift down with the wind or tide on the enemy is probably as old as naval warfare itself, but it reached its apogee of success in the wars of the latter half of the seventeenth century. Very large fleets, lacking manoeuvrability and tactical sophistication, fighting in restricted waters, made for situations which the fireship could exploit.

Any merchant ship or superannuated warship could do the job if filled with combustibles, but fireships became more sophisticated as time went on. Ingenious developments included methods of making the fire spread quickly, like grating decks and air funnels to create draught; downward-hinged gunports that would not fall closed when the fire burned through the port tackle; cofferdams below deck to prevent the masts catching fire and coming down prematurely; grappling irons on the yardarms to make it difficult for the target to free itself; and elaborate fusing systems and a large sallyport to allow the crew to escape at the last moment. This made the quick conversion of existing vessels more difficult, and late seventeenth-century navies tended to build specialist fireships, which could cruise as sloops until they were needed (1). This may seem like an expensive solution, since the ship was built to be 'expended' (the official term), but it might be seen as a forerunner of a modern guided missile—also expensive, but cost-effective if it destroys a far more valuable target.

The building of dedicated fireships died out in the Royal Navy at the end of the War of Spanish Succession in 1713, but was revived during the American Revolutionary War. In 1779 a combined Franco-Spanish fleet had dominated the Channel, and for most of the rest of the war Britain was on the strategic defensive at sea. In these circumstances fireships might prove an 'equaliser', and two of the leading tactical innovators of the time, Howe and Kempenfelt, were strong advocates of their aggressive employment. However, Kempenfelt pointed out to the Comptroller, Sir Charles Middleton (later the Lord Barham of the Trafalgar campaign), that one reason for earlier lack of success with fireships was that they were slow sailers, so any new ones needed to be fast enough to keep up with a fleet. This was the origin of the *Tisiphone* class of the 1780s, which were modelled on the lines of a highly regarded French prize of the 1740s (2).

Byam Martin, who commanded the name ship in the Mediterranean in 1793, confirms that they were considered fast-sailing ships. He could perhaps count himself lucky that he was not called upon to use his fireship in earnest, since two of her class-mates in Lord Hood's fleet were so employed at the evacuation of Toulon: *Vulcan* was 'expended' in the time-honoured fashion to set fire to a line of French battleships, but *Conflagration*, under repair and immovable, had to be burnt to avoid capture. Howe, as would be expected of a fireship partisan, had a number of these ships during his command of the Channel Fleet, although their presence was disguised by their cruising rating as sloops. There were no opportunities—and indeed no need—for deploying fireships in fleet actions, but they became an important part of British attempts to destroy various enemy squadrons trapped by an ever more effective blockade. The only other purpose-built fireship expended, the *Comet*, was sent into Dunkirk Roads with three converted sloops in July 1800 in an attempt to destroy four large frigates: the fireships set fire to nothing, but in the confusion the *Desirée* was cut out by the sloop *Dart*.

An increasing preoccupation for the Royal Navy from

2

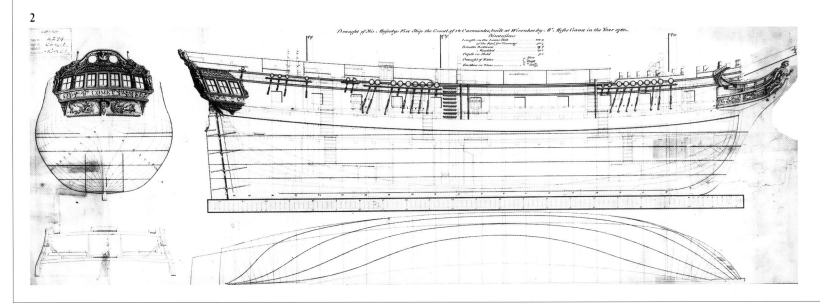

3

the mid-1790s was the assembly of would-be invasion craft across the Channel. Fireships might well be useful during an attempted crossing, but conceivably might also be employed against the shipping inside its harbours and anchorages if the opportunity presented itself. With this kind of operation in mind a number of smaller, shallower draught, merchant ships were converted as 'fire vessels' (3), but no opportunity had presented itself by the peace of Amiens and they were all paid off.

Unfortunately the peace lasted little more than a year, and the war took up where it had left off, with an invasion threat even more serious than that of 1801. Six fireships modified from the *Tisiphone* design (4) were laid down (although in the event all saw out the war as

sloops), but as a short-term measure more of the small fire vessels were taken up.

The last—and probably most infamous—set-piece use of fireships was Gambier's attack on the French squadron embayed in Basque Roads in 1809. Lord Cochrane led the attack, which included all the latest weaponry: cutters firing rockets, numerous fire vessels, a bomb, and three explosion vessels. The action became notorious because the initial success was not followed up, and provoked a very damaging public argument between Cochrane and Gambier. Leaving aside the rhetoric, it is worth noting that fireships and explosion vessels were rarely dangerous in themselves, but created panic that could be exploited by conventional forces.

1. The fire room of a fireship showing the elaborate system of wooden troughs carrying the fuses, which are led through the protective bulkhead L to the sallyport, I, where the train is lit as the crew escapes. H represents gunports for draught which were blown open by charges placed behind them, and had downward-hinged ports so that they would not close when the fire burnt through the port ropes.
From Falconer's Universal Dictionary of the Marine, *1815 edition*

2. As fitted draught of *Comet*, 1783, one of the few fireships of this era employed for her intended purpose. Admiralty Collection.
NMM neg 8229

3. 'Action between HMS Phosphorus and the French privateer L'Elize 14 August 1806', watercolour by Irwin Bevan, no date. In external appearance, the 'fire brig' was indistinguishable from any other small merchant vessel.
NMM ref PAD9481

4. Sheer draught for *Comet*, dated 10 October 1805, one of the 'repeat *Tisiphone*' class. Admiralty Collection.
NMM neg 6868

4

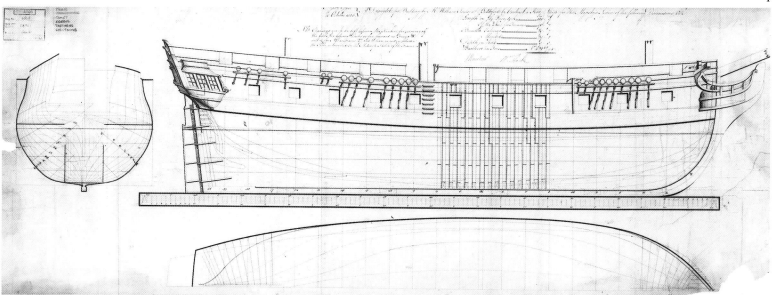

1

The Corsican campaign 1794

San Fiorenzo

After the fall of Toulon, Lord Hood moved the Mediterranean Fleet to Hyères Bay, east of Toulon, but, hearing that the republican troops on Corsica were short of supplies, he decided to make that island his base of operations. He had already opened communications with the Corsican leader General Pasquale de Paoli, who sought the removal of the French from the island and British support. Several ships were detached from the fleet to prevent the French being resupplied, one being the *Agamemnon*, 64, commanded by Captain Horatio Nelson. On 21 January 1794, a landing party from the *Agamemnon* destroyed a flour mill near the port of San Fiorenzo as part of this campaign of raiding against coastal traffic and defences.

Hood sailed from Hyères on 24 January, but a storm drove the fleet away from its destination of San Fiorenzo

Bay and it was forced to take shelter in Porto Ferrajo on Elba. From here, a squadron consisting of three 74s, *Alcide* (the flagship of Commodore Linzee), *Egmont* and *Fortitude*, and the 32-gun frigates *Lowestoffe* and *Juno*, with transports carrying troops under Major-General Dundas, sailed for Mortella Bay on Corsica, arriving on 7 February. The next day the tower at Mortella was attacked from both land and sea, but the small fort was so well defended that after two and one half hours the *Fortitude* and *Juno* were forced to break off their bombardment and withdraw out of range, the *Fortitude* having suffered sixty-two casualties and been set on fire. The tower surrendered the next day, having come under fire from guns landed from the ships (1) and its wooden breastwork set alight. The British then moved on to attack the Convention Redoubt, the main defence of San Fiorenzo itself, armed with twenty-one heavy guns, which after a two-day bombardment was stormed on 18 February.

2

The French fell back into San Fiorenzo (2), where they set fire to the frigate *Fortunée* and allowed the *Minerve*, 38, to sink as a result of damage she had taken from the British bombardment, and then retreated to Bastia. The town was occupied the same evening, and a few days later the *Minerve* was raised, being commissioned into the Royal Navy as the *San Fiorenzo* (3), there already being a ship named *Minerve* in service.

Bastia

The campaign continued with the British laying siege to the French garrison at Bastia (4, 5, 6). This was largely a naval affair, as Major-General Dundas felt unable to proceed after the fall of San Fiorenzo until reinforcements had arrived from Gibraltar. Hood, on the other hand, was eager to press on, and cruised with his squadron off Bastia until 5 March 1794 (7), when he returned to San Fiorenzo. Finding Dundas still unwilling to move without the 2000 new troops he was expecting, Hood decided to use the forces he had to hand, and sailed again for Bastia, landing there on 4 April. The landing force consisted of only 1248 men (although Corsican troops co-operated with them), with the seamen being commanded by Captain Nelson of the *Agamemnon*, whose own ship's company were very active in landing guns for the siege and manning the batteries established ashore.

By 11 April the preparations for the siege were complete, and Hood demanded the town's surrender, but the French governor General Lacombe Saint-Michel refused, resulting in a hard-fought siege of thirty-seven

3

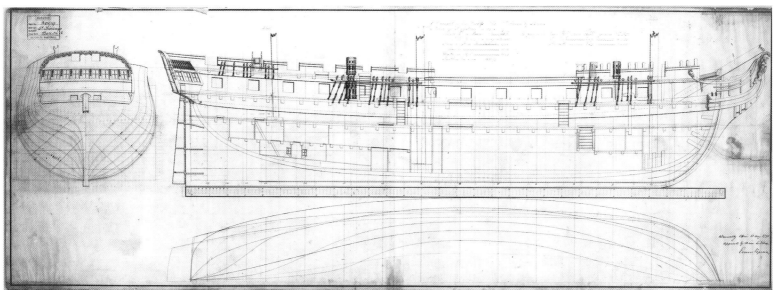

4

days, costing the British nineteen killed and thirty-seven wounded. The map (8) shows the British siege-lines. On 21 May, with provisions almost exhausted, the town surrendered, and two days later British troops marched through the gates. There had been some bad feeling between the navy and the army during these operations, and Nelson expressing frustration at the unwillingness of the army commanders to detach troops for the siege. As a result of the fall of Bastia, General Paoli formally transferred Corsica's allegiance from France to Great Britain on 19 June.

Calvi

The British then moved to attack Calvi on the north-western coast of the island, a stronger place than Bastia, defended by three forts. Again Nelson was put in charge of the naval forces involved, and Lieutenant-General The Hon. Charles Stuart commanded the troops. The squadron arrived off Calvi on 18 July 1794, but bad weather hampered the landing operations, a storm forcing the ships to stand out to sea on 22 June to avoid being wrecked, and it took some time to get the guns and supplies necessary for the siege ashore. Calvi held out for fifty-one days, the besiegers suffering badly in the heat of the Corsican summer, Nelson reporting at one point that half his force was sick. It was here, on 10 July, that Nelson received the injury that cost him the sight of his right eye (9), when he was hit in the face by stones and fragments from a shell bursting against the battery he was inspecting. Nine days later Fort Muzello, the main defence of the town, fell, and the British were thus able

5

6

7

1. 'Blue Jackets Landing Artillery and
Ammunition on Corsica',
anonymous grey and watercolour
pen and ink, c1794.
NMM ref PAH2355

2. 'View of the town of San Fiorenzo',
anonymous watercolour.
NMM ref PAH2349

3. Sheer draught of *Minerve*, as
captured. Admiralty Collection
NMM neg 2069

4. 'Bastia in the Island of Corsica,
drawn on the Spot by Captn Percy
Fraser RN 1794', coloured aquatint
engraved by Francis Jukes.
NMM ref PAH2314

5. 'A Southern View of Bastia in the
Island of Corsica from on Board His
Majesty's Ship Victory during the
Siege of that Town in May 1794',
watercolour by Ralph Willett Miller,
1794.
NMM ref PAH2324

6. 'Vue de Bastia en Corse',
anonymous graphite drawing, c1795.
NMM ref PAH2325

7. 'A View of Bastia', showing Admiral
Hood's squadron offshore in 1794,
aquatint engraved by Thomas
Medland from an original by Nicholas
Pocock, published by Bunny and
Gold, 1 July 1799.
NMM ref PAD5982

8. 'Siege de Bastia Par les Anglais et les
Corses Rebelles en 1794', etching by
Adam from an original by Fachot.
NMM ref PAD5469

9. 'Loss of His Eye Before Calvi',
etching by William Henry
Worthington from an original by
William Bromley, published by
Robert Bowyer, 1 March 1808.
NMM ref PAD5479

8

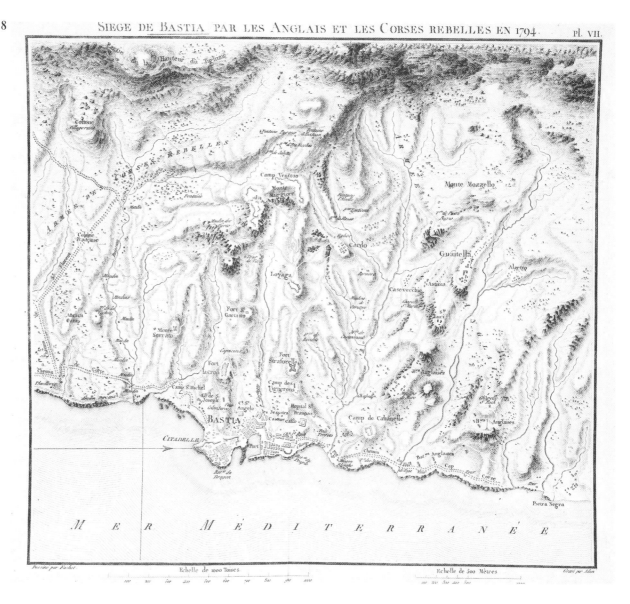

SIÈGE DE BASTIA PAR LES ANGLAIS ET LES CORSES REBELLES EN 1794. Pl. VII.

9

to bring their guns to bear upon Calvi itself. The French
commander negotiated a twenty-five day truce, promising to surrender if he had not received reinforcements
after that time, a ploy to exploit the sickness rife
amongst the besiegers, but the siege held and on 10
August Calvi surrendered. Two French frigates were
taken in the harbour, the 40-gun *Melpomène*, which was
taken into the Royal Navy as a 38, and the 32-gun
Mignonne, which was considered too small and unserviceable to be useful and was later burned at Porto Ferrajo.
After the siege, Nelson was worried that, as at Bastia, he
would not receive full credit for the part he had played
from the army, a symptom of the continued friction
between the two services in this campaign. He wrote:
'What degree of credit may be given to my services I cannot say. . . They hate us sailors; we are too active for
them. We accomplish our business sooner than they
like.' Corsica was held by the British until November
1796.

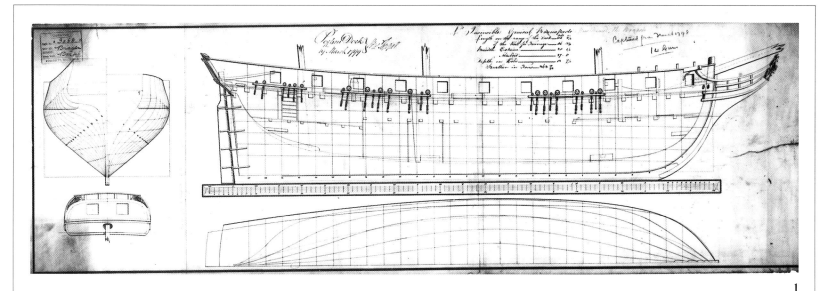

1

Ships of the Royal Navy: flush-decked ship sloops

IN NAVAL parlance, the word 'sloop' had a number of meanings, ranging from a single-masted rig to a rating—in effect, any vessel in the charge of an officer with the rank of Master and Commander (or Commander for short). Such ships were usually small cruisers, below the 20-gun post ships in size, but the rating also applied to vessels like a bomb or fireship when cruising, or even a ship of the line when armed *en flute* as a troopship or storeship.

The ancestry of the sloop of war can be traced back to the small craft—often little more than large boats—that accompanied sixteenth- and seventeenth-century fleets. In the eighteenth century, sloops grew in size and developed more ship-like characteristics, at the same time assuming more independent cruising roles. They were originally two-masted, but in the 1750s became ship rigged and in most respects small frigates, armed with fourteen or sixteen 6pdrs, although a few larger vessels carried eighteen. They proved more seaworthy, more habitable, longer-ranged and better armed than the old two-masted type, and the ship rig must have conferred some advantages in battle—three masts would have made them less vulnerable to damage aloft than two. But the one quality the new-style sloops did not possess was speed, and from the late 1770s the sloop category began to include faster and more weatherly brigs.

Quarterdecked ship sloops could be easily overtaken by far more powerful frigates and a number were captured under these circumstances: *Alert* and *Hound* in 1794, *Peterel* in 1798, *Cyane* and *Ranger* in 1805, and *Favourite* in 1806. Moreover, their sluggish sailing could result in the loss of other ships, like the *Africaine* in the Indian Ocean in 1810, surrendered because the British commodore could not assemble his force in time to prevent

2

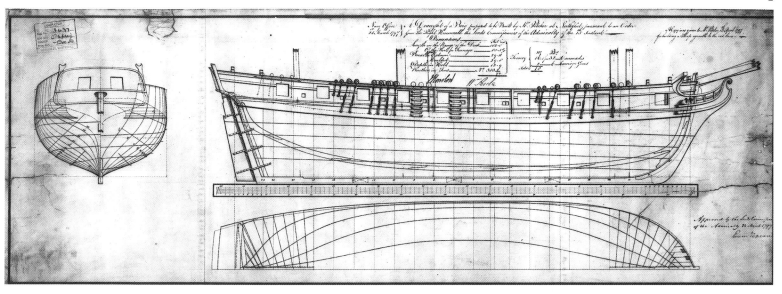

3

it, largely due to the slow progress of the *Otter*.

As a result it was rare for any ship sloop of the traditional type to be employed by the main fleets, and certainly not in frontline roles. They were not weatherly enough for the Channel blockade, and were not fast enough or powerful enough to act as scouts for the battlefleet. When attached to fleet commands, they were usually to be found detailed to convoy merchantmen within that command's jurisdiction. It is perhaps indicative of the official view of the quarterdecked ships that they tended to retain their long 6pdrs on the main deck, where the larger brigs were quickly converted to 32pdr carronades: the ship sloops seem to have been regarded as the smallest viable independent cruiser (for which a mixed armament was more useful), and patrol and convoy work, especially on more distant stations, was their usual lot for most of the war.

Almost all the sloops attached to the Channel Fleet in the early years of the war were brigs. However, a new type of flush-decked vessel was developed in the 1790s, initially entirely acquired by capture (1) but from 1797 purpose-built as well. These latter were essentially brig hull designs given three-masted rigs (2), whereas most of the French prizes were more ship-like, but lacking substantial upperworks were more weatherly and usually faster. The Channel Fleet's *Scourge* was of this design, while the 500-ton *Bonne Citoyenne* was a particular favour-

ite; she proved a very effective scout for the Mediterranean Fleet leading up to the battle of St Vincent, and in most respects was a good substitute for a frigate (3). As the Admiralty searched for new sources of supply, the shipbuilders of Bermuda offered their services, and in 1797 the first of a class of very sharp-hulled ship sloops were launched, using local cedar timber. Again, they were rather brig-like in their open flush deck, but a bow with a full set of headrails and false quarter galleries gave them the appearance of larger warships (4).

In this light it is instructive to look at the relative development of the two types of ship rigged sloops of war in the Royal Navy of this period.

Quarterdecked ship sloops

Year	No in Sea Service	No in Ordinary or Repairing
1794	32	1
1797	43	2
1799	38	0
1801	34	0
1804	19	2
1808	49	3
1810	54	2
1812	50	1
1814	43	1

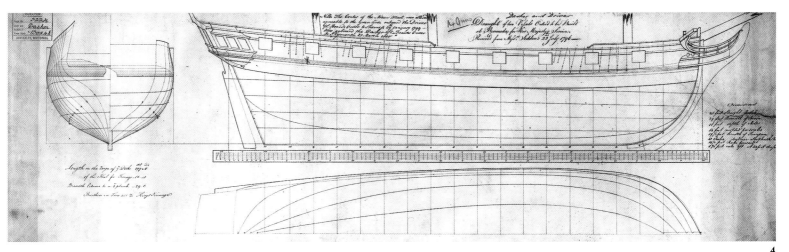

4

Flush-decked ship sloops

Year	No in Sea Service	No in Ordinary or Repairing
1794	0	0
1797	10	0
1799	23	0
1801	22	3
1804	37	0
1808	27	7
1810	19	2
1812	12	1
1814	9	1

The flush-decked ships grew in numbers in the French Revolutionary War just as the quarterdecked ships declined, reflecting the fleet concerns of the period, and the willingness of the Spencer Admiralty to back innovation in ship design (only one quarterdecked type was ordered after 1795). With sloops, as with so many other classes, a regression began with the St Vincent administration; the 1802 programme included fourteen quarterdecked ships to a design of 1795, and succeeding admiralties built even more. This period was obsessed with

the threat of invasion, and the good defensive qualities of the quarterdecked sloop may have seemed a better bet in the circumstances; certainly new building declined with the post-Trafalgar change in priorities. The flush-decked sloop also staged a small recovery later, thanks to the victories of the big American ship sloops in the War of 1812 forcing the construction of similar ships, for which the British reverted to the hull form of the highly regarded *Bonne Cityonne* (5).

1. Sheer draught of the *Brazen*, ex French privateer *Invincible General Bonaparte*, as taken off at Portsmouth Dockyard, 19 March 1799. Admiralty Collection. *NMM neg 3088-46*

2. Sheer draught of the *Osprey*, 21 March 1797, showing both the original brig rig, and the revised three-masted arrangement. Admiralty Collection. *NMM neg 3477-50*

3. 'Constantinople. North view, taken from the Artillery Quay (called Tophana) with H.B.M.'s ships Le Tigre and La Bonne Citoyenne under the command of Sir Sidney Smith', coloured aquatint engraved by J Jeakes after an original by John Thomas Serres, published by Edward Orme, 1 August 1805. *NMM neg B7136*

4. Sheer draught of the *Dasher*, as received from the builders, 22 July 1796. Admiralty Collection. *NMM neg 3224*

5. Sheer draught of the *Hermes* class sloops of 1810; those built as a response to the big American ship sloops in 1812 were slightly reduced versions, but with two extra gunports. Admiralty Collection. *NMM neg 2926*

5

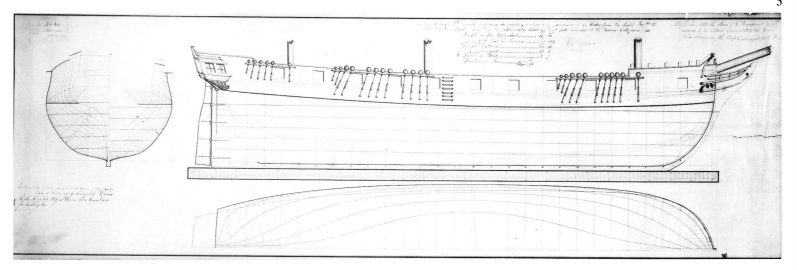

The Mediterranean Fleet under Hotham

2

LORD HOOD'S last service in the Mediterranean was to chase a French squadron that had escaped the Toulon holocaust into Gourjean Bay in June 1794. They were blockaded, but eventually escaped into their home port during a gale a few months later. Hood sailed for home in the *Victory* in November, turning over command to Vice-Admiral Hotham.

By early in 1795 the French had repaired enough of the Toulon damage to send a sizeable squadron to sea, and in February the 120-gun *Sans Culotte* (more famous to history under her later name of *L'Orient*), led three 80s, eleven 74s and half a dozen frigates on a mission to reconquer Corsica. British intelligence was very good, and Hotham's fleet—four three-deckers, seven 74s and two 64s—caught sight of them off Genoa on 13 March. The French had enjoyed a small victory a week earlier in capturing the jury-rigged *Berwick*, 74 which was strug-

gling to join the rest of the fleet at Leghorn, but showed no intention of taking on the whole Mediterranean Fleet. Hotham signalled 'general chase' and in their precipitate retreat the *Ça Ira* of 80 guns collided with another 80, the *Victoire*. The former lost her topmasts and was audaciously attacked by the frigate *Inconstant*, Captain Fremantle, but in an equally daring counter, with the British vanguard approaching, the French *Vestale* coolly took the stricken two-decker in tow.

First up was Nelson's *Agamemnon*, which skilfully tacked under the bigger ship's stern for three hours (1), by which time *Bedford* and *Edgar* were in action with the rear of the French line, including the giant *Sans Culotte*, but they were all recalled by the admiral. The pursuit was renewed at first light and *Ça Ira* was duly captured, along with *Censeur*, 74 which had taken over the tow from the gallant *Vestale* (2). The French made an attempt to rescue the prizes, but were thwarted by light winds, although *Illustrious* and *Courageux* were damaged. As in a number of these early fleet battles, the French fired red-hot shot, but to no great effect.

The day was yet young, and Nelson told his wife,

I went on board Admiral Hotham as soon as our firing grew slack in the Van, and the *Ça Ira* and *Censeur* had struck, to propose him leaving our two crippled ships, the two Prizes, and four frigates to themselves, and to pursue the enemy; but he, much cooler than myself, said 'We must be contented, we have done very well.' Now, had we taken ten sail, and allowed an eleventh to escape when it had been possible to have got at her, I would never have called it well done: we should have had such a day, as I believe the annals of England never produced.

Hood had received much the same response from Rodney after the Saintes in 1782, and it is interesting to speculate what Hood would have done in Hotham's place.

Having received a powerful reinforcement of nine of the line, including the famous *Victory*, in June Hotham sent the frigates *Dido*, 28 and *Lowestoffe*, 32 to investigate a report that the French fleet was at sea. By coincidence, the French frigates *Minerve*, 40 and *Artémise*, 36 had been sent on a similar mission, and the resulting action between the pairs of cruisers demonstrated the growing divide between British and French fighting skills. Although the smaller ship, the 9pdr-armed *Dido* as the senior officer's command chose to tackle the 18pdr-armed *Minerve*, at 1100 tons nearly twice the size of the British ship (3). Some support was supplied by the 12pdr *Lowestoffe* during the battle, but when *Minerve* surrendered it was the *Dido* which had done most of the damage. *Artémise* took little part in the action and fled when *Lowestoffe* was ordered in pursuit. *Minerve* became a favourite command in the Royal Navy, and carried Nelson's broad pendant during one famous clash with Spanish frigates in 1796.

Whatever his shortcomings, Hotham recognised Nelson's suitability for detached service, and in the following months the *Agamemnon*, with frigates and small craft in attendance, was often in action along French-held coastal territories. His squadron was chased by the

3

French fleet in July, but escaped to warn Hotham, who eventually brought them to one of his partial actions that so frustrated Nelson – on the 13th off Hyères he captured the *Alcide*, 74, but shortly after she struck, this prize caught fire and blew up, taking with her nearly half of her 615-man complement.

Nelson was more successful with his next detachment, in support of the Austrian campaign along the Gulf of Genoa, when he raided shipping in Alassio and Languelia Bays (4). He cut out a French corvette and a gunbrig, two galleys and five merchant ships, and destroyed two others, before his force escaped without loss.

4

1

Britain withdraws from the Mediterranean

UNDETERRED BY the minor defeats inflicted upon it by Hotham, the Toulon fleet sent very effective squadrons to sea on commerce-destroying missions under Richery and Ganteaume in the autumn of 1795. In November Hotham struck his flag and was replaced the following month by Sir John Jervis, a harsh disciplinarian but an effective and inspiring leader. Unfortunately for Britain, in March 1796 the French 'Army of Italy' was turned over to an even more effective young general, Napoleon Bonaparte, who began the phenomenal campaign that made him a household name throughout Europe.

For the Royal Navy, the first major blow was the French capture of Leghorn on 30 June (1), because this neutral port was a much-used rendezvous and a source of stores and victuals. One of the British ships in the harbour when French troops arrived was the frigate *Blanche*, whose complement included the American sailor-of-fortune Jacob Nagle, who left a description of a typical display of naval *sang froid*—followed with almost comic-book speed by a reversal of policy:

Early in the morning the French began to fire at us, but the guns from the batteries could not reach us by 15 or 20 yards though their guns was chock'd so that they could not recoil . . . we lay still and washed our

2

3

decks down as usual in the morning. At 8 o'clock we piped to breakfast. During this time, finding they could not reach us, they got a long gun from a tower on the S.W. side of the town and brought it to the nearest battery to us and began to open upon us. The very first shot went over us a quarter of a mile.

Immediately the hands were turned up to weigh anchor, got under way, and began to beat out, having a head wind from the westward. Our vessel being light, we fell to leeward and having to stretch along shore past all the batteries, they kept a continual fire upon us and we returning the salute till we were out of reach of their guns, which was not less than two hours.

After Leghorn the next French target was likely to be Elba, another possession of the Grand Duchy of Tuscany, which would provide an ideal springboard for the French recapture of Corsica. The British moved quickly and on 10 July Nelson's squadron occupied the heavily defended fortress town of Porto Ferrajo with the agreement of the local authorities (2, 3).

The British position in the Mediterranean worsened throughout the year, as one by one Britain's allies were

4

5

1. 'Entree des Francais dans Livourne, 30 Jun 1796', etching by Duplessi-Bertaux and Damburn after an original by Carl Vernet, no date. *NMM ref PAG8938*

2. 'To the Right Honble Earl Spencer, This View of Port Ferrajo from within the Bay', coloured aquatint engraved by Francis Jukes after an original by Captain James Weir, published by James Daniell, April 1814. *NMM ref PAF4682*

3. 'View of the West Side of Porto Ferrajo Bay, with positions of the Captain 74, Flora, Inconstant, Southampton Frigates', coloured aquatint engraved by Francis Jukes after an original by Captain James Weir, published by James Daniell, April 1814. *NMM ref PAH2433*

4. 'View of Coast of Spain ca. 1795', anonymous black and watercolour pen and ink, no date. *NMM ref PAG9685*

5. 'Capture of the Mahonesa Octr 13th 1796', coloured aquatint engraved by Thomas Sutherland after an original by Thomas Whitcombe (c1752-1824), published 1 November 1816. *NMM ref PAD5511*

6. Draught of *Mahonesa* as taken off in 1798. Admiralty Collection. *NMM neg 6207*

forced to sue for peace by French land victories. Spain's attitude hardened, and as a French squadron sheltered in Cadiz in August (4), an alliance with France was signed at San Ildefonso. This became a declaration of war in October, which raised the old spectre of Franco-Spanish domination of the Channel, as in 1779, followed by an invasion of Britain herself. The Mediterranean Fleet had to be positioned where it could rapidly reinforce the Channel, so the decision to withdraw from the Middle Sea was taken. This meant abandoning Corsica, and Nelson withdrew the garrison of Bastia in October and in November Jervis's fleet sailed from San Fiorenzo for Gibraltar, and eventually Lisbon. At this point there was not a single British battleship inside the Straits of

Gibraltar—even Nelson had to hoist his broad pendant in a frigate to evacuate the last British outpost, on Elba, in December.

While operating alongside the Spanish as allies, the British had formed a low opinion of their fighting efficiency, even if they never lacked bravery. This was confirmed on 13 October in the first clash between the new enemies, when after a battle of about an hour and a half the frigate *Mahonesa* surrendered to James Richard Bowen's *Terpsichore*, 32; Bowen had only four wounded, but Spanish casualties were around thirty dead and a similar number wounded (5). The prize was a fine big ship (921 tons), but was so badly knocked about in the action that she was never commissioned for British service (6).

6

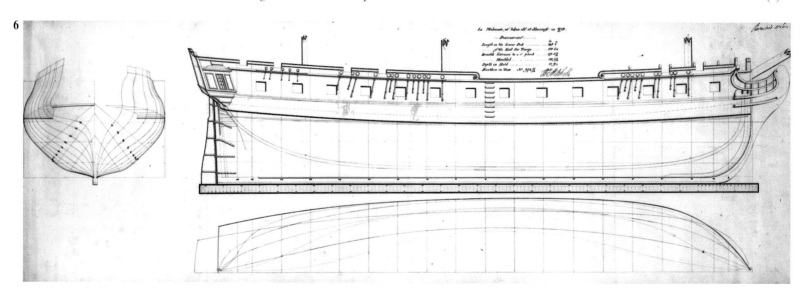

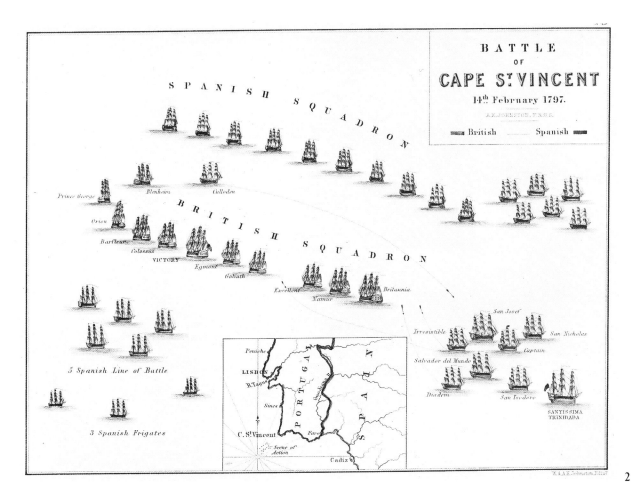

Battle of Cape St Vincent, 14 February 1797

AFTER ITS strategic withdrawal from the Mediterranean, the British fleet under Sir John Jervis (1) was based in the Tagus below Lisbon, where a sequence of accidents reduced its numbers to ten of the line, but a reinforcement of five from the Channel Fleet arrived early in 1797 and the combined fleet then included six powerful three-deckers. On 13 February Nelson's *Minerve*, having successfully evacuated Sir Gilbert Elliot, late Viceroy of Corsica, arrived with the news of sighting the Spanish fleet—indeed, the frigate had been vigorously chased by two 74s. Commanded by Admiral Cordóba, the Spanish force comprised seven three-deckers, two 80s and eighteen 74s, plus a dozen frigates.

Jervis, who once said 'men, not ships, win battles', was undaunted. He put to sea immediately, and on the morning of the 14th the Spaniards were sighted off Cape St Vincent heading for Cadiz in two loose groups. His view of the strategic situation was put simply and starkly to his captains—'a victory is very essential to England at this moment'—and he formed a single line of battle and steered for the gap in the opposing formation, by this time reduced to a total of twenty-five of the line. Through the early morning mist the Spanish took the British force to be no more than nine of the line, but as light winds cleared away the fog they saw their mistake and their danger.

The leeward squadron was actually the close escort for a small but highly valuable convoy carrying mercury for the all-important refining of silver, and Cordóba took his main body of seventeen ships downwind to close the gap. The better-disciplined British reached it first and a distant cannonade began as the fleets passed, and the British van then tacked in succession, led by the *Culloden*, to pass up the starboard, lee side of the enemy line, which closed the range and allowed the British line to keep in touch (2). One of the strengths of the Spanish fleet was its concentration of three-deckers, including six of 112 guns (3), each more powerful than the *Victory*, Jervis's flagship. At this point in the battle, one of these from the leeward group made an attempt to drive past the *Victory* to rejoin the main body. The incident is recorded in the usual laconic official style in the ship's log:

3

4

5

1. 'Admiral John Jervis (1735-1823), 1st Earl of St Vincent', oil painting after the style of John Hoppner (1758-1810). *NMM ref BHC3002*

2. 'Battle of Cape St Vincent 14th February 1797', coloured etching by W Johnston after an original by A K Johnston, published by William Blackwood & Sons, no date. *NMM ref PAH6270*

3. 'Vais [seau] Espagnol de 100 Canons, a la Cape', coloured engraving by Gaetano Canali after an original by Emeric, published 1794. *NMM ref PAH9399*

4. 'HMS Victory raking the Salvador del Mundo at the battle of Cape St Vincent, 14 February 1797', oil painting by Thomas Luny (1759-1837). *NMM ref BHC0484*

5. 'Historia de la Marina reale Espanola. La Funesta Battalla del Cabo de San Vincente . . . Santisima Trinidad', coloured lithograph engraved by Augusto de Belvedere and De Martinez y Ca., no date. *NMM neg no B9302*

6. 'Lord St Vincent's Victory, Feby 14th 1797', etching by Francesco Ambrosi after an original by William Wilkins, no date. *NMM ref PAF4683*

½ past [12], a Spanish Vice-Admiral attempted to pass ahead of the *Victory*. The *Culloden* and *Blenheim* on the larboard tack and passing to windward of our line . . . The Spanish Vice-Admiral forced to tack close under the *Victory*'s lee. Raked her both ahead and astern, he appeared to be in great confusion [and] bore up, as did six other of the enemy's ships.

forecastle and quarterdeck were joined and armed with an extra eight 8pdrs a side; she was also comfortably exceeded in dimensions and tonnage by the latest French 120-gun ships. Nevertheless, she was a very potent vessel and instantly recognisable, and although three other three-deckers were close by, she became the *Captain*'s target (5). The battle of manouevre was over and the contest of gunnery was about to begin (6).

This moment was caught very accurately by Thomas Luny's painting (4), except that at the time it was believed the opposing ship was the *Salvador del Mundo*; in fact, it was the flagship of Vice-Admiral Moreno, the *Principe de Asturias,* that received the double raking.

One by one, the British ships tacked, but the head of the Spanish line was far to the northeast of them, threatening to pass around the stern of the British formation and join up with the lee squadron. At this point Nelson, last but two in the British line, dramatically intervened: wearing his 74-gun *Captain* out of line, he recrossed the line ahead of *Excellent* (which then followed his manoeuvre) and steered across the van of the Spanish line, heading directly for the fleet flagship, the 136-gun *Santísima Trinidad*. This ship inspired awe, and not a few legends—a four-decker and the largest ship in the world—believed at the time and perpetuated by later historians. In fact, she was only a 'four-decker' by dint of a reconstruction shortly before St Vincent in which the

6

1

Nelson's Patent Bridge

ABOARD THE frigate *Lively* at St Vincent was Colonel John Drinkwater, a member of Elliot's staff from Corsica and the historian of the great siege of Gibraltar during the American War. Both men had begged Jervis to be allowed to sail with the fleet for the imminent battle, and he had obliged. Drinkwater therefore became an eye-witness, but, being on one of the frigates, at sufficient distance to appreciate the larger manouevres, and he later published the best contemporary account of the battle. Although he talked to many of those involved and collated reams of notes, he was particularly struck by Nelson, who came on board shortly after the fighting stopped and regaled him with the typically Nelsonic combination of charm and ego-

2

tism. Drinkwater's popular narrative was therefore responsible for fostering the idea that Nelson had, in effect, won the battle for Jervis.

Captain's dramatic intervention in the battle was certainly the most popular aspect of the battle with artists, and particularly the moment when the British ship crashed into the 84-gun *San Nicolas* which in turn collided with the 112-gun *San Josef* (1-4). The episode is best told in Nelson's own words:

The *Excellent* [Captain Collingwood] ranged up with every sail set, and hauling up his mainsail just astern, passed within ten feet of the *San Nicolas*, giving her a most awful and tremendous fire. The *San Nicolas* luffing up, the *San Josef* fell on board her, and the *Excellent* passing on for the *Santísima Trinidad*, the *Captain* resumed her situation abreast of them, close alongside.

At this time, the *Captain* having lost her fore topmast, not a sail, shroud, or rope standing, the wheel shot away, and incapable of further service in the line or in chase, I directed Captain Miller to put the helm a-starboard, and calling for the boarders, ordered them to board.

The soldiers of the 69th Regiment, with an alacrity which will ever do them credit, with Lieutenant Pierson, of the same regiment, were amongst the foremost on this service. The first man who jumped into the enemy mizen chains was Captain Berry, late my First Lieutenant. . . . He was supported from our spritsail yard, which hooked into the mizen rigging. A soldier of the 69th Regiment having broke the upper quarter-gallery window, jumped in, followed by myself and others as fast as possible. I found the cabin doors fastened, and the Spanish officers fired their pistols at us through the windows, but having broke open the doors, the soldiers fired, and the Spanish Brigadier (Commodore, with a distinguishing pendant) fell as retreating to the quarterdeck . . . Having pushed on to the quarterdeck, I found Captain Berry in possession of the poop, and the Spanish ensign hauling down. I passed with my people and Lieutenant Pierson on to the larboard gangway to the forecastle, where I met two or three Spanish officer prisoners to my seamen, and they delivered me their swords [5].

At this moment a fire of pistols or muskets opened from the admiral's stern gallery of the *San Josef*; I directed the soldiers to fire into her stern, and, calling to Captain Miller [his flag captain], ordered him to send more men into the *San Nicolas*, and directed my people to board the First Rate, which was done in an instant, Captain Berry assisting me into the main

3

chains. At this moment, a Spanish officer looked over from the quarterdeck rail and said they surrendered [6]; from this most welcome intelligence it was not long before I was on the quarterdeck, when the Spanish captain, with a bow, presented me his sword, and said the admiral was dying of his wounds below. I asked him, on his honour, if the ship were surrendered? he declared she was; on which I gave him my hand, and desired him to call his officers and ship's company, and tell them of it—which he did; and on the quarterdeck of a Spanish First Rate, extravagant as the story may seem, did I receive the swords of the vanquished Spaniards; which, as I received, I gave to William Fearney, one of my bargemen, who put them with the greatest sang-froid under his arm [7].

4

5. 'The San Nicolas and the San Josef Carried by Boarding February 14th 1797', engraving by Richard Golding after an original by Richard Westall, published by Thomas Cadell and William Davies, 15 November 1808. Supposed to be *San Josef* but more appropriate to *San Nicolas* perhaps (note Lieutenant Pierson).
NMM ref PAD5540

6. 'Nelson boarding the San Jose at the battle of Cape St Vincent, 14 February 1797', oil painting by George Jones (1786-1869). Shows exact moment Spanish officer (top left) hailed to announce their surrender.
NMM ref BHC0492

5

To capture two ships in succession in a such a fashion was unique in the Royal Navy's long and illustrious history, and the exploit was soon known in the fleet as 'Nelson's Patent Bridge for Boarding First Rates'.

Needless to say, there were others who saw their efforts diminished by Nelson's capture of the limelight, if not all the prizes. Some argued that *Culloden* was already coming up with the leading Spanish group, when *Captain* arrived in such an operatic, and unauthorised, fashion, while others felt that Nelson had actually taken *their* prizes. In truth, the whole fleet fought very well, but it suited Britain to elevate Nelson's achievement to the level of the extraordinary—it boosted public morale at a dark time, and was another step on the ladder towards establishing the Royal Navy's aura of invincibility in the minds of its enemies.

Given the odds, the final haul of prizes—the 112-gun *Salvador del Mundo* and *San Josef*, the 84-gun *San Nicolas* and the 74-gun *San Isidro*—was extraordinary, but before

6

7. 'Commodore Nelson receiving the Sword of the Spanish Admiral', engraving published by J & J Cundee, 1813. Although crude, it shows all the main features.
NMM ref PAD7691

8. 'San Nicolas 84 guns', watercolour by William Innes Pocock, no date but presumably 1797.
NMM ref PAF0603

9. 'The San Isidro 74 Guns', watercolour by William Innes Pocock, no date but presumably 1797.
NMM ref PAF0604

Jervis could get them home he had to ward off a threatened rescue attempt by Cordóba's undamaged ships, but they did not press home the attack. The prizes were splendid trophies—especially the three-deckers, which were only rarely captured in battle—but they were not much of an addition to the strength of the Royal Navy. The two-deckers were rather old, the *San Nicolas* (8) built at Cartagena in 1769 and the *San Isidro* (9) a year earlier at Ferrol; they were portrayed on their voyage to the Tagus, battle-scarred and under jury rig, by Lieutenant William Innes Pocock, son of the famous Nicholas, but he lacked his father's talent as a marine artist. As a stopgap measure they were all retained with the British fleet until October, but after they returned to Britain for survey, none was found suitable for sea service. Spanish ships had a reputation for heavy sailing—at least partly based on experience with the 80-gun *Gibraltar* captured in the previous war—but the *San Josef* was refitted in 1801, probably as a quick replacement for the *Queen Charlotte* which had caught fire and blown up the previous year. Fittingly, she was earmarked as Nelson's flagship, but this appointment was overtaken by events.

Following the battle, the honours were generous for the victors, Jervis henceforth being known as the Earl of St Vincent; two junior admirals were made baronets, and Nelson became a Knight of the Bath. Conversely, Cordóba and his second in command were cashiered and stripped of titles, and half a dozen Spanish captains dismissed or reprimanded.

The naval officer: recruitment and advancement

TOWARDS THE end of the war that stern disciplinarian Admiral St Vincent, reflecting on changes in the Navy, expressed strong reservations to the King about what might be called the gentrification of the officer corps. There had always been a few aristocrats in the service, but as the Navy became more successful, and as its standing in the country rose, more and more young gentlemen sought to make a career at sea. The experience of having a son in the Navy became a common one for many families—some of Jane Austen's few overt references to the war she lived through occur in *Persuasion*; the naval officers might be drawn from life since she had two brothers who became prominent in the service. In this common experience the caricaturist Cruickshank found a ready market, and in a popular series published after the war, he satirised the process of turning callow youths into naval officers.

His hero is Master William Blockhead, shipping as a Midshipman aboard HMS *Hellfire* and destined for the West Indies (1). He is seen in childish mood (a new Mid was often some way short of his teens when first going to sea) chasing his sister with the dirk that marked his rank, as a sword would do when he became more senior. His mother weeps, as mothers always do, at the prospect of losing him, while his father surveys with obvious dis-

taste the mountain of bills for the various requirements of a young naval gentleman. These items, scattered about his sea-chest, include luxuries like preserved meats and cherry brandy, but since the ship is off to the dangerous West Indies there are also medicines and 'rags for wounds'.

5

6

7

It is clearly a well-to-do household, and Blockhead's first sight of the licensed bedlam of the Midshipmen's berth is a shock (2). The boisterous cheek-by-jowl existence, the noisy merriment, and lack of privacy is evident, although if he had been educated at an English public school and not by private tutor he would hardly have noticed the difference. The artist even manages to convey something of the smell of the place, with the hatch to the noisome hold open. His introduction to his duties is no more encouraging, keeping the middle watch in cold, rainy conditions (3), but the inevitable youthful clashes with authority bring even less pleasant retribution (4). Sending malefactors to the masthead for long periods was a common punishment for even minor misdemeanors, and since the caption says he is 'enjoying the fresh air for the 304th time', he is frequently in trouble. The accompanying dialogue, the cause of his punishment, will be recognisable to any schoolchild who has ever faced the unreasonable and arbitrary exercise of adult power:

Lieutenant:	Pray Mr B, did you call the Master?
B:	No, Sir. I *thought* . . .
Lieutenant:	You thought Sir! How dare you *think* Have you marked the Board?
B:	No, Sir. I didn't think . . .
Lieutenant:	Didn't think; why *didn't you think* Sir!!! Up to the Masthead directly . . .

Midshipmen were officers in the making, and were given nominal authority over far older and more experienced seamen from early in their careers. In ships of the line they might command a part of a gun deck, and a boarding action could find them in the thick of hand-to-hand fighting. They had to grow up quickly, and as the caption suggests, Blockhead has already reached Soldier in Shakespeare's Seven Ages of Man, 'seeking the bubble reputation, even in the cannon's mouth' (5). In fact, a midshipman could not seek more, since his promotion depended on passing an examination, for which (in theory at least) he could not be entered until he was at least nineteen years of age and had six years of certified sea-time. It was an ordeal, but once successfully negotiated it brought with it, after 1812 at least, a splendid epaulette to set off the new uniform and a dress sword (6).

However, further promotion, and even an appointment, thereafter depended on 'interest'—who one knew or who the family might be connected to. Calling at the Admiralty in person was the last resort, and its waiting room (7) was the graveyard of many an ambition. This lively conclusion to the series depicts a very mixed collection of officers, civilians and even a seaman, through which the proud new Lieutenant Blockhead struts. One man, perhaps a half-pay officer, spells out 'DAMNA . . .' in dust on the floor, and an ominous piece of graffitti on the wall declares:

In sore affliction, tried by God's commands
Of patience, Job, the great example stands
But in these days, a trial more severe
Had been Job's lot, if God had sent him here.

1-7. Coloured aquatints engraved by George Cruickshank, published by Thomas McLean, 1 August 1835.

1. 'Midshipman Blockhead. Fitting out Mastr. Willm Blockhead HM Ship Hellfire West India Station'. *NMM ref PAD4721*

2. 'Master B finding things not exactly what he expected'. *NMM ref PAD4722*

3. 'Master B on the Middle watch, cold blows the wind & the rain's coming on'. *NMM ref PAD4723*

4. 'Mr B mastheaded or enjoying the fresh air for the 304th time'. *NMM ref PAD4724*

5. 'Mr B seeking the bubble reputation'. *NMM ref PAD4725*

6. 'Mr B Promoted to Lieut. & first putting on his uniform'. *NMM ref PAD4727*

7. 'Waiting room at the Admiralty (no misnomer)'. *NMM ref PAD4726*

1

Blockade of Cadiz

FOLLOWING ITS smashing victory over the Spaniards off St Vincent, Jervis took the fleet back to the Tagus, where the most damaged vessels, including the *Victory*, were dispatched home and the remainder refitted. Reinforcements included the brand-new *Ville de Paris*, the first 110-gun ship in the Royal Navy and named after de Grasse's flagship captured at the Saintes in 1782. With middle and upper deck batteries of 24pdrs and 18s, she was more than a match for the Spanish 112-gun ships with their 18pdrs and 12s, although not quite as large as the *San Josef*. She became the flagship of the newly ennobled Admiral St Vincent, and led the fleet of twenty-one of the line to sea on 31 March 1797 to blockade Cadiz (1).

The sheltered Bay of Cadiz (2) still contained twenty-six ships of the line, now under the command of Mazzeredo, and the British fleet trailed its coat off the port for six weeks, but could not draw them out (3). On

19 May St Vincent established a close blockade, anchoring off the town in a crescent formation (4), with an Advanced or Inshore Squadron under Nelson right in the mouth of the harbour (5). However, there was also what a military man might call a 'forlorn hope', in the shape of the frigate *Blanche* whose crew still included Jacob Nagle, last noticed off Leghorn, and he left a record of his ship's thankless and forgotten duty:

Jervis's fleet lay at an anchor outside, then Nelson with a squadron of seven sail of the line lay inside of them, and we were stationed within the whole, laying off and on from one shore to the other, all hands at quarters during the night with the hatches laid over that no one was allowed to go below, and let us stand on the one tack or the other, we would have a shot or shell flying over us during the night. The reason was to keep the gunboats off from annoying the line of battle ships. The gunboats would come out and lay off and keep firing at the ships laying at their anchors, but when we were inside we could cut them off, but the batteries on either shore could fire at us. We remained on this station about a fortnight, then we were relieved . . .

Having failed to shame the Spanish fleet into action, St Vincent resolved to bombard the town, which seemed likely to provoke some defensive moves. Nelson, now a rear-admiral, was given the task and on the night of 3 July the bomb vessel *Thunder* with gunboats and the boats of the fleet stood in towards the tower of San Sebastian. The Spanish countered with gunboats and other small craft and Nelson was involved in a savage hand-to-hand fight with the boat of the Spanish commander, Don Miguel Tyrason, as recounted by one of the sailors present (see the next section for illustration):

John Sykes was close to Nelson on his left hand, and he seemed more concerned for the Admiral's life than his own: he hardly ever struck a blow but to save his gallant officer. Twice he parried blows that must have been fatal to Nelson. . . . It was cut, thrust, fire, and no load again—we had no time for that. The Spaniards fought like devils, and seemed resolved to win from the Admiral the laurels of his former victory; they appeared to know him, and directed their particular attack towards the officers.

Twice had Sykes saved him; and now he saw a blow descending which would have severed the head of Nelson . . . but Sykes saved him—he interposed his own hand! We all saw it . . . and we gave in revenge one cheer and one tremendous rally. Eighteen of the Spaniards were killed, and we boarded and carried her; there not being one man left on board who was not either dead or wounded.

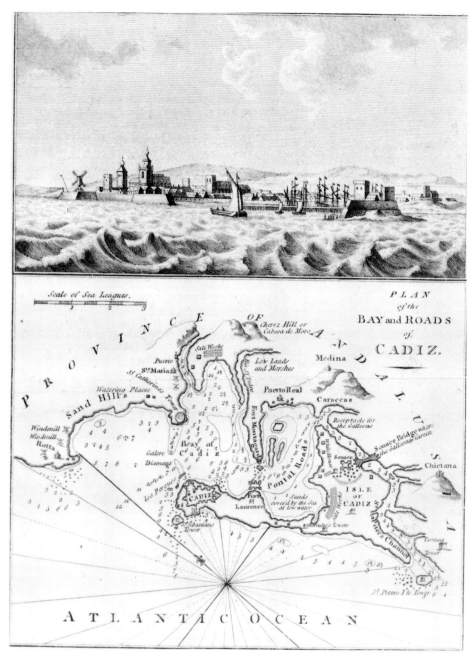

2

3

4

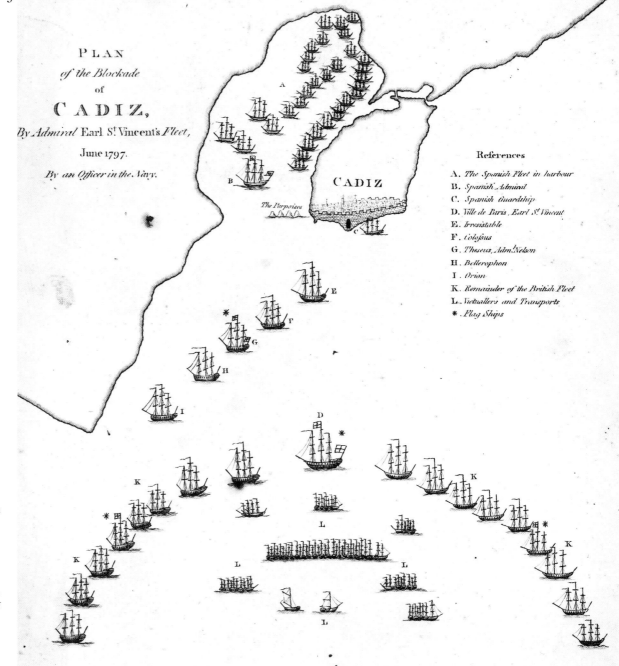

5

1. 'Earl St Vincent leaving Lisbon in the Ville de Paris 31 March 1797', grey wash by Thomas Buttersworth (1768-1842). *NMM ref PAH9502*

2. 'View of Cadiz in Spain from the West. European Magazine. Plan of the Bay and Roads of Cadiz', engraving by J Cary, published by I Fielding, 1 January 1783. *NMM ref PAD1662*

3. 'The inshore blockading squadron at Cadiz, July 1797', oil painting by Thomas Buttersworth (1768-1842). *NMM ref BHC0499*

4. 'A View of the Blockade off Cadiz by the British Fleet under the Command of the Right Honble Earl St Vincent', anonymous watercolour, no date. *NMM ref PAF4685*

5. 'Plan of the Blockade of Cadiz, by Admiral Earl St Vincent's Fleet June 1797. By an Officer in the Navy', engraving, no date. *NMM ref PAD5519*

6. 'Blockade of the Port of Cadiz August 1797 by the Fleet under the Command of Adm. Sir John Jervis – with the Advanced Squadron', watercolour by Thomas Buttersworth (1768-1842). *Peabody Essex Museum, Salem MA neg 15121*

7. 'Representation of the advanced Squadron under the command of Rear-Admiral Lord Nelson during the Blockade of Cadiz exhibiting a View of the Harbour and Fortifications taken from the Original Drawing by T Buttersworth now in his Lordship's Possession', published by T Williamson, London, 1 July 1802. *NMM ref PAG7151*

PLAN
of the Blockade
of
CADIZ,
By Admiral Earl St Vincent's *Fleet*,
June 1797.
By an Officer in the Navy.

CADIZ

The Porpoises

References

A. *The Spanish Fleet in harbour*
B. *Spanish Admiral*
C. *Spanish Guardship*
D. *Ville de Paris, Earl St Vincent*
E. *Irresistable*
F. *Colossus*
G. *Theseus, Adml Nelson*
H. *Bellerophon*
I. *Orion*
K. *Remainder of the British Fleet*
L. *Victuallers and Transports*
✱ . *Flag Ships*

6

Besides the commandant's launch, the British captured two mortar boats, but the bombardment was a failure, as was a more powerful attack with three bombs two days later. The frustrated Nelson was dispatched on the even more disastrous Santa Cruz expedition later in the month.

Meanwhile the blockade went on. That the events of this period are so well illustrated is largely due to Thomas Buttersworth, who was serving as a seaman in the fleet and must have observed at first hand the incidents he illustrates—his depictions of the Advanced Squadron, for example, both as original watercolours (6) and as prints (7).

St Vincent withdrew the main fleet to the Tagus in the autumn, but a squadron of observation was kept cruising off Cadiz during the winter.

7

Santa Cruz de Tenerife

URING THE blockade of Cadiz, rumours reached Earl St Vincent that a Spanish treasure ship, the *Principe de Asturias*, carrying £7 million in gold from Manila, had taken shelter in Santa Cruz de Tenerife in the Canary Islands. The loss of this bullion would be a crippling blow to Spanish finances, an important boost for the British exchequer, and, not least, a fabulously rich prize for the admirals and captains responsible for its capture.

On 15 July 1797 a squadron commanded by Rear-Admiral Nelson sailed for Tenerife (1). It comprised Nelson's flagship *Theseus*, the *Culloden* and *Zealous*, all 74s, the *Leander*, 50, the frigates *Seahorse, Emerald* and *Terpsichore*, the cutter *Fox* and a mortar boat. The ships arrived off Tenerife on the 20th, but bad weather and contrary currents prevented an immediate landing and the element of surprise was lost. The island turned out to be far more strongly defended than expected, and a landing on the 22nd was abandoned without loss when the heights above the town of Santa Cruz were found to be too strongly held to be taken.

However, Nelson did not give up, and on 24 July attempted another attack, this time against the defences of the harbour entrance, with the *Fox* and a number of the other ships' boats, Nelson himself in command. It was far from usual for a rear-admiral to participate directly in small boat actions, but it was Nelson's practice to lead from the front, as at St Vincent and later at Cadiz when he was involved in a battle with a Spanish launch, (2) where one of his sailors had saved his life three times in vicious hand-to-hand fighting. But this time he was not to be so lucky. The attack was met by heavy fire, the *Fox* being sunk by three direct hits. The boats managed to reach the mole head, but Nelson was hit in the right elbow as he stepped out of his boat (3), fell back into it and was carried back to the *Theseus*, where his arm had to be amputated.

Meanwhile, the battery at the mole head had been taken and its guns spiked, but almost the entire attacking force was then either killed or wounded by fire from the citadel and the houses nearby. Among those killed was Captain Richard Bowen (4) of the *Terpsichore*, who had distinguished himself after the battle of Cape St Vincent by pursuing and engaging the famous 136-gun *Santísima Trinidad* in his 32-gun frigate, only breaking off when other Spanish ships appeared. Other boats had managed to put their men ashore elsewhere, but the surf was so high that many had had to put back, and the men who were landed had their ammunition ruined by water. By dawn there were some 340 sailors and marines ashore, under the command of Captain Thomas Troubridge of the *Culloden*, facing a reported 8000 Spaniards. Amazingly, Troubridge was able to negotiate a withdrawal, the Spanish governor, Don Antonio Guttierrez, permitting the British to re-embark, even providing them with boats and rations, in return for a promise of no further attacks on any of the Canary Islands.

The expedition had been very costly. The British had lost 141 men killed, 95 of these drowned when the *Fox* was sunk, and 105 wounded. By comparison, only seventy-three men had been killed aboard British ships at the battle of Cape St Vincent. Nelson had been lucky to escape with his life.

1. 'View of Santa Cruz', coloured aquatint engraved by T Medland from an original by W Alexander, published by Messrs Cadell and Davies, 4 June 1806. *NMM ref PAD1949*

2. 'Nelson in conflict with a Spanish Launch, July 1797', oil painting by Richard Westall, 1806. *NMM ref BHC2908*

3. Nelson wounded at Tenerife, 24 July 1797', oil painting by Richard Westall, 1806. *NMM ref BHC0498*

4. 'Captain Richard Bowen 1761-1797', stipple engraving by H R Cook, published by J Gold, 31 May 1810. *NMM ref PAD3035*

3

4

Part IV

IRELAND AND THE CHANNEL 1795–1797

BY THE Treaty of Basel in April 1795 Prussia had made peace with France. With the end of fighting on the mainland, French military planning could concentrate on plans against the Britain Isles. The combined naval forces of France, Spain and the Netherlands, if they could find the means to co-operate well together and overcome the training and supply problems of the French, and the manpower shortages of the Spaniards, would be a formidable force in the Channel. Unlike the Duc de Vergennes, who had refused to contemplate the large-scale invasion of England during the American War because he feared the reverberations throughout Europe such a marked change in the balance of power would cause, the revolutionary government had nothing to lose by invading the British Isles. The need to counter the danger of invasion was to to be a major factor in British defence planning until in 1805 that option was decisively closed for the enemy. The events of 1796 and 1797, however, were to show how inadequate the naval resources of France, even when allied to Spain and the Netherlands, were for the task.

The stimulus for invasion of Ireland came from the United Irishmen, led by Lord Edward Fitzgerald. After a preliminary sounding of the ground in Paris, he and Arthur O'Connor met General Hoche at Basel to discuss a plan. Hoche and Admiral Truguet were in close agreement on the value of an operation to undermine Britain's position by outflanking her in Ireland, and in October 1796 Villaret-Joyeuse was ordered to fit out the Brest fleet to land a French army under General Hoche at Bantry Bay. Discipline had been restored in the fleet, but the dockyards were still desperately short of supplies, and the men lacked the training and experience to inspire confidence.

Villaret-Joyeuse said so, and was replaced by Admiral Morard de Galles.

The Irish nationalist Wolfe Tone had developed the plan of operations with Hoche, and now accompanied the expedition. It was intended that the Brest fleet should avoid naval action. The army was to be landed at Bantry Bay in southwest Ireland, and it was to make a quick movement to Cork where the Royal Navy victualling stores would have been easily taken. There was next to no British military force ashore in Ireland.

De Galles was able to sail his fleet of seventeen ships of the line, and nineteen light craft with seven transports and a powder ship, from Brest without opposition because Vice-Admiral Colpoys was not on station, but he lost a ship, *Séduisant*, 74, which ran on a rock. Indeed, it was the inadequacy of French seamanship, and the fact that the ships were supplied for only a few weeks, which was to defeat the expedition. The frigate *Fraternité*, aboard which were the admiral and General Hoche, became separated from the rest of the squadron, which made its way under Admiral Bouvet but missed its proper landfall and spent days beating against gale-force easterlies into Bantry Bay. The fleeting opportunities which occurred to put the army ashore were missed by General Grouchy acting in the absence of Hoche, and the continued easterly wind and shortage of supplies made it unhealthy to remain long in the Bay when Bridport could be expected to appear with the Channel Fleet.

In fact, however, the operational inadequacy of Spithead as the base for Channel Fleet operations was made abundantly clear by the difficulty Bridport experienced in getting to the westward when ordered to sea by the Admiralty. His own indolence was a contributing factor, and he also had bad luck when several of his ships collided on leaving the anchorage. He did not even get far enough down Channel to meet de Galles on his way back to Brest.

A straggler from the fleet, *Droits de l'Homme*, was engaged in heavy weather by Captain Sir Edward Pellew with two frigates, the 44-gun *Indefatigable* and the 36-gun *Amazon*. The high sea, and the fact that *Droits de l'Homme* had lost her fore and main topmasts which prevented her putting up sails to steady her roll, made it impossible for her to use her lower deck guns. *Indefatigable* was armed with long 24pdr guns on the lower deck, and 42pdr carronades on the upper, so she was a formidable opponent.

During the whole of this long engagement, [wrote William James] the sea ran so high, that the people on the main decks of the frigates were up to their middles in water. So violent, too, was the motion of the ships, that some of the *Indefatigable*'s guns broke their breechings four times; some drew their ring-bolts from the side, and many of the guns, owing to the water having beaten into them, were obliged to be drawn immediately after loading.[1]

In the murk, navigation became inexact. When land was sighted close under their lees all three ships broke off their fight to claw themselves clear, but only *Indefatigable* saved herself from the rocks in Audierne Bay.

Part of the Toulon fleet under Vice-Admiral Villeneuve had followed Jervis out of the Mediterranean, passed him at Gibraltar during the gale which had caused him such heavy losses, and safely reached Brest. At the end of June 1797 there were nineteen fully armed ship of the line at Brest, and many armed *en flûte* for use as transports. These were to co-operate with the movement of the Dutch fleet to escort an invasion force from the Texel to England. However, the Battle of Cape St Vincent had discouraged the combined Franco-Spanish fleet seeking action in the Channel. A political convulsion in Paris which temporarily eclipsed the power of the Directory brought the dismissal of Admiral

1. Jemes, Vol 2, p20.

2. I bid, p32.

Truguet from the naval ministry. He was replaced by M. Pléville-de-Peley who was inexperienced with naval affairs but was able to execute the instruction to disarm the Brest fleet and sell some of the frigates. The Directory recovered its power in September and ordered the rearming of the fleet at Brest, but it was to take all winter before it was again in a condition for sea.

The threat from the small navy of the Netherlands became critical when on 15 April 1797 the seamen and marines at Spithead refused to sail until their grievances about pay, victuals, and treatment of sick and wounded were met. 'The spirit of mutiny,' wrote William James, 'had taken deep root in the breasts of the seamen, and, from the apparent organisation of the plan, seemed to be the result of far more reflection, than the wayward mind of a jack-tar is usually given credit for.'[2] Against this well-organised collective action the government was powerless, and to his credit Spencer did not compound the problem by attempting the use of force. Instead, Parliament rushed through a bill on 10 May agreeing to the seamen's demands, and the King signed a pardon for all the sailors involved. About half of the officers whom the seaman had sent ashore were relieved of their duty. The popular Lord Howe was called out of retirement to meet the seamen's delegates and respond to their demands. The affair ended in a mood of rejoicing and the fleet went to sea.

A more violent sequel broke out at the Nore on 15 May and spread to the North Sea squadron at Yarmouth. Vice-Admiral Adam Duncan kept control of his own flagship, *Venerable*, and regained control of *Adamant* when he intervened personally and held at arm's length overboard the only sailor who dared contest his authority, but the rest of the ships sailed to join the mutineers at the Nore.

Spencer found it impossible to negotiate with these delegates, and their leader Richard Parker, because they did not have clearly defined objectives, and were too emotional. Even the seamen at Spithead expressed their concern about the events at the Nore. The mutineers stopped merchant shipping entering or leaving the Thames in the hope of forcing the government's hand.

Eventually the supply of victuals to the fleet was cut off, the forts at Tilbury, Gravesend and Sheerness were prepared to fire red-hot shot, and the buoyage in the estuary was removed to deter attempts to take the ships to the Texel. Gradually the ships' companies turned against their leaders, fights broke out, and finally one by one the ships sailed away to surrender. Parker and twenty-eight delegates were hanged, and others were flogged round the fleet.

Duncan had kept up the blockade of the Texel with his flagship and *Adamant*, anchoring in the mouth of the harbour when the wind blew from the east so that the Dutch could sail. False signals were made to suggest that the main force was just across the horizon. Soon he was reinforced by six ships from the Channel Fleet under Sir Roger Curtis, and the Russian squadron put in an appearance. Finally the chastened mutineers returned to their duty.

In July the army was embarked on the Dutch transports, but as Wolfe Tone recorded dismally in his journal, the wind was steadily foul for departure. The invasion plan was abandoned when Hoche died, but Admiral de Winter was nonetheless ordered to seek action at sea. The opportunity occurred in October when Duncan was in Yarmouth. The battle which followed, known as the battle of Camperdown, was exceptionally hard-fought. The stubborn courage of the Dutch was a marked contrast to the performance of the

French Marine since the revolution. The Dutch, however, were at a disadvantage because their ships were small, and because the armament of the British ships included carronades which increased the weight of shot that could be fired.

De Winter took a position close to the shoals. To prevent him slipping to leeward into such shallow water that the deeper-draught British ships could not follow, Duncan sought to break through the Dutch line and engage from the leeward. He attacked in two divisions which concentrated on the Dutch van and rear, and his captains managed to break through in several places. His approach tactics exposed his leading ships to fire they could not immediately return, but when the ships in the rear of the columns came to the support of the leaders their superior gunnery carried the day. The former mutineers, who greatly respected their admiral, showed no reluctance to fight and die for their King and country. Unlike actions with the French and Spaniards, who sought to immobilise their enemy by firing into their rigging, the Dutch and British both concentrated on firing into the enemy gun decks, and at the waterline, to destroy their fighting capability.

At the end of 1797 the Directory again took up the idea of invading Britain, and General Bonaparte, back from Italy was put in command of the Army of England. He surveyed the embarkation ports and ordered the construction of troop-carrying gunboats, but his advice to Paris was that invasion was impossible without command of the sea. Rather than persevere in a campaign which was likely to be the end of his career, if not to cost him his life, he suggested that he be sent with an army, first to conquer Egypt, and then from that base to co-operate with Tipu Sultan in India. His modest goal was the conquest of Asia.

1

Close blockade

BECAUSE THE Channel Fleet was not permanently on station off Ushant, the close blockade of Brest was entrusted to detached squadrons of ships of the line (1) and frigates, although even this degree of attention was neither consistently nor rigorously applied. While major movements of the French fleet might not escape attention for long, it was less difficult for small divisions of the battlefleet, and especially frigate squadrons, to slip out undetected.

In April 1795 a squadron of five of the line and three

2

frigates under Rear-Admiral Sir John Colpoys discovered and chased three French frigates. These split up, leaving the 32-gun *Astraea* to pursue and bring to action the 36-gun *Gloire* on the evening of the 12th. They were well matched 12pdr-armed ships, although without any carronades the British ship had a lower broadside weight of fire, and as usual high-trajectory French fire damaged the top-hamper of her opponent (which lost all her topmasts), whereas the British fired into the hull, causing about 40 casualties before *Gloire* struck her colours (2). One of the other frigates, *Gentille*, was taken by the 74-gun *Hannibal* the following morning.

The independent Channel cruiser squadrons were also active in hunting down frigates that escaped the watch off the ports. By 1796 they contained some very powerful ships that under Sir Edward Pellew, for example, consisting of the cut-down 64 (or *rasée*) *Indefatigable*, a 24pdr-armed ship rated at 44 guns, the 44-gun two-decker *Argo*, the big, ex-French *Revolutionnaire*, 38, and the 36-gun *Amazon* and *Concorde*. In April they pursued and captured the *Unité*, 36 guns, and no sooner was the prize dispatched than another strange sail was sighted and the squadron set all sail in pursuit. The stranger was very fast, but Pellew had insisted that *Indefatigable* retain her full-sized spars when cut down a deck and this powerful rig gave her an advantage over her consorts. After a 15-hour chase covering 168 miles, she brought to action the French 40-gun frigate *Virginie*; the ensuing battle lasted nearly two hours and although heavily outgunned the French ship only surrendered when *Amazon* joined *Indefatigable* (3).

By this stage in the war the Channel was a dangerous

3

cruising ground for French commerce raiders, and neither mid-winter darkness nor bad weather offered any respite, as the *Nereide* discovered in December 1797. She was pursued all of the 27th and into the night by the *Phoebe*, 36 and in a somewhat confused battle in the darkness forced the French ship to surrender. One of Whitcombe's more dramatic compositions (4) shows the *Phoebe* charging past her quarry, who has tacked without the British ship noticing. It proved another engagement where ships of nominal force—36 guns—were actually heavily mismatched, the British 18pdr-armed frigate having a significant advantage in firepower over her 12pdr opponent, reflected in the French casualties which were six times those of the *Phoebe*.

4

1. 'A Squadron standing along a coast under Easy Sail, A Cutter under the Stern of the Commodore for Orders', engraving produced and published by Robert Dodd, London, 21 February 1793.
NMM neg B3858

2. 'Capture of La Gloire April 10th 1795', coloured aquatint engraved by Thomas Sutherland after an original by Thomas Whitcombe (c1752-1824), 1 June 1816.
NMM ref PAD5488

3. 'The Indefatigable of 44 Guns Capt. Sr Edward Pellew engaging and capturing La Virginie of 44 Guns', coloured engraving, published by C Sheppard, 1 June 1797. This is both crude and inaccurate as a depiction of the battle—the ships went into action carrying more canvas and they never seem to have passed on opposite tacks —but the *Indefatigable* is correctly shown as having the stern gallery on the level of the quarterdeck, a legacy of her origins as a 64-gun two-decker.
NMM ref PAD5498

4. 'Capture of La Nereide Decr 21st 1797', coloured aquatint engraved by Thomas Sutherland after an original by Thomas Whitcombe, 1 May 1816.
NMM ref PAD5533

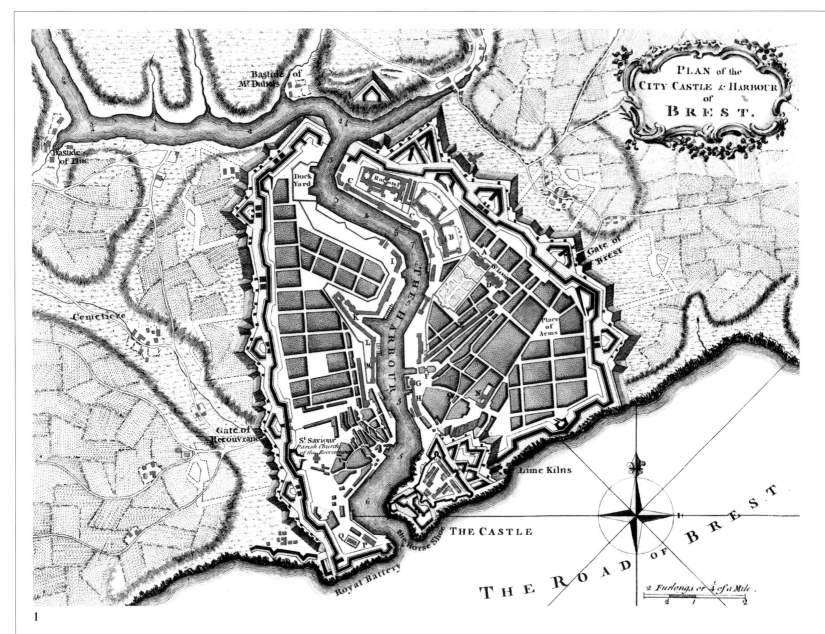

Plan of the
CITY CASTLE & HARBOUR
of
BREST.

1

French naval bases: Brest

BREST HAD been France's major Atlantic base since the time of Louis XIV, with a dockyard set up by Colbert and fortifications by Vauban (1). A century later it was to be Revolutionary France's main base against Britain. The dockyard installations (2, 3) were set on the banks of the little river Penfeld, with the massive bulk of the castle overshadowing its mouth (4).

Outside the river mouth lay an enormous area of sheltered water—the *Rade de Brest* (Brest roads)—which led out to sea through the narrow gap of the *Goulet* (literally the Gullet). This gap was both a great advantage, as it was narrow enough to be commanded by batteries on both sides and therefore any enemy could be prevented from coming into the *Rade* and threatening Brest itself, but also it was a major disadvantage as the prevail-

ing westerly wind blew directly into it, and made access to the open sea difficult, particularly in the face of a blockading fleet, and there were severe navigational difficulties in using the passages immediately outside, especially in bad visibility or by night when trying to obtain surprise.

The ironbound coast of western Brittany tested to the utmost the skill of the British ships charged with the close blockade of the French Brest fleet. Illustration (5) shows the view from a blockading ship penetrating as close to the *Goulet* as was possible without risking total destruction. However, usually only the inshore squadron was actually off Brest, the rest of the blockading fleet being out to sea or in reasonably well-sheltered bays, knowing that the French would find it very difficult to

get out through the *Goulet* without adequate warning being given to catch them. An onshore gale might make it necessary for the blockading fleet to run for the shelter of Torbay, but would equally pin the French in port, and any change in the wind would bring the blockading fleet back, just as it would help the French emerge.

Geography imposed other problems on Brest. At the extreme western end of the comparatively barren Breton peninsula, its land communications with the rest of France were poor, and local supplies quite inadequate to support such a major base. The obvious supply route was by sea, and was strangled by the same blockad-

ing squadron that kept an eye on the Brest fleet. Napoleon initiated plans for a canal from Nantes to Brest which would bypass the blockade, but it was completed far too late to be of assistance in his wars.

From the very start of the Revolution in 1789 there was conflict in and around Brest with mutinies by parts of the Army garrison and (in 1790) by the fleet as well. The fleet was still in a state of indiscipline shading into outbreaks of actual mutiny in 1793. By this year Brest had become an island of republicanism in a Brittany almost entirely given over to counter-revolution. Troops from the port gained a narrow victory over local

4

1. 'Plan of the City Castle & Harbour of Brest', etching by T Jefferys, 1761. *NMM ref PAD1500*

2-4. Etchings of the Port of Brest by Yves Maire Le Gouaz after originals by Nicolas Marie Ozanne, 1776.

2. 'Le Port de Brest. Vu de la cale de construction atenant au Bureau general. Reduit de las Collection des Ports de France dessines pour le Roi en 1776. Par le Sr. Ozanne Ingenieur de la Marine Pensionnaire de sa Majeste', *NMM ref PAD1502*

3. 'Le Port de Brest. Vu du Chenal devant le nouveau quai aux canons. Reduit de las Collection des Ports de France dessines pour le Roi en 1776. Par le Sr. Ozanne Ingenieur de la Marine Pensionnaire de sa Majeste'. *NMM ref PAD1503*

4. 'Le Port de Brest. Vu du Magazin des vivres en face de la Chaine. Reduit de las Collection des Ports de France dessines pour le Roi en 1776. Par le Sr. Ozanne Ingenieur de la Marine Pensionnaire de sa Majeste'. *NMM ref PAD1504*

5. 'View of Brest Harbour', aquatint engraved by Robert Pollard after an original by Nicholas Pocock (1740-1821), published by Burney & Co, 1 February 1799. *NMM ref PAD1505*

royalists, but for some time Brest was even more isolated than usual. Famine and epidemics ravaged the population, and, whilst the escape of the French grain convoy from America in 1794 may not have saved the country, it probably did rescue Brest from starvation. In the circumstances the fact that the fleet at Brest managed to achieve anything at all is more surprising than that it did not do well. Its difficulties were added to by the fact that in 1792 much of its reserves of timber and naval stores were moved to Toulon in anticipation of a war restricted to the Mediterranean, and were lost there a year later.

The British blockade of Brest was fairly effective in strangling the port; and, though it had been the chief centre for naval shipbuilding for Atlantic France in the eighteenth century, during the last decade of the Napoleonic wars most new major warships were building at Antwerp, Cherbourg, or in the Mediterranean.

5

1

The Irish Guard

IN THE allocation of big frigates, the Irish squadron based at Cork and commanded during this period by Vice-Admiral Kingsmill, was probably second only in priority to the Channel Fleet. Not only did it have the Atlantic coast of Ireland to patrol and the shipping in the Western approaches to defend, but Ireland itself was a frequent target for invasion. Apart from Kingsmill's near-stationary flagship, ships of the line could not be spared permanently to guard against this eventuality and so large frigates were the next best thing—they possessed sufficient seakeeping for boisterous Atlantic conditions, and were weatherly enough to claw off the

2

3

many lee shores of the command's cruising grounds. Kingsmill's frigates proved active and successful, and were almost the only ships in a position to oppose Hoche's abortive Bantry expedition in the winter of 1796-7, the British battle squadrons being completely wrong-footed.

June 1796 proved a particularly successful month for the Irish Guard. On the 8th the 18pdr 32-gun *Unicorn* and 12pdr 36-gun *Santa Margarita* sighted part of a French cruiser squadron that had escaped from Brest a few days earlier; having lost touch with the *Proserpine* it now comprised the 36-gun frigates *Tribune* and *Tamise*, and the corvette *Légère*, 18. The French squadron formed a bow and quarter line, but as the British frigates came into range, the *Légère* hauled up to windward and passed asern at long range (far right in '1'). The struggle soon dissolved into two separate single-ship engagements,

the *Santa Margarita*, a prize from the Spanish, taking on the *Tamise*, the ex-British *Thames* captured by the French in 1793. There was little difference in firepower between the ships, but after a fierce 20-minute exchange *Tamise* surrendered and was returned to her original owner-ship. As a tribute to the efficiency of Captain Byam Martin's ship, she lost only 2 dead and 3 wounded to the enemy's 32 killed and 19 wounded. *Santa Margarita*, an active cruiser under Martin's command, had been the subject of a sketch by Nicholas Pocock while lying in the Cove of Cork earlier in the year (2).

The other fight was not so quickly ended; in fact, *Unicorn* was involved in a running battle, covering over 200 miles before, with the onset of night, the wind dropped and the British ship carrying every fair-weather sail was able to creep up on the *Tribune*'s weather quarter, stealing her wind. This moment is the subject of one of

Pocock's most dramatic renderings of single-ship engagements (3), with the British ship lit from within by the fire of her first broadside and the chaotic mass of flapping canvas silhouetted against the sky. The *Tribune* was well handled by her *émigré* American captain, but not well fought, and when she struck her colours, with 37 dead and 18 wounded, she had not inflicted a single casualty on her, admittedly more powerful, opponent.

A few days later another of Kingsmill's cruisers was in action, and the target was the missing frigate from the same French squadron, *Proserpine*, 40. She was chased and captured after a similarly one-sided action by the 18pdr-armed *Dryad* (4). Even the *Légère* was snapped up on 22 June by the frigates *Apollo* and *Doris* so all the units of this French raiding group had been eliminated in a matter of days.

---

1. 'To Captain Thomas Byam Martin This Print representing the Engaging and Taking La Tamise French Frigate, by His Majesty's Frigate Santa Margaritta', aquatint engraved by Robert Pollard after an original by Nicholas Pocock (1740-1821), published by the artist 4 June 1796. *NMM neg no C626*

2. 'His Majesty's Ship Santa Margarita J. B. Martin Esq. Commander as she appeared on the morning of 14th Jany 1796 at the Cove of Cork. J. C. From a sketch by Mr Pocock June 1811', grey wash. *NMM ref PAD8650*

3. 'To Captain Sir Thomas Williams, This Print representing The Capture of the French Frigate La Tribune by His Majesty's Ship The Unicorn on the 8th June 1796', aquatint engraved by Francis Chesham after an original by Nicholas Pocock (1740-1821), published by the artist 14 August 1797. *NMM neg no B3226*

4. 'Capture of La Prosperpine, June 13th 1796', coloured aquatint engraved by J Jeakes after an original by Thomas Whitcombe, published 1 May 1816. *NMM ref PAD5501*

4

1

The naval officer: life at sea

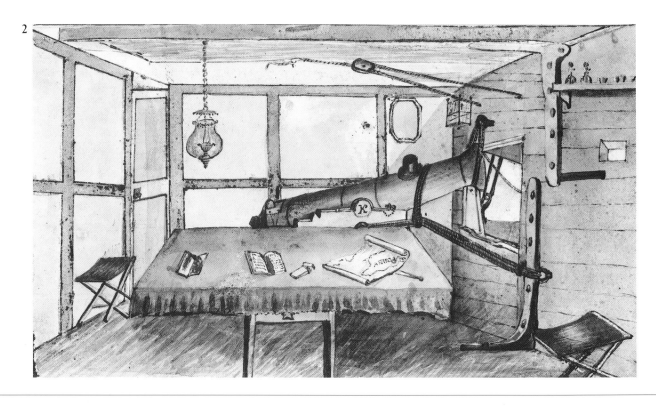

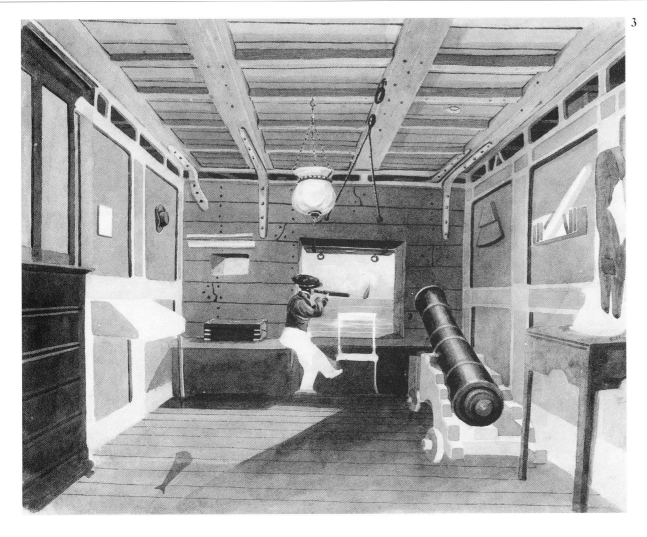

3

For the younger sons of gentlemen, life at sea in the Royal Navy was no less arduous than that of the ordinary seamen and, relative to the comforts in which they had invariably been raised, a great deal more uncomfortable. A career at sea for a young man nevertheless often had more to attract him than the alternative professions: the church, the army, medicine or trade. The attraction of escape to an adult world exploring foreign ports, with all the temptations they offered, was the poorer man's version of the nobility's grand tour. Moreover it held out the prospect, where patronage was available, of a career that in some cases led to distinction and even affluence. For, although wage payment was always in arrears, the proportion of prize money shared among officers—one quarter between the commissioned and warrant officers—ensured each of them a significant proportion that in a few cases amounted to small fortunes.

The young gentlemen who succumbed to these attractions would find, however, that sea life had a great deal more to endure than, in their original enthusiasm, they had foreseen. So much depended on patronage: initial entry and, even having proved courage and ability,

being recommended and obtaining appointments. Employment was likely in wartime, but even in the eighteenth century, peace prevailed for just as many years as wars lasted. There were therefore long periods of waiting and writing for appointments, which equally

4

balanced the activity afloat. Even there, calculations show that ships of war spent as long in port as cruising at sea. And, even at sea, an officers' life in a small ship, where much fell to one officer, was very different from that in larger ships of the line, where duties were more specialised.

For young officers a berth in a ship of the line, with the prospect of notice and promotion, was more attractive to those wishing to rise in the service. In these large vessels, the working of the ship, changes of watch, cleaning of decks, meal times, taking navigational sights at noon, occasional punishments and weekly divine service, when there was a chaplain or taken by the captain, who also read the Articles of War, all formed a framework within which sea officers pursued their existence. A large part of their time was spent in supervising sections of the crew to which they were allotted on a divisional system in which midshipmen assisted lieutenants in supervising sub-sections. At sea gun drill ensured seamen were trained for action, while in port they were invariably occupied in repairing, painting, mending or shifting equipment and stores.

Sea life was essentially communal for the lower ranks (1), but in larger ships a berth of their own was provided for the senior lieutenants (2) and warrant officers where they could occasionally gain moments of privacy, to read and write. Their officially required production of a daily journal always involved them some of the time in calculating positions—note the sextant case on the bulkhead of the master's cabin in (3)—and recording events. Otherwise they enjoyed games of backgammon (4), cards, even fishing. Some admirals enjoyed music and had musicians among their crews for regular soirees. Other musical officers who played instruments had to avoid unpopularity with watch-keeping messmates trying to sleep. But their playing complemented the dancing and singing of crewmen and introduced a cultivated element to the atmosphere of a ship primarily concerned with working at sea. Even literary endeavours were not unknown—indeed, Captain Edward Thompson was a nationally recognised poet.

Among officers, for much of the time socially isolated together, meal times provided a focus of their communal life. Officers dined in the wardroom (5). The wealth of the participants determined quality of diet and accessories like wine; just to take a place at this table demanded income sufficient to dress appropriately and pay the wardroom bills. Boorish drunken behaviour was on the decline by the late eighteenth century, while honour—the mark of a gentleman—self-discipline and sociably pleasing conduct were points of recommendation, while skill at conversation was a quality increasingly prized. Those meals with the captain present, or when invited in turn to the admiral's table, were high points in an officer's life. For a captain himself, living in the god-like isolation of the great cabin (6), such socialising was often the only relief from the proverbial loneliness of command.

For an officer with permission, the ability to leave the ship and enjoy days or longer on shore in port provided relief and access to wives, families or other society. In the Mediterranean some took the opportunity, for example, to visit sights of classical antiquity. In England there were theatres and concert rooms. However, in port some captains brought their own women on board, and tolerated the wives of a few warrant or petty officers sailing and berthing with the crew. Childbirth on board was not uncommon, while the presence of children as well as animals created something of a domestic environment.

The smaller vessels—frigates, brigs, sloops and gun vessels—were more usually detached on services distant from the main fleet, which offered greater variety of tasks and movement between coasts. Officers on such vessels had less space and fewer companions, which

5

6

reduced the variety of social activities and increased crowding. In bad weather officers as well as seamen became wet and cold, as much from water leaking through decks as from working on watch (7). Winters at sea, poorly prepared food, blockade or routine convoying, with little prospect of immediate relief or patronage could be demoralising. An important role of senior officers was accordingly the maintenance of morale among their juniors as much as in the crew. For it was upon these subordinates that the reputations of sea officers were built.

1. 'Life on the ocean: midshipman's berth in a British frigate at sea', oil painting by Augustus Earle (*fl*1806-1838).
NMM ref BHC1118

2. 'Study of accommodation in a vessel. 3rd Officer's Mess Room Wexford 1809. 10. 11', watercolour by Charles Copland 1809. This is actually an East Indiaman but gives a good impression of the cramped space, often containing a gun, and the partitions of canvas stretched over a wooden frame, all of which had to be taken down when clearing for action.
NMM ref PAF2387

3. 'Master's cabin 1825', watercolour attributed to the Reverend Thomas Streatfield. Although the details are accurate, the proportions are woefully wrong, appearing to give far more space (and particularly more headroom) than was ever the case.
NMM ref PAD8627

4. 'Sketch of Thomson and Harris playing backgammon on board Andromeda', anonymous black & wash, grey pen & ink sketch probably by a naval officer, no date, but about 1790.
NMM ref PAH4903

5. Officers at dinner in the wardroom. From a sketchbook of Edward Pelham Brenton, 1801-2.
NMM ref PAF8407

6. 'Interior of a ship's cabin ca. 1819', anonymous watercolour of the nineteenth- century British school, 1820.
NMM ref PAD5857

7. Midshipman at the wheel learning to steer the ship. Anonymous watercolour, undated.
NMM ref 4886

7

1

Inshore warfare in the Channel

2

WARFARE IN the Channel was a matter of overlapping layers of defence. The main fleet was usually retained in Torbay or Spithead, with the occasional cruise off Ushant, the closer blockade being maintained by detached squadrons and frigates. However, there was a more advanced element that took the war right up to the enemy's high-water line. France could be greatly inconvenienced by interference with her coasting trade, or *cabotage*, since the road and canal network of the western departments was not well developed. The British became adept at daring boat attacks—'cutting-out' expeditions they were called—and many a small vessel was surprised, boarded and carried from harbours and anchorages (1). The prospect of a descent on any small port increased the

sense of insecurity and drew off troops for coast-defence duties that might have been more dangerously employed elsewhere. An urgency was added to British actions from 1795-96 with the threat of invasion, and many of the small craft assembled in the French Channel ports for a possible landing became a higher priority target.

These inshore squadrons were usually commanded by frigate captains, and none was more active than Sir Sidney Smith (2). The exploits of his *Diamond*, 38, including the audacious reconnaissance of Brest, added to a reputation already established by burning part of the French fleet at Toulon. Even frigates drew too much water for many of these activities, and the square rig of conventional ships did not make them sufficiently handy. As a result, much of the burden

Published 30th April, 1806, by J. Gold, 103, Shoe Lane, Fleet Street.

3

4

5

fell on cutters and luggers, many of which were hired or purchased rather than purpose-built by the navy. One of the best known was the lugger *Aristocrat*, which had fought an epic action lasting eighteen hours off the Channel Islands in July 1795, when she had finally escaped from the French flotilla of nine ships that had surrounded her (3). Along with the brig *Liberty*, she volunteered to join Sidney Smith's squadron in a typical attack on Herqui in March of the following year, where a 16-gun corvette, and her convoy of four brigs, two sloops and one armed lugger were burnt and destroyed. As he said in his report, 'I was much pleased by the conduct of Lieutenant Gosset in the hired lugger.'

These actions often involved landings and attacks on shore batteries and were very high-risk ventures. Sidney Smith's luck ran out the following month when a night attack on a lugger off Le Havre went horribly wrong. The official account, printed in the Annual Register for 1796, set out the details (4):

> Advice was received at the Admiralty, brought by Lieutenant Crisp of the cutter *Telemachus*, of the capture of the enterprising Sir Sidney Smith, commander of HMS *Diamond*, on the coast of France, having on the 18th instant, boarded and taken a lugger privateer belonging to the enemy, in Havre de Grace har-

bour, by the boats of his squadron, then on a reconnoitring expedition; and the tide making strong into the harbour, she was driven above the French forts, which the next morning, the 19th, discovering, at break of day, the lugger in tow by a string of English boats, immediately made the signal of alarm, which collected together several gun-boats and other armed vessels, that attacked the lugger and British boats, when, after an obstinate resistance of two hours, Sir Sidney had the mortification of being obliged to surrender himself prisoner of war, with about sixteen of his people, and three officers with him in the lugger.

In these circumstances, the shallow draught gunboats, with their single or paired big guns and the manoeuvrability endowed by their sweeps (large oars), were particularly effective (5). The Annual Register continued:

> The *Diamond* frigate is safe, but could afford her commander no assistance, there not being a breath of wind during the whole of this unfortunate transaction. . . . When the officers on board the *Diamond* heard of the disaster which had befallen their gallant commander, they sent a flag of truce into Havre, to discover whether he was wounded, and entreating that

he might be treated with kindness. The governor returned for answer that Sir Sidney was well, and that he should be treated with the utmost humanity and attention.

However, the authorities did not honour the governor's promises. Sir Sidney should have been exchanged quickly with a French officer of similar rank, as was the standard custom of the day, but his incendiary activities at Toulon had earned him the special animosity of the French government and he was consigned to the notorious Temple prison in Paris. His eventual escape and return to service in May 1798 only added to his public reputation.

However active the British inshore flotillas, it was impossible to bottle up permanently every small French harbour, and privateers continued to pose a significant threat to British commerce. Most captures of merchantmen were too mundane to attract artists, but the French were obviously proud of the capture of the cutter *Swan* by the *Unité* in January 1797 (6). *Swan* was not a naval vessel but may have been a revenue cutter.

1. The cutting out of a French brig, possibly la *Chevrette*. Black and wash, grey pen and ink sketch by P J de Loutherbourg, undated.
NMM ref PAH8407

2. 'Sir William Sidney Smith 1764-1840', stipple engraving after an original by Daniel Orme, no date.
NMM ref PAD3504

3. 'The Aristocrat armed Lugger engaging a French Flotilla, consisting of nine sail. Captain Wilkins got away from 9 French vessels after a running fight of 18 hours 15 July 1795', aquatint engraved by Hall after an original by John Thomas Serres, published by Joyce Gold, 30 April 1806.
NMM ref PAD5497

4. 'His Majesty's frigate the Diamond . . . off Cape La Heve . . . to cut out a French lugger named Le Vengeur . . . 18 April 1796 . . . was boarded . . . but the cable cut by one of the prisoners . . . swept . . . into the River Seine . . . surrender', coloured aquatint engraved by J Jeakes after an original by J Boxer and J T Serres, published by Edward Orme, September 1803.
NMM ref PAH7892

5. 'A French Gun Boat', engraving by J Tomlinson after an original by J Flight, published by J Stratford, 24 November 1804.
NMM ref PAD5500

6. 'Combat du Corsaire Francais L'Unite contre le cutter Anglais Le Swan (Janvier 1797)', lithograph engraved by Ferdinand Victor Perrot and Roger et Cie, after an original by Perrot, no date.
NMM ref PAD5516

6

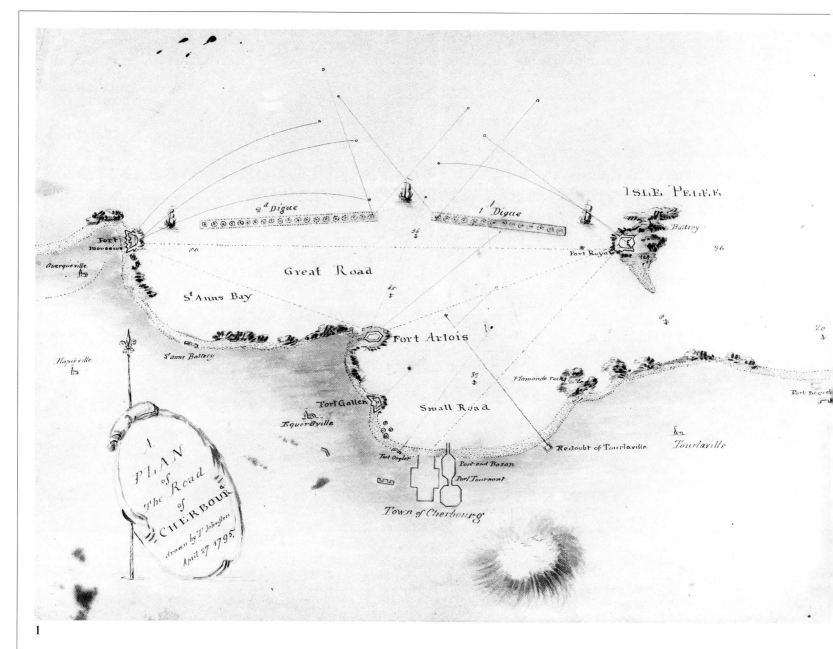

1

French naval bases: Cherbourg

IN ANY war with Britain France was badly handicapped by having no natural large, sheltered, anchorages or good deepwater ports on her Channel coast to compare with Falmouth, Plymouth and Torbay, and, particularly, the shelter provided by the Isle of Wight and Portsmouth harbour. The French channel ports were on river mouths, difficult of access, cramped and usually unsuited to larger vessels. Ports like Saint Malo, Le Havre and Dieppe were fine for merchantmen, privateers and even frigate squadrons, but were unsuitable for even one or two ships of the line, let alone fleets of these vessels. Projects for constructing an artificial haven opposite the English coast were raised from time to time and these usually involved the port of

Cherbourg, situated at the top of the Cotentin peninsula. During the reign of Louis XIV the great French engineer Vauban had made plans which did not get very far, his half-complete fortifications being demolished for fear that the British would land and occupy the Cotentin.

A century later, in 1776, just before France joined in the American War of Independence in support of the North American colonists, work was begun on modernising and enlarging the port. This was masterminded by Captain de la Bretonnière and involved the construction of a couple of basins (the 'Port Tornant' of the 1795 map (1)). This was followed by an ambitious attempt to form a protected anchorage by sinking a series of enormous cones (2), made of wood and filled with stones, to form a protective breakwater between the west end of St. Anne's Bay to Pelée Island. These were to be in two lines (*1st Digue* and *2nd Digue* in (1)). These massive and extremely expensive constructions were meant to serve as forts as well as a sea defence, and had they been successful would have provided a large and secure anchorage. Louis XVI made an unprecedented trip to see the sinking of one of the cones, an event marred by a fatal accident. The whole project was, in any case, doomed. The cones began to disintegrate as soon as they were emplaced, and, by the time of the summoning of the Estates General in 1789 it had become obvious that they were not working.

During the Revolutionary War, Cherbourg was a base for privateers, and had some importance as a centre of shipbuilding, particularly for invasion barges. Napoleon began a programme of port improvement, which included the construction of a mole, but the work was far from complete at his downfall and was not finished until 1853, in the reign of his nephew Napoleon III. However the large basin capable of holding a fleet of line of battle ships was ready by 1813, when Cherbourg was formally opened as a naval port, and Cherbourg had for some time been noted for building frigates, and as a base for that type of vessel.

1. 'A Plan of the Road of Cherbourg', watercolour by Thomas Johnston, 27 April 1795.
NMM ref PAD1488

2. 'View of a Cone Constructed in the Year 1785 being conducted to its place in the Road of Cherbourg, in order to be sunk', engraving by Thomas Pratten, published by John Sewell, 1 April 1794.
NMM ref PAD1489

2

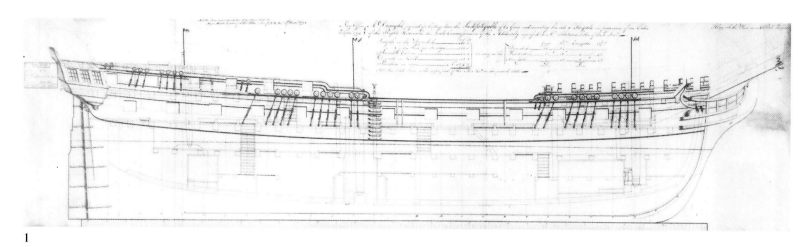

1

Droits de l'Homme, 13-14 January 1797

SIR EDWARD Pellew was perhaps the most success-ful British frigate captain of the early years of the war, and in the heavy frigate *Indefatigable* he had a command worthy of him. She had been built as a 64-gun line of battle ship and then cut down to a 38-gun frigate (1). As a result both her main armament (24pdr guns) and her construction were much heavier than a stan-dard frigate of nominally the same number of guns—or a 36-gun ship such as her consort, the *Amazon*, both of which had 18pdr guns as their main armament. The two ships together formed a powerful fighting force, but not one, in ordinary circumstances, which could have suc-cessfully taken on a 74-gun line of battle ship, though that is what they successfully did in one of the most dra-matic actions of the war.

At the end of 1796 a French expedition intended to land in Ireland escaped from Brest under cover of dark-ness, but in considerable disorder—a disorder which was worsened by Pellew's intervention with the *Indefatigable*, firing false signals and assisting in the scattering of the French fleet. This dispersal ensured that no landing took place, as the frigate carrying both the land and sea com-manders failed to rejoin the majority of the force which contrived to gather off the Irish coast before being dis-persed again by a storm. Meanwhile Pellew was return-ing to his watch off Brest, accompanied by the *Amazon*. Early in the afternoon of 13 January 1797 with 'the wind . . . blowing hard, with thick hazey weather . . .' he sight-ed a French warship some 50 leagues off Ushant and immediately steered to cut her off. This was the *Droits de*

2

3

l'Homme, a 74-gun ship, with over 700 soldiers aboard, returning from the Irish coast. She was an experimental vessel, without a poop and longer and lower than usual. As the British ships approached she became further handicapped by carrying away both fore and main topmasts, which made her roll heavily. It seems that, partly because of this and her design, and because she was heavily laden with soldiers and military supplies, that she could not use her heaviest guns on the lower deck. These were too close to the water to open the gun ports safely. When this was tried she nearly sank. This meant that the French ship was now only capable of firing a broadside of roughly the same power as the *Indefatigable* by herself, though the massed musket fire of the troops made her more dangerous at close quarters. As night fell Pellew's ship caught up (2), ranged up alongside, and then, after her enemy had nearly succeeded in ramming and boarding her, surged ahead. The *Amazon* then came up into action (3). Through the night the two frigates, stationing themselves on either bow of the 74 and yawing to fire broadsides, harried the French ship, which would occasionally herself yaw to reply. By about 4am the *Droits de L'Homme* was virtually out of ammunition and almost unrigged, with her opponents not in a much better state: 'The sea was high, the People on the main Deck were up to their middles in water, some Guns broke their Breechings four times over . . . All our masts were much wounded, the Maintopmast completely unrigg'd and sav'd only by uncommon alacrity . . .'

Breakers were sighted, and Pellew, thinking he was in the Bay of Brest, turned north. He was, in fact, in the next bay south, Audierne Bay, and was saved by his Breton Royalist pilot shouting 'Non, non mon Capitaine, the oder way'. As the *Indefatigable* managed to claw her way off the lee shore she sighted her opponent, aground on a shoal (4). Pellew escaped by the skin of his teeth, and consummate seamanship, but *Amazon* was less lucky. She went aground, though nearly all of her crew escaped to land and captivity. The major tragedy was the fate of the French ship they had harried to her doom. She had already lost some 103 dead and 150 wounded, and it took four days for the weather to moderate enough for help to reach the wreck. The total loss was perhaps in the region of 1000 troops and crew.

1. Sheer plan of *Indefatigable*. The dotted line shows the original outline of her upperworks before she was cut down to a frigate in 1795. *NMM neg 6199*

2. 'Destruction of the Droits de l'Homme, 14 January 1797', oil painting by Ebenezer Colls (*fl*1852-1854), no date. *NMM ref BHC0482*

3. 'Destruction of the Droits de l'Homme', anonymous oil painting of the nineteenth-century British school, no date. *NMM ref BHC0483*

4. 'Destruction of Le Droits de l'Homme . . . Frigates in Hodierne Bay near Brest, with the Indefatigable . . . throwing up rockets . . . 13 Jan 1797', coloured aquatint engraved by Robert Dodd after his own original, published by I Brydon, February 1798. *NMM ref PAG7155*

4

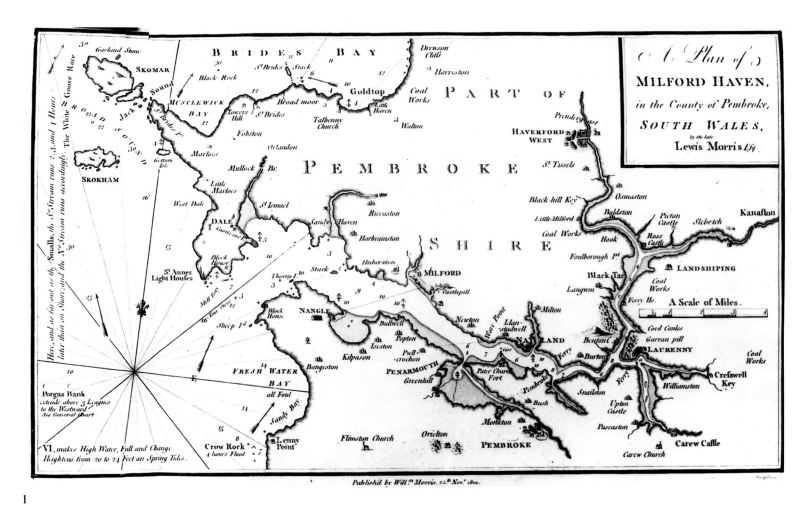

A Plan of MILFORD HAVEN, in the County of Pembroke, SOUTH WALES, by the late Lewis Morris Esq.

1

The Black Legion invades Wales

MOST BRITONS believe that their islands have not been invaded since the Norman Conquest in 1066, but although none has forced an unwilling change of government on the population, since then there have been forty-two successful military landings. None, however, was as bizarre as the last: a force of 1800 galley slaves and convicts, rejoicing under the name of the Black Legion, commanded by a revolutionary American, were put ashore in February 1797 in the extreme west of Wales and surrendered without a fight.

Originally conceived as a diversion during the landings in Ireland, the plan was to land and burn Bristol (or hold it to ransom), the country's second port and one with virtually no fixed defences. Like the main invasion it was confounded by the weather. The whole force was embarked in the big new frigates *Résistance* and *Vengeance*, the corvette *Constance* and a lugger, but even these weatherly vessels could not beat up the Bristol Channel in the face of an easterly gale, and eventually the 'troops' were put ashore at Fishguard. There was little of strategic value in the area, except perhaps the shipbuilding around Milford Haven (1), and it is difficult to find any

logic in their final choice of target. Despite the fervour of a few Jacobin officers, the jailbirds had no stomach for a fight, and soon surrendered to the local militia, led by Lord Cawdor, and were marched off to prison in Haverfordwest. A persistent legend in Wales holds that a number of inquisitive local women, in the traditional garb of red cloak and tall black hat, lined the cliff, and were mistaken for regular soldiers by the Black Legion, which convinced them of the folly of resisting.

While the incursion was another embarrassment for the Royal Navy, the French frigates did not reach port unmolested. When in sight of Brest, two of Bridport's frigates, the 18pdr-armed *San Fiorenzo* and the 12pdr *Nymphe*, intercepted *Résistance* and *Constance*; a running fight of half an hour ended with the capture of both. The frigate, at 1180 tons, was one of the biggest and newest ships of her type, an experimental vessel with a unusual hull form (3). She was renamed *Fisgard*, the usual contemporary spelling of the invasion port, and made a considerable name for herself under the active command of Thomas Byam Martin. *Constance* was similarly purchased as a 22-gun Sixth Rate post ship.

2

1. 'A Plan of Milford Haven in the County of Pembroke, South Wales, by the late Lewis Morris Esq.', published by William Morris, 25 November 1800. *NMM neg A129*

2. 'The capture of the Resistance and Constance by HMS San Fiorenzo and Nymphe, 9 March 1797', oil painting by Nicholas Pocock (1740-1821), no date. *NMM ref BHC0495*

3. Sheer draught of *Résistance*, as captured. Admiralty Collection. *NMM neg 1917*

3

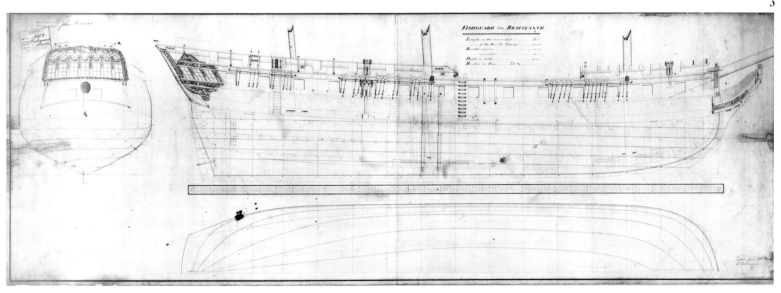

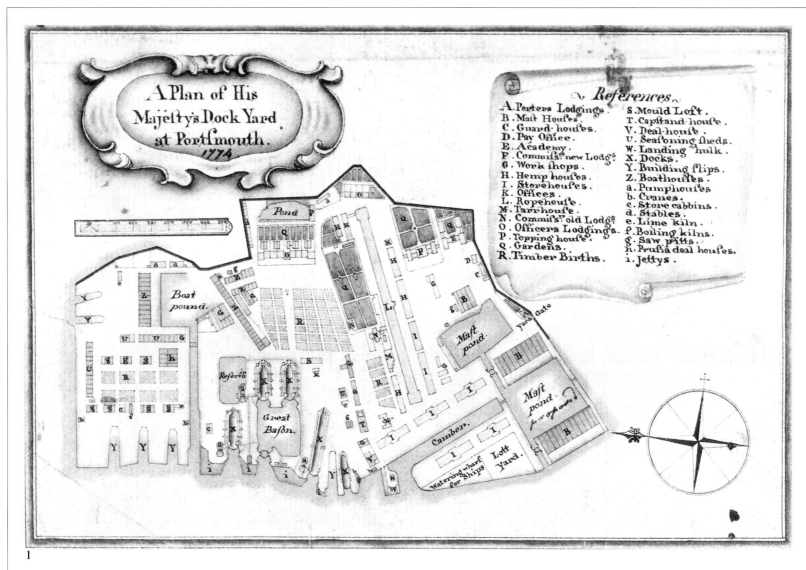

A Plan of His Majesty's Dock Yard at Portsmouth. 1774

~ References ~

A. Porters Lodgings.
B. Mast Houses.
C. Guard-houses.
D. Pay Office.
E. Academy.
F. Commiss.r new Lodg.s
G. Work shops.
H. Hemp houses.
I. Storehouses.
K. Offices.
L. Ropehouse.
M. Tarr house.
N. Commiss.r old Lodg.s
O. Officers Lodgings.
P. Topping house.
Q. Gardens.
R. Timber Births.

S. Mould Loft.
T. Capstand house.
V. Deal-house.
U. Seasoning sheds.
W. Landing hulk.
X. Docks.
Y. Building slips.
Z. Boathouses.
a. Pumphouses.
b. Cranes.
c. Store cabbins.
d. Stables.
e. Lime kiln.
f. Boiling kilns.
g. Saw pitts.
h. Prussia deal houses.
i. Jettys.

1

Portsmouth – key to the Channel

BETWEEN 1793 and 1815 Portsmouth was the Royal Navy's principal naval base and Spithead the main anchorage of the Channel Fleet and departure point for many of the fleets and convoys despatched all over the world. Sheltered from south-westerly winds by the Isle of Wight, Spithead had long been an assembly point for expeditions. In a stretch of water over three miles by eight miles, fleets and a multi-tude of transports and storeships could assemble with-out danger of collision, their main departure route southwest around the point of St Helens on the eastern point of the island, but in the event of emergency west-ward through the Solent and into the English Channel past the Needles. However, in the 1790s, with the policy of distant blockade of Brest, it was too far to the west-ward for an ideal base for the main fleet, and Torbay was often used as the fleet's preferred anchorage.

With such a capacious and convenient anchorage, Portsmouth had been a storage and distribution point for naval expeditions since the twelfth century. A dock was ordered to be dug at Portsmouth by Richard I as early as 1194, and a wall to enclose the excavation was ordered by King John in 1212. However, it was not until 1495-96 that the dockyard took shape when King Henry VII acquired more land along the eastern side of Portsmouth Harbour within which was constructed the first reinforced dry dock to be built in England, and new building slips. The *Mary Rose* was laid down at Portsmouth in 1509 and it was from there that the fleet set out to drive off the French fleet in 1546 when the *Mary Rose* sank in sight of the land off Portsea.

Portsmouth dockyard was little used after 1560 and during the early seventeenth century, when the Spanish Netherlands and Holland harboured the nearest ene-mies. Then the dockyards along the Rivers Thames and Medway had greater strategic value. However, as France became increasingly powerful, Spithead and the dock-yard at Portsmouth became more important. There was a need for a base from which warships could defend the south coast and western approaches, especially when easterly winds confined ships in the Thames estuary and River Medway. Stores were also needed further west, at a harbour of refuge for ships returning hard pressed from the Atlantic. Oak timber was readily available close by in the New Forest, and the route from London to Portsmouth relatively direct. During the years of the Commonwealth after 1650 new docks and building slips were created, and after the Restoration in 1660 a commissioner's house and a rope house. Further facilities were created after 1698 and the yard was pre-eminent among the six home dockyards by 1739 (1).

Fire, rather than a wartime enemy, was the main danger at this time. In 1760 a fire totally destroyed two large hemphouses containing hemp, tar, oil and other stores connected with rope-making. Another even more damaging fire occurred in the ropehouse in 1770, causing damage valued at £149,000; and a third fire in 1776, allegedly ignited by a thief sympathetic to the American cause, known as John the Painter. The fires resulted in a rearrangement of storage for all inflammable material, and new storehouses for hemp were erected away from the rope houses (2).

Ironically, as the eighteenth century proceeded and ships became larger, the harbour itself became a problem for the fleet refitting and repairing in time of war at Spithead. Ships had to come into harbour to receive new masts at the sheerhulk or to be taken into dock for work on their hulls. Yet a bar of shallow water stretched across the mouth of the harbour, providing only 14ft of water at low tide, with another 12ft to 15ft in spring tides (3). Ships of the line accordingly had to remove their guns and reduce their draught outside the harbour before entering and even then had to ride in on high tides, the reverse procedure happening as they were taken out.

This was not always easy as eddies ran across the harbour mouth on both sides of the bar. Yet the removal of ships outside the harbour was generally imperative for, as the fleet became larger, the small amount of deep water within the harbour became inconveniently crowded (4).

For by the time of the American War the harbour was also the location of a naval victualling yard, gunpowder stores and ordnance wharves. Victualling premises—a bakery, slaughterhouse, meat store and storehouse—were scattered in various places around the town of Portsmouth. But a good supply of fresh water had permitted the Victualling Board to establish a brewery on the western, Gosport, side of the harbour, opposite the dockyard, which also included a large cooperage. North of the victualling yard, also on the western side of the harbour, was the gunpowder magazine managed by the Board of Ordnance. The magazine, enclosed within walls of immense thickness, was laid out in 1773 and had capacity for around 4500 barrels of powder. Known as Priddy's Hard, the magazine was complemented by gun wharves storing actual ordnance close to the harbour mouth, just south of the dockyard.

Also on the Gosport side of Portsmouth Harbour, but facing Spithead, was Haslar Naval Hospital. Ordered to be built in 1745 as an alternative to the more expensive method of contracting sick seamen out to private houses and public hospitals, Haslar was completed in 1761 and was the largest purpose-built medical establishment then in existence. Initially designed for 1500 patients, the design was enlarged to 1800 in 1754, and the hospital actually housed 2100 patients in 1779. A survey in 1780 revealed it had 84 general medical and surgical wards, including isolation wards for consumption, fever and smallpox. Haslar Hospital has remained the main centre of medicine in the Royal Navy.

1. 'A plan of His Majesty's Dock Yard at Portsmouth 1774', anonymous coloured etching, published post-1785.
NMM ref PAD1077

2. Model of Portsmouth Dockyard.
NMM neg D539D

3. Chart of Portsmouth 1785.
NMM neg 2533

4. 'Le Port de Portsmouth Vu du cote de l'Est. Reduit de la Collection des Ports d'Angleterre dessines par Milton et graves par Suntache l'annee 1788', etching by Antoine Suntache after an original by Thomas Milton, 1788.
NMM ref PAD1056

2

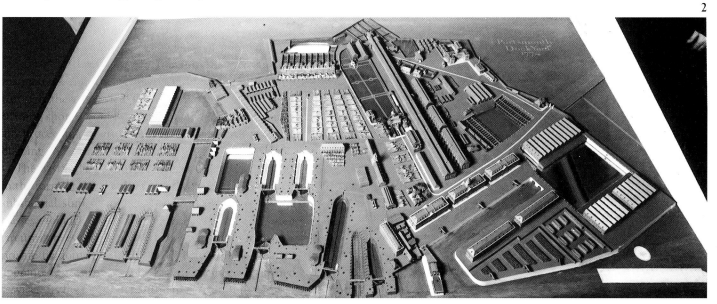

3

4

1

The Great Mutinies of 1797

AT THE outbreak of war in 1793, there had officially been 45,000 seamen and marines in service in the Royal Navy, but by 1797 this had increased to 120,000. By this time, the Navy had had to resort to any means necessary to obtain men. The Quota Acts of 1795 obliged counties to provide set numbers ('quotas') of men, and naturally judges and magistrates took the opportunity to hand over beggars, minor offenders and other social nuisances to the fleet, which resulted in the Navy receiving large numbers of untrained and unruly landsmen on board their ships. Coupled with the bad conditions aboard these ships, the low level of wages, which for many were years in arrears, poor rations and the almost complete lack of shore leave (unsurprising in a fleet manned in part by pressed men and criminals, where desertion was rife), unrest was inevitable, particularly at a time of social and political turmoil following the French Revolution.

Although there had been mutinies aboard individual ships in previous years, 1797 saw a series of organised 'strikes' aboard the ships of the Channel Fleet at its various anchorages. On 15 April 1797 the men of Lord Bridport's fleet at Spithead refused to put to sea, each ship's company appointing delegates to speak for them and on 17 April submitted a list of their grievances. The fleet flagship *Queen Charlotte* was the headquarters of the mutineers. They wanted an increase in pay to reflect the increased cost of living, better quality rations in fair measures, better treatment for the sick and wounded, and shore leave to visit their families. As seamen's wages had last been set in 1653, there was considerable justice in their demands, and within the week a pay rise had been given and a pardon issued to all mutineers. However, the failure of the Admiralty to meet the seamen's demands regarding rations caused the crew of the *London* to continue their resistance to orders at St Helen's in early May, and shots were fired, five seamen being killed. The mutiny spread to other ships, but Lord Howe, who was highly respected by the men, came to negotiate with them and on 16 May the fleet put to sea as ordered. At the end of the mutiny, there was a celebration at Portsmouth, with the ships' crews saluting Lord Howe

3

The DELEGATES in COUNCIL or BEGGARS on HORSEBACK.

2

4

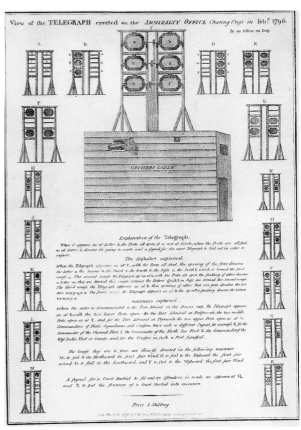

5

1. 'A View of the Queen Charlotte Man of War, of 100 guns, laying at Spithead , wherein the Ship's Company is represented Manning the Yards, in order to Salute the Admiral coming aboard', aquatint published by John Fairburn, London, 24 December 1796.
NMM ref PAF7981

2. 'The Delegates in Council or Beggars on Horseback', by Cruickshank, published by J W Forest, London, 9 June 1797.
NMM ref PAF3899

3. 'Parker the Delegate, Sketch'd by a Naval Officer', coloured etching published by W Holland, London, June 1797.
NMM ref PAD3033

4. 'Richard Parker, President of the Committee of Delegates, tendering the List of Grievances to Vice-Admiral Buckner, on board the Sandwich at the Nore', mezzotint published by G Thompson and L Evans, London, 3 July 1797.
NMM ref PAG6424

5. 'View of the Telegraph erected on the Admiralty Office Charing Cross in Feby 1796, By an Officer on Duty', published by S W Fores, London, 26 March 1796.
NMM ref PAH2206

6. 'Escape of HMS Clyde from the Nore Mutiny', oil painting by William Joy (1803-1866), no date.
NMM ref BHC0496

7. 'HMS Clyde arriving at Sheerness after the Nore Mutiny, 30 May 1797', oil painting by William Joy (1803-1866), no date.
NMM ref BHC0497

6

by manning the yards as he was rowed through the fleet, as shown in this earlier picture of the fleet flagship (1).

The Spithead mutiny appears to have been entirely concerned with the men's complaints about their conditions of service, and their petition stressed their loyalty to their country, despite the government's fears of radical agitation in the fleet. However, the next outbreak was not only more serious and more violent, but also believed to be more influenced by radicalism, as the cartoon by Cruickshank shows (2), with the opposition leader Charles James Fox and the French under the table leading the simple seamen astray. On 20 May, the ships at the Nore elected delegates to present grievances very similar to those which had been largely settled at Spithead, and elected one Richard Parker as their overall leader. Parker (3) was a man of some education—in fact, a naval officer disrated for disobedience—who was trusted by the men and chosen to present their demands to Vice-Admiral Buckner (4), the local commander.

By the end of the month all the ships save Admiral Duncan's flagship *Venerable* had joined the mutiny, leaving him to maintain the blockade of the Texel with this single ship of the line. Duncan was a powerful man and had retained control of his flagship by holding the one sailor who had defied his authority over the side of the ship and threatening to let go unless he returned to duty. The situation escalated dangerously when the mutineers moved their ships to blockade the Thames, but the government began to set up batteries on shore and move other ships to threaten the mutineers. Throughout the crisis, the Admiralty in London kept in constant touch with the Nore by means of the chain of

shutter telegraph stations which linked the major fleet anchorages to London (5). Fearing reprisals, ships' companies began to desert the 'strike', the first being the *Clyde*, 38, which slipped away into Sheerness on the night of 30 May (6, 7). By 13 June all the ships had surrendered, without any concessions being gained from the Admiralty. In the aftermath, Parker and thirty-five others were hanged, with many more being flogged or imprisoned. The Nore Mutiny had come at a time of great danger to Great Britain, but her enemies had failed to exploit the situation quickly enough, although they were well informed of developments.

There were numerous outbreaks of mutiny aboard single ships in later years, but nothing to equal these mass uprisings. The harshness of the punishments for mutiny, however, continued to show the Admiralty's fear of disobedience amongst its crews.

7

1

'Dangers of the sea': grounding

THE ROYAL Navy expected to be able to take its ships anywhere there was water to float them, but this last consideration often posed a problem. With little more than sounding rods and lead-lines for tools, marine surveying was at best an inexact science, with the charting of coastal waters very variable in the quality of printed information available. Furthermore, states—and particularly navies—regarded charts as restricted if not secret documents, and it was not until the next century that the Admiralty's hydrographic office made the Navy's greatest contribution to maritime history by not only systematically charting the world's waters but also releasing the charts to the world's mariners irrespective of nationality or creed.

The power of the wind was also uncertain, and currents and tides similarly unstudied, so even the most experienced seaman might find himself putting a ship aground from time to time. Depending on conditions this need not cause major damage, and unlike a modern steel ship the full facilities of a dockyard were not always

2

3

necessary. In fact, a wooden warship was remarkably self-sufficient and could repair all but the most serious damage itself. These points are demonstrated by a series of watercolours showing the grounding and subsequent refloating and repair of the frigate *Thetis* in the winter of 1795-96 off the American coast, an incident of no great significance in itself but typical of the ingenuity and self-reliance of the service.

Thetis, 38, was on the North America station, probably patrolling the American coast to prevent supplies of food reaching France, when she ran aground off Currituck Inlet, North Carolina a few days before Christmas 1794. The first view shows the ship with anchors carried out astern to warp herself off (1). Two of her boats in the foreground are sounding, using lead-

lines to discover the surrounding depth of water, and her consort, the 32-gun *Cleopatra*, is standing by. Having got the ship off a week later, with topmasts struck she is towed by *Cleopatra* into the Chesapeake, attended by *Thisbe*, 28 and *Lynx* sloop (also of the squadron) and the pilot schooner *Sally* of Norfolk, Virginia (2).

The next view (3) shows the squadron riding out bad weather in Lynhaven Bay, just inside the entrance to the Chesapeake, before the *Thetis* can be moved up to Gosport to be hove down and the underwater damage inspected and repaired (4). Gosport had minimal facilities at this time and the repairs were effected by the ship's crew, taking over a month. The ship cannot have suffered badly from her ordeal, since she was in service until 1814.

4

1-4. A series of watercolour originals by George Tobin, dated 1795, which have the feel of first-hand experience.

1. 'No.1. Thetis on shore near Currituck Inlet, North Carolina Dec 23rd 1794 . . . Cleopatra at anchor near her, Thisbe and Lynx answering private signals'.
NMM ref PAG9750

2. 'No.2. Dec 31st 1794, The Cleopatra towing the Thetis towards the Chesapeake, Lynx and Thisbe attending . . . A Virginian pilot boat the Sally of Norfolk in the foreground'.
NMM ref PAG9751

3. 'No.3. January 2nd 1795, Thetis, Cleopatra and Thisbe at anchor in Lynhaven Bay at the mouth of the Chesapeake'
NMM ref PAG9752

4. 'No.4. Thetis Feby 1795 - Repairing at Gosport in Virginia'. Another pilot schooner, the Hamilton of Norfolk, sails in.
NMM ref PAG9753

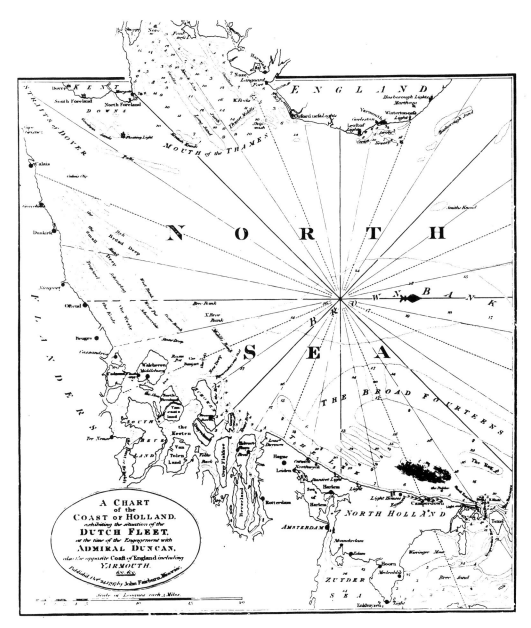

A CHART of the COAST of HOLLAND. *exhibiting the situation of the* DUTCH FLEET. *at the time of the Engagement with* ADMIRAL DUNCAN. *also the opposite Coast of England including* YARMOUTH. &c. &c.

Published Oct 24 1797 by John Fairburn Minories

2

From the London-Gazette Extraordinary, October 16, 179

Venerable, off the Coast of Holland, October 13, 1797.

IN the Morning of the 11th, I got Sight of the Enemy, forming in a Line on the Larboard receive us, the Wind at North West. As we approached near, I made the Signal for the Squa thorten Sail, in order to connect them. Soon after, I saw the Land between CAMPERDOWN and Eg about Nine Miles to Leeward of the Enemy; and, finding there was no Time to be loft in mak Attack, I made the Signal to bear up, break the Enemy's Line, and engage them to Leeward, ea her Opponent; by which I got between them and the Land. The Action commenced about For Minutes paft Twelve, and lafted near Two Hours and a Half; when I obferved all the Mafts of the Admiral's Ship to go by the Board: She was, however, defended for fome Time in a moft gallant M but, being overpowered by Numbers, her Colours were ftruck, and Admiral De Winter was foon on-board the Venerable. On looking around me, I obferved the Ship bearing the Vice-Admiral was alfo difmafted, and had furrendered to Vice-Admiral Onflow, and that many others had ftruck were in Nine Fathoms Water, and not farther than Five Miles from the Land. One of the Enemy caught Fire in the Action, but was extinguifhed, and fhe is One of the Ships in our Poffeffion Squadron has loft a Number of Men, but in no Proportion to that of the Enemy. The Twe Admiral Ships had no lefs than Two Hundred and Fifty Men killed and wounded in each Ship.

Signed, ADAM DUN

LIST OF SHIPS TAKEN.

Vryheid,	Adm. De Winter, 74 Guns, 550 Men.		*Alkmaar,*	Capt. Kraft,	56 Guns, 35	
Jupiter,	Vice-Ad. Reyntjes, 74	550	*Delft,*	Capt. Verdoorn, 56	3	
Gelykheid,	Capt. Ruyfen, 68	450	*Maanikrendam,*	Capt. Lancafter, 44	27	
Haerlem,	Capt. Wiggers, 68	450	*Ambufcade,*	Capt.-Lieut. Huys, 32	27	
Adm. Devries,	Capt. Zegers, 68	450				
Waffenaer,	Capt. Holland, 64	450				
Hercules,	Capt. Van Ryfoort, 64	450				

N. B. Another Line-of-Battle Ship reporte taken, Name unknown.

Difpofition of the British Squadron, in the Order of Battle, October 11, 1797.

LARBOARD, or LEE DIVISION.
Rd Onflow, Efq. Vice-Admiral of the Red, Commander
Guns. Men.
1 Ruffel, Henry Trollope, Capt.   74   590
2 Director, William Bligh, Capt.   64   491
3 Montagu, John Knight, Capt.   74   590
4 Veteran, George Gregory, Capt.   64   491
5 Monarch, V.-Ad. Onflow, E.O'Bryen, Capt. 74   590
6 Powerful, William O'Bryen Drury, Capt. 74   590
7 Monmouth, James Walker, Capt.   64   491
8 Agincourt, John Williamfon, Capt.   64   491

Carried over, 552 4355
REPEATERS.
Beaulieu Frigate. — Cutters Rofe, King George, Active, Diligent. — Speculator Lugger.

STARBOARD, or WEATHER DIVISI
Adam Duncan, Efq. Admiral of the Blue, an mander-in-Chief, &c. &c. &c.
Gu
Brought over, 5
9 Triumph, William Henry Effington, Capt.
10 Venerable, Ad. Duncan, W.G. Fairfax, Capt.
11 Ardent, Richard R. Burgefs, Capt.
12 Bedford, Sir Thomas Byard, Capt.
13 Lancafter, John Wells, Capt.
14 Belliqueux, John Inglis, Capt.
15 Adamant, William Hotham, Capt.
16 Ifis, William Mitchell, Capt.

Total, 104
REPEATERS. — Circe Frigate. — Martin

Lift and Difpofition of the Dutch Fleet, October 11, 1797.

VAN.
Vice-Admiral Reyntjes, Commander.
Guns. Men.
1 Cerberus, Capt. Jacobfon,   68   45
2 Delft, Capt. Verdoorn,   56   37
3 Jupiter, V.-Ad. Reyntjes and R.-Ad. Meures, 74   55
4 Alkmaar, Capt. Kraft,   56   30
5 Haerlem, Capt. Wiggerts,   68   45
6 Munnikkendam, Capt. Lancafter,   44   2
7 Helden, Capt. Duminitle L'Eeftrille,   32   2
8 Daphne Brig, Lieutenant Fredericks,   18   9

CENTRE.
Admiral De Winter, Commander-in-Chief.
9 Waffenaer, Capt. Holland,   64   4
10 Batavier, Capt. Souters,   56   55
11 Vryheid, (the Liberty,) Ad. De Winter, Van Roffen,   74   550
12 States General, Rear-Admiral Story,   74   550

Carried over, 684 4675

Brought over, 6
13 Leyden, Captain Mufquetier,
14 Mars, Capt. Kolft,
15 Wakkfaamheid, Capt.-Lieutenant Nicrop,
16 Minerva, Capt. Eilbrecht,
17 Galatea Brig, Lieutenant Rivery,
18 Atalanta Brig, Lieutenant Plets,

REAR.
Rear-Admiral Bloys, Commander.
19 Admiral Devries, Capt. Zegers,
20 Hercules, Capt. Van Ryfoort,
21 Brutus, Rear-Admiral Bloys,
22 Beschermer, Capt. Hinxtt,
23 Gel-kheid, (the Equality,) Capt. Ruyfen,
24 Ambufcade, Capt.-Lieutenant Arkenbout,
25 Haasje, (Atilo,) Lieutenant Hartenfeld,

Total, 120

Lift of killed and wounded on board Admiral Duncan's Squadron.

Venerable, 13 Seamen, 2 Marines, killed; 6 Officers, 23 Seamen, 4 Marines, wounded,   To
Monarch, 2 Officers, 34 Seamen, killed; 9 Officers, 79 Seamen, 12 Marines, wounded,
Bedford, 2 Midshipmen, 16 Seamen, 2 Marines, killed; 1 Lieutenant, 37 Seamen, 3 Marines, wounded,
Powerful, 8 Seamen, 2 Marines, killed; 4 Officers, 74 Seamen and Marines, wounded,
Ifis, 1 Seaman, 1 Marine, killed; 3 Officers, 18 Seamen, wounded,
Ardent, 2 Officers, 53 Seamen, 6 Marines, killed; 8 Officers, 85 Seamen, 11 Marines, 3 Boys, wounded
Agincourt, none killed or wounded.
Belliqueux, 2 Officers, 20 Seamen, 5 Marines, killed; 3 Officers, 63 Seamen, 11 Marines, wounded,
Lancafter, 3 Seamen killed; 2 Officers, 13 Seamen, 3 Marines, wounded,
Triumph, 25 Seamen, 3 Marines, 1 Boy, killed; 5 Officers, 50 Seamen and Marines, wounded,

Total of the killed and wound

The North Sea Squadron

IN 1795 HOLLAND was added to the number of Britain's enemies. The country had been overrun by the French, whose cavalry even captured a frozen-in Dutch fleet by galloping over the ice. The commander given the task of blockading the Dutch fleet was the impressive figure of Admiral Adam Duncan (1), who had quelled the mutiny aboard the *Venerable*.

Duncan's fleet was very much a cinderella force, scraped together at a time when most ships of the line in good condition were already allocated to the Channel, Mediterranean or West Indies stations. Most of the North Sea ships were not only in a poorer state, but also tended to be the older and smaller vessels: much of this squadron was made up of 64-gun ships and 50s, the latter definitely too weak for the line of battle, and the former now widely regarded as less than ideal. Apart from the stretched nature of the Navy's resources, the main arguments for the allocation of such ships to Duncan were that his cruising ground was never far from a British base, so maintenance was easily accessible (in theory) for old and decrepit ships; but primarily, because the Dutch navy was itself comprised of ships that were small for their rate. Traditionally, the shoal conditions of the Netherlands coast are given as the reason for Dutch warships being small, but during the eighteenth century both the administration and ship design of the Dutch admiralties had failed to keep up with developments abroad.

The major part of the Dutch fleet was based in the Texel (2), and it was off this port that Duncan's blockading force, originally including some Russian ships, cruised. The shallow waters and shifting sandbanks of the southern North Sea made such a task very difficult, and from time to time the blockading squadron would be blown off station or have to return to its base at Great Yarmouth for re-supply. On one of these occasions, in February 1796, a small force of two Dutch 64s, two small two-deckers and some other ships escaped. They later came across an inferior British force whose only major ship was the 56-gun *Glatton*, but failed to take advantage of their superiority.

The *Glatton* was a curious ship, converted whilst building from an East Indiaman, and armed, at her captain's (Henry Trollope) insistence, entirely with short-ranged carronades, firing a very heavy shot for their weight, but with a short effective range (68pdrs on the lower deck, 32pdrs on the upper). The former had muzzles so wide they were virtually restricted to firing directly on the broadside, whilst there were no long guns at all and none of the carronades could be brought into position to be used as chasers, firing directly forward or aft.

Later the same year, off the Dutch coast, *Glatton* came across a squadron of eight French ships and boldly took them all on (3). The identification of these ships is not certain but they seem to have included the *Brutus*, a 74 cut down to a frigate, the *Rassurante*, an 18pdr frigate, the *Républicaine*, a 12pdr frigate and the *Incorruptible*, an experi-

3

mental 'frigate sloop' armed with 24pdrs, with between two and four smaller vessels. The *Glatton* seems to have done considerable damage with her heavy carronades and it was presumably their power that frightened the French off. They should have been able to stand off out of range and shoot the audacious British ship to pieces. Instead the *Glatton* was left with only two men wounded and her masts and rigging in a bad state (4). She had not had enough men to fire both broadsides at once and her crew had been divided into two with a group of loaders who loaded the guns on one side and then the other, the carronades being aimed and fired by a second group of picked men who also rushed from side to side.

The summer of 1797 saw most of Duncan's ships in a state of mutiny. At one time he only had his flagship, the *Venerable*, 74 and the 50-gun *Adamant* together with a cutter, to maintain the blockade, and he was forced to keep up the pretence of signalling to imaginary ships over the horizon to keep the Dutch in port. Fortunately they remained there until well into the autumn.

---

1. 'Admiral Adam Duncan (1731-1804), 1st Viscount Duncan', oil painting by Sir William Beechey (1753-1839), no date.
NMM ref BHC2668

2. 'A Chart of the Coast of Holland exhibiting the situation of the Dutch Fleet at the time of the Engagement with Admiral Duncan, also the opposite coast of England including Yarmouth', coloured etching by W T Davies, published by John Fairburn, London, 24 October 1797.
NMM ref PAG8953

3. 'To the Right Honorable Earl Spencer . . . This Plate representing His Majesty's Ship Glatton . . . attacking a French Squadron consisting of six Frigates, a brig and a Cutter, on the night of the 15 July 1796', aquatint engraved by Robert Dodd, dated 19 December 1796.
NMM ref PAH7901

4. 'This Portrait of His Majesty's Ship Glatton . . . shewing her situation after Defeating the French Squadron, on the Night of the 15th July 1796', coloured aquatint engraved by Robert Dodd, dated December 1796.
NMM ref PAH7903

4

1

The battle of Camperdown, 11 October 1797

FRENCH PLANS for 1797 had included an invasion of Ireland covered by the Brest fleet, joined by the Dutch fleet from the Texel. By October of that year that plan was in abeyance, but the Dutch fleet, under Admiral De Winter, left the Texel notwithstanding. It is not clear whether he was going to join the Brest fleet, or merely to try conclusions with Duncan's fleet, most of which had recently been in a mutinous state; the most likely explanation is that the Dutch higher command were determined to make a gesture, against De Winter's

2

												Place
Venerable	Montagu	Russell	Glatton	Ardent	Repulse	Nassau	Beliqueux	Monmouth	Standard	Isis Inflexible		Main
Albatross	Iris	Garland	Apollo	Stork	Warrier	Astrea	Vestal Kite	Sea Gull Martin	Bulldog William	Circe		Main
Ganges Pylades	Champion Formidable	Caesar Endymion	Triumph Hydra	Swan	Around Powerful	Hawke	Nautilus	Redoubt Veteran	Naiad	Lancaster Amphrete		Mizen
Bedford Zion	Bedford Hart	Gincourt	Iris Tisiphone	Braakel				Weazle Proserpine	Director	Ranger		Fore
Trial	Coburg	Rose	Active Venus Black Joke	Spiegle Comet Adamant Tremant		Nancy	Leopard Agamemnon	Liberty	Rambler	Fox		Main

3

4

5

better judgement. His own fleet was not in the happiest of states either. It is not generally realised that there had been an aborted revolution in the Netherlands just before the French Revolution took place; but the result of this had been that there was a strong republican party in the country which were prepared to throw in their lot with the invading French. A substantial proportion of Dutch naval officers, including De Winter, were of this persuasion, but the great majority of the sailors were of the traditionalist party which supported the rule of the exiled Orange family. In the event the fighting power of both fleets does not seem to have been affected by these ideological splits, and both fought with the wholehearted (but far from vindictive) pugnaciousness that seems to have characterised battles between the British and Dutch.

The opportunity for the Dutch break out had arisen because Duncan and most of the fleet had retired to Yarmouth Roads to victual and refit, leaving a small observation squadron. It was there on 9 October that a hired cutter with news of the escape reached them (1). Duncan got under way immediately, and early on 12 October sighted the enemy fleet off their own coast near the village whose Dutch name, englished to Camperdown, is given to the battle. Neither fleets were in a neat formation, so both began forming a line of battle. The Dutch, however, were edging away into shallow water, and Duncan decided he had no time for careful

manoeuvring and signalled for his fleet to 'pass through the Enemy's Line and Engage from Leeward', after first hoisting the flags for 'General Chase' (2 shows the distinguishing pendants of the various ships of Duncan's fleet). With one exception (*Agincourt*, whose captain was court-martialled) his ships proceeded to engage the enemy as closely as possible, the general spirit being summed up by the short-tempered Scots Captain of

6

(appropriately) the *Belliqueux* who said: 'Damn . . . Up wi' the hel-lem and gang into the middle o'it'. They swept down in two groups, one led by Duncan's *Venerable*, the other by his second-in-command, Richard Onslow in the *Monarch* (3). As De Winter said later to Duncan: 'Your not waiting to form line ruined me . . . '. As it was the Dutch had managed to form a line, unusually (and sensibly) positioning frigates and brigs (in numbers of which they had an advantage) behind gaps in the line to help rake the British vessels as they came into action.

It was Onslow in the *Monarch* who first cut through the Dutch line. He then became involved in a battle with the Dutch *Jupiter*. Eventually nine of his ships came into action with five Dutch and overwhelmed them. Duncan's *Venerable* had aimed to break the Dutch line between the flagship *Vryheid* and her next astern, the *States General*, but the latter closed that gap, and so the *Venerable* went under her stern, firing a damaging raking broadside as she did so (4), and then ranged up alongside her originally intended opponent (5). Initially three other Dutch ships supported their admiral in this battle of the flagships, and *Venerable* had to withdraw from close action. By this time, however, the large British 74 *Triumph*, which had already battered the *Wassenaar* into surrender had come up and the 64 *Ardent* was also fighting De Winter (she lost more casualties than any other British ship as a result). Later Bligh's *Director* came up to fire the final broadsides against the much-battered *Vryheid* (6). William Bligh did well in this battle, though he is usually only remembered for his leading role in the *Bounty* mutiny.

With her masts gone (7) the embattled and surrounded Dutch admiral (8, 9) finally had to surrender. He had by then been abandoned by the remaining uncaptured Dutch ships which, seeing the British clearly winning, withdrew to the Texel.

7

1. 'HM Armed Cutter the Active J Hamilton Commander, Communicating by Signal to Admiral Duncan in Yarmouth Roads the intelligence of the Dutch Fleet being at Sea which led to the Glorious Victory of Camperdown', aquatint engraved by Edward Duncan after an original by John William Huggins, published 1830.
NMM ref PAG8957

2. 'Flag Table of the English Ships at Camperdown', watercolour by Nicholas Pocock (1740-1821), no date.
NMM ref PAD8873

3. 'An exact Representation of the Engagement & Defeat of the Dutch Fleet, by Admiral Lord Duncan', engraving and etching by Pass after an original by Godefroy, published London 13 January 1798.
NMM ref PAG7061

4. 'Battle of Camperdown, 11th October 1797', by Thomas Luny (1759-1837), 1803.
NMM neg no 9757

5. 'The battle of Camperdown, 11 October 1797', oil painting by Thomas Whitcombe (c1752-1824), signed and dated 1798.
NMM ref BHC0505

6. 'Director firing her last broadside, to which the Vreyheid struck', watercolour with etched base by Samuel Owen, 1798.
NMM neg no A3429

7. 'The battle of Camperdown, 11 October 1797', oil painting by Phillippe-Jacques de Loutherbourg (1740-1812), signed and dated 1801.
NMM ref BHC0504

8. 'Zeeslag. Tusschen de Bataafsche en Engelsche Vlooten op de Hoogte van Egmond den Elfdn. October 1797', etching by Reiner Vinkeles after an original by Gerrit Groenewegen, published by J Allart, no date.
NMM ref PAF4687

9. 'Battle of Camperdown, 11 Oct 1797', grey wash by Nicholas Pocock (1740-1821), no date.
NMM ref PAF5875

Camperdown: end of the battle

THE BATTLE had resulted in a series of individual fights between single ships and small groups. There were many dramatic moments. The Dutch *Hercules* caught fire and, though the conflagration was put out, had to throw her gunpowder over the side. Left defenceless she surrendered. The *Venerable* had her colours shot away, which were replaced by a young seaman, John Crawford (1). However, perhaps the most human moment of the entire battle was when, on the quarterdeck of the *Venerable* (2) Admiral De Winter offered his sword to Duncan, who refused it and shook his hand instead (3). De Winter then remarked on the extraordinary fact that both huge men, prominent upon the exposed quarterdecks of their heavily-engaged flagships during a very bloody action, had both escaped without a scratch.

The British fleet had consisted of seven 74s (the Dutch had three, plus a 72), seven 64s (the Dutch had the same number of roughly equivalent vessels, five 68s and two 64s), and two 50s (the Dutch three 56s and two 44s, one of them a cut-down vessel). By now most navies considered the 64 as rather small for the battle-line, and the small two-deckers of less than 60 guns as totally obsolete for that purpose. Both sides were roughly equal in numbers, but the Dutch ships were generally smaller and weaker. The British had more and heavier guns and slightly more men. The fact that the Dutch had considerably more small vessels (two large frigates, two 34s, four brigs and one despatch vessel as against one heavy

John Cranford, of   Sunderland, Durham.

The Sailor who nailed the Flag to   the Main Top Gallant mast head.
board the Venerable, Lord   Duncan's Ship, after being
Shot away by the Dutch Adm.ᵉ   de Winter.

...awn by M.ʳ Orme on board for the Express   purpose of Introducing into his
...ture of L.ᵈ Duncans Victory now Engraving by   Subscription & which includes Portraits
...he Admirals & Officers who so Gloriously   Distinguished themselves on the
...r Memorable 11.ᵗʰ of October 1797.

Proposals may be had & Subscriptions   Received by M.ʳ Orme.

...according to Act of Parliament Nov.ʳ 21 1797 by M.ʳ Orme N.º 23 ...

1

2

3

1. 'John Crawford of Sunderland, Durham, The Sailor who Nailed the Flag to the Main Top Gallant mast head, on board the Venerable, Lord Duncan's ship, after being Once shot away by the Dutch Admiral de Winter', coloured etching by Daniel Orme after his own original, published by the artist and Edward Orme, London, 21 November 1797. NMM ref PAD3447

2. A view of the quarterdeck and poop of HMS *Venerable*, brown pen & ink by John Little, dated 6 March 1799. The *sauve-tête* netting was rigged in action to protect the crew from debris falling from aloft. NMM ref PAF7977

3. 'The battle of Camperdown, 11 October 1797: Duncan receiving the surrender of Admiral de Winter', oil painting by Samuel Drummond (1765-1844), no date. NMM ref BHC0506

4. 'To the . . . Lords Commissioners . . . this representation of the Dutch Prizes . . . with the Flagships of the Admirals Visc. Duncan and Sir Richard Onslow, Bart, as stationed in the River Medway previous to the intended Royal Review', coloured aquatint and etching by J Wells after his own original, published by Robert Pollard, 29 December 1798. NMM ref PAH7912

frigate, one 28 and four hired cutters) did not compensate for this, despite their intelligent use of them during the battle. The result of the battle was that the British captured seven ships of the line, two 56s (of which one was then wrecked) and two frigates. Both frigates then went ashore, one of them being wrecked and the other recaptured and salved by the Dutch.

It was very noticeable that the Dutch had concentrated their fire on the hulls of the British ships, whose rigging was virtually undamaged, but whose hulls and crews had suffered considerably. British casualties were 244 killed or mortally wounded and 796 wounded, the Dutch figures being 540 and 620 respectively. The heavier Dutch casualties and the fact that all the prizes were dismasted when captured, or their rigging was so damaged that they became so soon afterwards, would argue that British gunnery was even more effective than the Dutch. It should be remembered, however, that the British had on balance heavier guns and more stoutly-built ships than their opponents. Certainly the hulls of all the prizes were considerably shattered and none of them was of much use for first-line service afterwards (4). However, Dutch ships, intended for use in shallow home waters, were built with flatter bottoms, shallower draught, and usually both of lighter construction and smaller size than nearly all their contemporaries. This made them of lesser interest and use to the Royal Navy than French or Spanish prizes.

4

1

A global war

FOR MUCH of the nineteenth century in Britain, the period 1793-1815 was usually known as 'The Great War'—until eclipsed by an even more terrible conflict after 1914—for it was a truly global struggle, with naval warfare occurring in the remotest corners of Europe untouched by land fighting, and almost every place on the planet where European powers had colonies. After 1803 if anything it became even wider, but even in the early years its scope was remarkable. These pages feature a selection of actions away from the main theatres of war to demonstrate this geographical spread.

While convoying a small number of merchantmen to

2

3

Smyrna, the 50-gun ship *Romney* spotted the French frigate *Sybille*, 40 guns, Commodore Rondeau, lying with three armed merchant ships in the bay off the Greek town of Mykonos. On 17 June 1794 Captain Paget anchored near the French frigate and demanded her surrender, but although her main battery was only 18pdrs compared to the British ship's 24pdrs, the French vessel decided to fight. The opponents then battered each other at close range for over an hour until *Sybille* surrendered with 46 killed and 112 wounded; British loses were 10 and 28 respectively (1, 2, 3). Because she mounted extra carronades and could fight an extra main deck gun in a spare port, the theoretical firepower of the French frigate was not much less than that of the British 50 (380lbs to 414lbs), but the real advantage of a two-decker in concentrated fire can be seen in the very different casualties. The *Sybille* was a relatively new Toulon-built ship of 1091 tons which enjoyed a long active career in the Royal Navy under the same name (4).

4

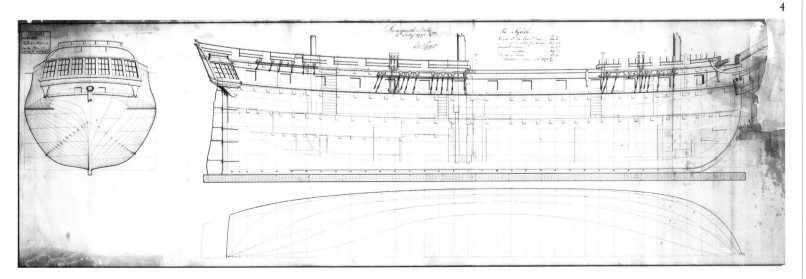

5

6

Nearly a year later, in May 1795, the British frigates *Thetis*, 38 and *Hussar*, 28 intercepted five armed storeships off Chesapeake Bay on the coast of the United States. The French squadron formed line of battle and one hoisted a commodore's broad pendant, giving the appearance of regular warships armed *en flûte* (with part of the armament, usually from the lower deck, unshipped). Nevertheless, the British attacked and captured the *Prévoyante* of 803 tons and the smaller *Raison* (5). Both prizes were commissioned as cruisers, but enjoyed only short careers; they were really only storeships and did not have the sailing qualities for a more active role.

French involvement in the Netherlands which lead to the establishment of the Batavian Republic and the flight of the Stadholder to Britain produced a range of new opportunities from January 1795. The political fiction was that Britain supported the legitimate government so no state of war could be declared, but orders were issued nevertheless to detain Dutch ships and occupy colonies belonging to the Netherlands, these being held in trust until the victory of the old regime. Dutch possessions stretched as far as modern Indonesia and Dutch trade was still among the most important in Europe. Part of this round-up of Dutch merchant ships included the taking of five rich East Indiamen off the South Atlantic way-station of St Helena on 14 June 1795 (6).

Traditionally, Dutch economic strength was heavily dependent on Baltic and northern trade, and on 22 August 1795 a Dutch commerce protection squadron of two 36-gun frigates and a cutter was discovered off Norway and pursued towards the port of Egeroe by a superior British force—the *Vestal*, 28, *Stag*, 32, and *Isis*, 50, under the command of Captain James Alms of the *Reunion*, 36. It was a complicated little action, and when Nicholas Pocock was commissioned to produce a painting of the event he first sketched a plan (7) showing how the cutter and the frigate *Argo* escaped into harbour, while *Reunion*, *Vestal* and *Isis* were forced to go about quickly to avoid running ashore; *Stag*, however, cut off and captured the Dutch frigate *Alliante*, 36, and Pocock's sketchbooks include two alternative compositions for a painting (8,9).

Similar encounters were occurring in the East Indies and the Indian Ocean, and probably the only sea free from any conflict by this time was the uncolonised vastness of the Pacific.

---

1. 'The Romney captures La Sybille 17 June 1794', anonymous pen & ink and watercolour, no date.
NMM ref PAG9683

2. 'Action of the Romney Captain the Honble. Wm Paget & La Sybille & 3 armed vessels—Commodore Rondeau June 17th 1794', black and watercolour pen & ink by J Livesay, no date.
NMM ref PAG9743

3. 'Action between Romney and Sibylle off Miconi, Grecian Archipelago, 17 Jun 1794', grey wash by Robert Cleveley, dated 1796.
NMM ref PAF5826

4. Sheer draught of *Sibylle* as captured. Admiralty Collection.
NMM neg 6139-33

5. 'To Capt the Honble A F Cochrane of . . . Ship Thetis, Captain Beresford of the Hussar . . . representation of their action with five . . . French Ships of War near Cape Henry June 17th [*sic*] 1795', coloured aquatint engraved by J Wells after an original by Nicholas Pocock (1740-1821), published by Nicholas Pocock 1 January 1801.
NMM neg no A4901

6. 'The Honble East India Company's Ship, General Goddard . . . with His Majesty's Ship Sceptre and Swallow Packet Capturing Seven Dutch East Indiamen off St Helena on the 4th of June 1795', coloured aquatint engraved and published by Robert Pollard, 21 January 1797, after an original by Thomas Luny (1759-1837).
NMM ref PAH7885

7. 'Plan of engagement between Isis, Reunion, Stag and Vestal and the Dutch frigate Alliante, 22 Aug 1795', pen & ink by Nicholas Pocock (1740-1821), dated 1795.
NMM ref PAD0397

8. 'Capture of the Alliance by the Stag Captain the Hon J S Yorke, 22 Aug 1795', graphite and wash by Nicholas Pocock (1740-1821), dated 1795.
NMM ref PAD0398

9. 'Action between the Stag Captain Yorke and two Dutch Frigates in which the Alliance was captured, 22 Aug 1795', graphite by Nicholas Pocock (1740-1821), dated 1795.
NMM ref PAD0399

8

9

POSTSCRIPT

THE FIRST five years of the war between revolutionary France and Britain had not presented the Royal Navy with difficulties comparable to those experienced during the war of the American Revolution. It was the triumphs of the French army ashore, especially its conquests in Italy, which caused the navy its greatest strategic problems. The near disaster of the French expedition to Ireland in 1796 was a salutary lesson in the need for a complacent service to rethink its fundamentals.

Ireland continued to present the French with an opportunity to knock Britain out of the war, but subsequent attempts to co-operate with the Irish independence movement were to be on a smaller scale, and were no more successful. The Irish rebel leader, Fitzgerald, was arrested before he could coordinate the plans for a military rising, which when it occurred was defeated before the French could bring support. In August of 1798 four of the line carried a small army of crack troops to Killala Bay in northern Ireland, but they were unable to keep the field on their own when a much larger British army was brought against them. In September another attempt was made, by Rear-Admiral Bompart with *Hoche* of 74-guns, and eight frigates. Thanks to the prompt action of Captain Keats in reporting the sailing to Bridport who was then at Torbay, Bompart was intercepted by Rear-Admiral Sir John Warren with three 74s and five frigates before he could get to Lough Swilly. In a rising gale and heavy sea a running fight developed and *Hoche* was forced to surrender. In her, Wolfe Tone was taken prisoner, and committed suicide to avoid being executed.

In 1800, when Admiral the Earl St Vincent took command, the Channel Fleet began continuous close blockade of Brest, in flexible formations which watched L'Orient, Rochefort, and the Spanish ports of Corunna, Ferrol and Cadiz. The powerful position which it thereby acquired over naval movement was more within reach because the British fleet had expanded rapidly, partly through capture from the enemy. In 1795 the Royal Navy had 512,000 tons of shipping compared to 284,000 tons in the French navy. In 1800 it was to have 569,000 tons compared to 204,000 tons in the French Marine. However, Spain's entry into the war in 1796 with a navy of 227,000 tons affected that calculation, although the operational consequences were not in proportion because of the tremendous difficulty Spain experienced in manning its fleet.[1] Probably more significant than the tonnage calculations was the experience St Vincent had had keeping the Mediterranean squadron at sea off Toulon and Cadiz. His careful attention to the health of his men reduced one of the principal dangers of blockade.

The opening years of the war had been all but disastrous for the French Marine. In the first five years it had lost twenty-six ships of the line to the enemy and another nine to accidents. Fifteen of them had been taken into service with the Royal Navy. Their Dutch allies had lost eleven taken by the enemy, of which ten had been commissioned in the Royal Navy, and the Spaniards had lost eight, of which five had been taken into the Royal Navy. Gradually, from 1796, the French Marine began to recover its discipline, and the dockyards began to recover their ability to send fleets to sea properly provisioned and fitted. The fleet which carried Napoleon to Egypt in 1798 was to be much more capable, even though it was to be defeated by Nelson at the battle of the Nile. When Napoleon came to power in France, he was able to attract back into the service some of the officers of the old regime who had resigned during the revolutionary years.

It was to be Napoleon who would provide Britain with its greatest challenge. To defeat a popular uprising 18 Fructidor 1796, General Hoche had used troops intended for the Irish expedition, supported by displaced military officers. Thereafter, the government had become increasingly vulnerable to the army it no longer fully controlled. The generals who had conquered in Italy and Germany ignored their instructions to return the occupied territories, preferring instead to set up vassal 'Republics' under their personal command. This prevented the Directory concluding a durable peace. On his return from his abortive Egyptian campaign, Napoleon succeeded in displacing the Directory itself, taking the reigns of power as 'First Consul', and then as 'Emperor'.

---

1. Jan Glete, *Navies and Nations: Warships, Navies and State Building in Europe and America, 1500–1860*, Stockholm: Almqvist & Wiskell, 1993, II, table 23; 35, p376.

SOURCES

Intoduction and general
William Laird Clowes, *The Royal Navy*, 7 vols (London 1897-1903)
Julian S Corbett (ed), *The Private papers of George, second Earl Spencer, 1794-1801*, Vols 1 & 2 (London 1914 & 1914)
William S Cormack, *Revolution and Political Conflict in the French Navy 1789-1794* (Cambridge 1995)
Patrick Crowhurst, *The French War on Trade: Privateering 1793-1815* (Aldershot 1989)
Norman Hampson, *La Marine de l'an II: Mobilisation de la Flotte de l'Océan, 1793-1794* (Paris 1959)
William James, *Naval History of Great Britain*, 6 vols (London 1837)
E H Jenkins, *The History of the French Navy* (London 1973)
G J Marcus, *A Naval History of England. The Age of Nelson* (London 1971)
Brian Tunstall (edited by Nicholas Tracy), *Naval Warfare in the Age of Sail: The Evolution of Fighting Tactics, 1650-1815* (London 1990)

The Nootka Sound crisis 1789-1790
William James, *Naval History of Great Britain*, Vol 1
William Kingsford, *The History of Canada*, Vol 7 (London 1894)
William Laird Clowes, *The Royal Navy*, Vol 4 (London 1898)
J Holland Rose, *William Pitt and National Revival* (London 1911)

First shots of the naval war
William Laird Clowes, *The Royal Navy*, Vol 4
William James, *Naval History of Great Britain*, Vol 1

The Low Countries, 1793-1794
J W Fortescue, *British Campaigns in Flanders 1690-1794* (London 1918)
William James, *Naval History of Great Britain* (London 1837), Vol 1
John Watkins, *A Biographical Memoir of His Late Royal Highness Frederick, Duke of York and Albany* (London 1827)

Ships of the Royal Navy: the First Rate
Brian Lavery, *The Ship of the Line*, 2 vols (London 1983-1984)
David Lyon, *The Sailing Navy List* (London 1993)

The Glorious First of June: preliminary skirmishes/the battle/aftermath
Oliver Warner, *The Glorious First of June* (London 1961)
David Cordingly, *Nicholas Pocock, 1740-1821* (London 1986)
Rear-Admiral T Sturges Jackson (ed), *Logs of the Great Sea Fights, 1794-1805*, Vol 1 (London 1899)
Michael Lewis (ed), *A Narrative of my Professional Adventures, 1790-1839 by Sir William Henry Dillon*, Vol 1 (London 1953)

A ship of the line in action
Brian Lavery, *Nelson's Navy: The Ships, Men and Organisation 1793-1815* (London 1989)
Michael Lewis (ed), *A Narrative of my Professional Adventures, 1790-1839 by Sir William Henry Dillon*, Vol 1

The Glorious First of June: the prizes
Jean Boudriot, *The 74-gun Ship*, Vol 3 (Rotherfield 1987)
David Lyon, *The Sailing Navy List*

'Dangers of the sea': fire
Captain Edward Pelham Brenton, *The Naval History of Great Britain*, 2 vols (London 1837)

Michael Lewis, *A Social History of the Navy, 1793-1815* (London 1960)

The Channel Fleet, 1794-1795
James Dugan, *The Great Mutiny* (London 1966)
Michael Lewis, *A Social History of the Navy 1793-1815* (London 1960), Ch XI
Colin Pengelly, *The First Bellerophon* (London 1966)

Bridport's action, 23 June 1795
Brian Tunstall (edited by Nicholas Tracy), *Naval Warfare in the Age of Sail*

The Channel frigate squadrons
James Henderson, *The Frigates* (London 1970)
William James, *Naval History of Great Britain*, Vol 1

Ships of the Royal Navy: the 18pdr frigate
Jean Boudriot, *The History of the French Frigate 1650-1850* (Rotherfield 1993)
Robert Gardiner, *The Heavy Frigate*, Vol 1 (London 1994)

West Indies 1793-1794/1795-1797
William Laird Clowes, *The Royal Navy*, Vol 4
Michael Duffy, *Soldiers, Sugar, and Seapower: The British Expeditions to the West Indies and the War against Revolutionary France* (Oxford 1987)
William James, *Naval History of Great Britain*, Vols 1 & 2

Commerce warfare in the West Indies
William James, *Naval History of Great Britain*, Vols 1 & 2

Capture of the Cape, 1795
William Laird Clowes, *The Royal Navy*, Vol 4
William James, *Naval History of Great Britain*, Vol 1

East Indies, 1793-1796
William Laird Clowes, *The Royal Navy*, Vol 4
William James, *Naval History of Great Britain*, Vol 1
C Northcote Parkinson, *War in the Eastern Seas, 1793-1815* (London 1953)

London, commercial capital of the world
R Davis, *The Rise of the English Shipping Industry in the Seventeenth and Eighteenth Centuries* (Newton Abbot 1962)
C Northcote Parkinson (ed), *The Trade Winds. A Study of British Overseas Trade during the French Wars, 1793-1815* (London 1948)
G Rude, *Hanoverian London, 1714-1808* (London 1971)

The cruise of a frigate
John Harland and Mark Myers, *Seamanship in the Age of Sail* (London 1984)

The Naval Officer: duties and privileges
W Falconer and W Burney, *A New Universal Dictionary of the Marine* (London 1815, reprinted London 1974)
W E May, *The Dress of Naval Officers* (London 1966)
N A M, Rodger, *Naval Records for Genealogists* (London 1988)

Occupation of Toulon
Political tangles
Evacuation of Toulon
John Barrow, *The Life and Correspondence of Admiral Sir Sidney Smith*, 2 vols (London 1848)
Brian Lavery, *The Ship of the Line*, Vol 1, App XI
J Holland Rose, *Lord Hood and the Defence of Toulon* (Cambridge 1922)

Lord Russell of Liverpool, *Knight of the Sword: The Life and Letters of Admiral Sir Sidney Smith* (London 1964)

The original Martello tower
Quentin Hughes, *Military Architecture* (Liphook 1991)

Fireships
W Falconer and W Burney, *A New Universal Dictionary of the Marine*
Robert Gardiner (ed), *The Line of Battle* (London 1992), Ch 5 [fireships]
Sir Richard Vesey Hamilton (ed), *Letters of Sir Thomas Byam Martin*, Vol 1 (London 1902)

Corsican Campaign, 1794
William Laird Clowes, *The Royal Navy*, Vol 4
James Hewitt (ed), *Eye-Witnesses to Nelson's Battles* (Reading 1972)
William James, *Naval History of Great Britain*, Vol 1
Tom Pocock, *Horatio Nelson* (London 1987)

Ships of the Royal Navy: flush-decked ship sloops
Robert Gardiner (ed), *The Line of Battle*, Ch 3

The Mediterranean Fleet under Hotham
James Hewitt (ed), *Eye-Witnesses to Nelson's Battles*

Britain withdraws from the Mediterranean
John C Dann (ed), *The Nagle Journal, 1775-1841* (New York 1988)

Battle of Cape St Vincent
Nelson's Patent Bridge
Colonel J Drinkwater Bethune, *A Narrative of the Battle of St Vincent* (second edition, London 1840)
Rear-Admiral T Sturges Jackson (ed), *Logs of the Great Sea Fights, 1794-1805*, Vol 1
Christopher Lloyd, *St Vincent and Camperdown* (London 1963)
Nicholas Tracy, *Nelson's Battles: The Art of Victory in the Age of Sail* (London 1996)

The Naval Officer: recruitment and advancement
Brian Lavery, *Nelson's Navy*
Michael Lewis, *A Social History of the Navy, 1793-1815*

Blockade of Cadiz
John C Dann (ed), *The Nagle Journal, 1775-1841*
James Hewitt (ed), *Eye-Witnesses to Nelson's Battles*

Santa Cruz de Tenerife, 1797
William Laird Clowes, *The Royal Navy*, Vol 4
James Dugan, *The Great Mutiny*
James Hewitt (ed), *Eye-Witnesses to Nelson's Battles*
William James, *Naval History of Great Britain*, Vol 2
Tom Pocock, *Horatio Nelson*

Close blockade
William James, *Naval History of Great Britain*, Vols 1 & 2

French naval bases: Brest
J Meyer & M Acerra, *Marines et Revolution* (Rennes 1988)
Simon Scharma, *Citizens* (London 1989)

The Irish Guard
William James, *Naval History of Great Britain*, Vols 1 & 2

The Naval Officer: life at sea
N A M Rodger, *The Wooden World. An Anatomy of the Georgian Navy* (London 1986)

Inshore warfare in the Channel
John Barrow, *The Life and Correspondence of Admiral Sir Sidney Smith*
William James, *Naval History of Great Britain*, Vols 1 & 2
Lord Russell of Liverpool, *Knight of the Sword: The Life and Letters of Admiral Sir Sidney Smith*

French naval bases: Cherbourg
J Meyer & M Acerra, *Marines et Revolution*
Simon Scharma, *Citizens*

Droits de l'Homme, 1797
C N Parkinson, *Edward Pellew, Viscount Exmouth* (London 1934)

The Black Legion invades Wales
Édouard Desbrière, *Projets et Tentatives de Débarquements aux Iles Britanniques*, Vol 1 (Paris 1900)
James Dugan, *The Great Mutiny*

Portsmouth—key to the Channel
J Coad, *Historic Architecture of the Royal Navy. An Introduction* (London 1983)
————, *The Royal Dockyards, 1690-1850. Architecture and Engineering Works of the Sailing Navy* (Aldershot 1989)
R J B Knight (ed), *Portsmouth Dockyard Papers 1774-1783: The American War* (Portsmouth 1987)
R A Morriss, *The Royal Dockyards during the Revolutionary and Napoleonic Wars* (Leicester 1983)

The Great Mutinies
James Dugan, *The Great Mutiny*
Conrad Gill, *The Naval Mutinies of 1797* (Manchester 1913)
Brian Lavery, *Nelson's Navy*

'Dangers of the sea': grounding
John Harland and Mark Myers, *Seamanship in the Age of Sail*

The North Sea squadron
Battle of Camperdown
Camperdown: end of the battle
Rear-Admiral T Sturges Jackson (ed), *Logs of the Great Sea Fights, 1794-1805*, Vol 1
Christopher Lloyd, *St Vincent and Camperdown*

A global war
William James, *Naval History of Great Britain*, Vols 1 & 2

Notes on artists, printmakers and their techniques
E H H Archibald, *Dictionary of Sea Painters* (Woodbridge, England 1980)
E Bénézit, *Dictionnaire critique et documentaire de Peintres, Sculpteurs, Dessinateurs et Graveurs* (Paris 1976)
Maurice Harold Grant, *A Dictionary of British Etchers* (London 1952)
Ian Mackensie, *British Prints: Dictionary and Price Guide* (Woodbridge, England, 1987)
Lister Raymond, *Prints and Printmaking* (London 1984)
Ronald Vere Tooley, *Tooley's Dictionary of Mapmakers* (New York and Amsterdam 1979)
Ellis Waterhouse, *The Dictionary of 18th Century Painters in Oils and Crayons* (Woodbridge, England 1980)
Arnold Wilson, *A Dictionary of British Marine Painters* (Leigh-on-Sea, England 1967)

Notes on Artists, Printmakers and their Techniques

These brief notes cover most of the artists and printmakers who appear in the volume, as well as the principal printing techniques. They are intended only to put the artists in context with the period and readers wanting further information on their art and lives should turn to the sources; in many cases there is little more to tell.

Alexander, William *(1762-1816)* English watercolourist and architectural illustrator known mainly for his series on China which he visited in 1792. In 1807 he was appointed Professor of design at the Military College at Great Marlow.

Alken, Samuel *(1750-1815)* English engraver of acquaints (*qv*) of topographical scenes and sporting scenes.

Ambrosi, Francesco *(fl mid-late eighteenth century)* Italian engraver who produced mainly topographical views, but who also worked after Nicholas and Pierre Ozanne (*qv*) and Claude Vernet (*qv*).

Anderson, William *(1757-1837)* Scottish marine painter who trained as a shipwright. He is known principally for his small river and estuarine scenes around Hull, but he also executed large-scale set pieces such as 'The battle of the Nile' and 'Lord Howe's Fleet off Spithead'. The British Museum hold sketch books of the battles of the Nile and Copenhagen.

Andrews, George Henry *(1816-1898)* English watercolourist of marine subjects who was trained as an engineer. He also did drawings of a number of journals such as the *Illustrated London News* and the *Graphic*.

Aquatint A variety of etching (*qv*) invented in France in the 1760s. It is a tone rather than a line process and is used principally to imitate the appearance of watercolour washes. The process involves the etching of a plate with acid through a porous ground of powdered resin. The acid bites small rings around each resin grain and gradations of tone are achieved by repetition of the biting process and the protection of areas of the plate with varnish.

Bailey, John *(fl late eighteenth and early nineteenth centuries)* English engraver of aquatints (*qv*) of topographical views and naval subjects after his contemporaries.

Baines, John Thomas *(fl late eighteenth and early nineteenth centuries)* English marine painter. As well as his naval subjects, such as 'Action between *Blanche* and *Pique*', he also painted views derived from a trip to Australia in 1855-56.

Baugean, Jean-Jérôme *(1764-1819)* French painter and prolific engraver best known for his collection of shipping prints, *Collection de toutes des Éspeces de Bâtiments*, which went through numerous editions in the early nineteenth century. Also well known is his depiction of 'The Embarkation of Napoleon onboard *Bellérophon*'.

Beechey, Sir William *(1753-1839)* English portrait painter who studied under Zoffany. He was made portrait painter to Queen Charlotte in 1793 and for the rest of his career produced a steady output of fashionable subjects. A contemporary portraitist, James Opie, said of his pictures that they 'were of that mediocre quality as to taste and fashion, that they seemed only fit for sea captains and merchants'.

Bendorp, Carel-Frederik *(fl mid-late eighteenth century)* Flemish painter and engraver who worked at Rotterdam and produced topographical views and historical and naval subjects.

Bowles, Carington *(fl late eighteenth century)* London engraver and publisher of decorative and allegorical subjects and topographical views.

Bowles, John *(fl mid-late eighteenth century)* English draughtsman and line engraver of topographical views.

Boydell, John *(1752-1817)* English engraver, publisher and print seller who was patron of most of the painters of his day whose works he engraved and supplied to every European market. This export market made him a considerable fortune and in 1790 he became Lord Mayor of London.

Boydell, Josiah *(1752-1817)* English mezzotint (*qv*) engraver mainly of portraits, and the nephew of John Boydell (*qv*) whose partner he became.

Briggs, Henry Perronet *(1792-1844)* English portrait and history painter who became a member of the Royal Academy in 1832.

Bromley, William *(1769-1842)* English engraver. He worked for the British Museum but is remembered principally for his portraits of Wellington and Napoleon.

Brown, Mather *(1761-1831)* American portrait and history painter, who settled in England in 1781 where he became a pupil of Benjamin West (*qv*). As well as portraits of members of George III's Court, he also painted military and naval subjects such as his depiction of 'Howe on the Deck of the *Queen Charlotte*'.

Buttersworth, Thomas *(1768-1842)* English marine painter who served in the Royal Navy from 1795 until he was invalided out in 1800. His vivid watercolours of the battle of St Vincent and the blockade of Cadiz, painted while he was at sea, suggest first-hand experience. After leaving the Navy he devoted himself fulltime to his painting and created a very considerable body of work.

Cadell, Thomas *(1742-1802)* London publisher and bookseller, amongst whose publications was *Cook's Voyages, 1773-77*.

Carey, J *(fl late eighteenth century)* English engraver, principally of decorative subjects.

Cauvin, Thomas *(1762-1846)* French geographer and archaeologist.

Chesham, Francis *(1749-1806)* English draughtsman and engraver, principally of topographical views and naval subjects.

Cleveley, John the Elder *(c1712-1777)* English marine painter and father of John the Younger (*qv*), Robert (*qv*) and James, who became a ship's carpenter. He worked in Deptford Dockyard and may have

learnt his painting skills from the dockyard painters responsible for external ship decoration. He is best known for his scenes of dockyards and shipbuilding.

Cleveley, John the Younger *(1747-1786)* English marine painter, son of the shipwright and painter John Cleveley the Elder (*qv*), and twin brother of Robert Cleveley (*qv*). He was brought up in the Deptford Dockyard and learned his craft from his father and the watercolourist John Sandby. He travelled with Joseph Banks as draughtsman on his exhibition to Iceland in 1772, and again to the Arctic in 1774, and it is for his depictions of the Arctic that he is best known.

Cleveley, Robert (1749-1809) English marine painter, son of John Cleveley the Elder (*qv*) and twin brother of John Cleveley (*qv*). He was Captain's Clerk in the *Asia* and served on the North American and West Indies stations in the 1770s. He is known mainly for his history paintings of the American Revolutionary War.

Colls, Ebenezer *(fl mid nineteenth century)* English marine painter of coastal and naval subjects.

Cook, Henry R *(fl the first half of the nineteenth century)* English engraver, mainly of portraits.

Cruickshank, George *(1792-1878)* English draughtsman and etcher and temperance preacher, celebrated for his caricatures and political and social satires. He produced an immense volume of work during his long life, following the tradition of Hogarth, Gillray and Rowlandson.

Daniell, James *(fl late eighteenth and early nineteenth centuries)* English mezzotint (*qv*) engraver and publisher, mainly of naval scenes, many after Singleton.

Daniell, Samuel *(1775-1811)* English draughtsman and engraver and younger brother of William Daniell, the eminent topographical, marine and architectural artist, for whom he worked.

Dodd, Robert *(1748-1815)* English marine and landscape painter and successful engraver and publisher, best known for his portrayals of the naval battles of the Revolutionary American and French Wars. His is also known for his formal portraits of ships in which three views are included in a single image.

Doumet, Zacherie-Félix *(1761-1818)* French marine painter, born in Toulon, who left that port during the siege to move to Corsica and then Lisbon, before returning in 1806.

Drummond, Samuel *(1765-1844)* English landscape painter and portraitist who served in the Royal Navy for seven years. Self-taught, and with first-hand experience of naval warfare, he painted a small number of naval subjects including the well-known 'Death of Lord Nelson'.

Drypoint Intaglio *(qv)* engraving *(qv)* technique in which the image is scratched into a copper plate with a steel needle which is held like a pen. Ridges —burr— are created around the lines which give drypoint its characteristic fuzzy effect. The burr is delicate and quickly wears away during the printing process so that print runs are short.

Duncan, Edward *(1803-1882)* English landscape painter and engraver of marine and sporting subjects as well as topographical scenes after his contemporaries.

Duplessi-Bertaux, Jean *(1747-1819)* French engraver and painter whose principal body of work depicted the events of the French Revolution.

Dutton, Thomas Goldsworth *(c1819-91)* Prolific English draughtsman and lithographer of ships and shipping scenes, after his own watercolours and those of his contemporaries. His huge and varied body of work gives a vivid impression of nineteenth-century shipping.

Durand-Brager, Jean-Baptiste-Henri *(1814-1879)* French marine painter and traveller. As well as official history paintings for the French Government of naval scenes, he also accepted commissions from the Czar and the Austrian Emperor.

Earle, Augustus *(fl early nineteenth century)* American-born history and marine painter who travelled widely to the United States, New Zealand and the Mediterranean in search of subjects. He was the draughtsman onboard the *Beagle*.

Edy, John William *(fl early nineteenth century)* Danish painter and engraver of topographical views and naval scenes after both his contemporaries and his own designs.

Elliott, Thomas *(fl late eighteenth and early nineteenth centuries)* English marine painter who worked in and around Portsmouth in the last decade of the century.

Elmes, William *(fl late eighteenth and early nineteenth centuries)* English draughtsman and engraver who made caricatures much in the manner of Cruickshank *(qv)*, including two of Napoleon, published between 1811 and 1816.

Emeric, F J *(fl late eighteenth century)* French naïve ship portrait painter.

Engraving The process of cutting an image into a block or metal plate which is used for printing by using a number of techniques such as aquatint *(qv)*, drypoint *(qv)*, etching *(qv)*, or mezzotint *(qv)*. An engraving is a print made from the engraved plate.

Etching An intaglio *(qv)* engraving process by which the design is made by drawing into a wax ground applied over the metal plate. The plate is then submerged in acid which bites into it where it has been exposed through the wax. An etching is a print made from an etched plate.

Evans, Benjamin Beale *(fl early nineteenth century)* English engraver, principally of portraits, who did work for John Boydell *(qv)*.

Faden, William *(1750-1836)* English cartographer and publisher, and the partner of Thomas Jeffereys *(qv)* whose business he ran in the Charing Cross Road after the latter's death in 1771. He is best known for his *North American Atlas*, published in 1777, *Battles of the American Revolution* and *Petit Neptune Français*, both of 1793.

Fairburn, John *(fl late eighteenth and early nineteenth centuries)* London publisher and geographer and map seller whose works include *North America* (1798) and *Spain and Portugal* (1808).

Flight, J *(fl late eighteenth and early nineteenth centuries)* English miniaturist painter who worked in London and exhibited regularly at the Royal Academy between 1802 and 1806.

Gear, Joseph *(1768-1853)* English marine painter, born in Portsmouth, who became marine painter to the Duke of Sussex and is best known for his views of the 'Grand Review at Spithead' (1815). He moved to America at an unknown date where he continued to paint, principally depictions of British ships.

Golding, Richard *(1785-1865)* English engraver, principally of portraits and genre subjects after his contemporaries.

Groenewegen, Gerrit *(1754-1826)* Dutch marine painter and etcher who trained as a ship's carpenter. After losing a leg he turned to drawing ships' draughts and then to watercolour paintings and etching *(qv)*. Author of a famous collection of etchings of shipping and craft entitled *Verzameling van Vier en tachtig stuks Hollandsche schepen* (Rotterdam 1789).

Huggins, John William *(1781-1845)* English marine painter who spent his early years at sea with the East India Company until around 1814 when he established himself as a painter. He produced an enormous number of ship portraits, many of them engraved by his son-in-law, Edward Duncan *(qv)*, as well as a number of large-scale naval battles, in particular the battle of Trafalgar. In 1836 he was made marine painter to King William IV.

Jeakes, Joseph *(fl early nineteenth century)* English engraver of aquatints *(qv)*, notably of topographical scenes, naval engagements after his contemporaries, particularly Thomas Whitcombe *(qv)* and his own designs.

Jefferys, Thomas *(c1710-1771)* English cartographer and publisher, and one of the most important map publishers of the eighteenth century. His huge output included *The Maritime Ports of France* (1761), and between 1751 and 1768 he produced important maps of America and the West Indies. After bankruptcy Robert Sayer *(qv)* acquired many of his interests and published much of his work posthumously, notably his *North American Pilot* and *West Indies Atlas* in 1775.

Jones, George *(1786-1869)* English history painter, particularly of battle scenes of the Napoleoenic Wars, for example 'Nelson Boarding the *San Josef* at the Battle of St Vincent'.

Joy, William *(1803-1866)* English marine painter who worked mainly in collaboration with his brother John Cantiloe, and the two are often referred to as the 'brothers John'. As well as paintings of naval incidents they were commissioned by the Government in the 1830s to record and make drawings of fishing craft.

Jukes, Francis *(1747-1812)* English painter and etcher of aquatints. As well as his popular 'Views of England' and his sporting prints he was a prolific exponent of marine subjects.

Livesay, J *(fl late eighteenth and early nineteenth centuries)* English marine watercolour painter.

Livesay, Richard *(1750-1823)* English landscape and genre painter and pupil of Benjamin West *(qv)*. He was appointed the drawing master of the Naval Academy, Portsmouth, in 1796, and his first marine painting, 'Cornwallis's Retreat', was exhibited at the Royal Academy that year.

Loutherbourg, Philippe Jacques de *(1740-1812)* Born in Strasbourg, he moved to London in 1771 at the instigation of David Garrick, the actor, who employed him as scenic director at the Drury Lane Theatre. Though principally a landscape painter, his dramatic naval works and seascapes, notably the vast 'Battle of the Glorious First of June 1794', had considerable influence on marine artists in the early years of the nineteenth century, particularly J W M Turner.

Lithograph A print made by drawing a design on porous limestone with a greasy material. The stone is then wetted and ink applied to it which adheres only to the drawn surfaces. Paper is then pressed to the stone for the final print. Lithography was discovered only at the very end of the eighteenth century but quickly developed into a highly flexible medium.

Luny, Thomas *(1759-1837)* One of the leading English marine painters of his generation. A pupil of Francis Holman *(qv)*, he served in the Royal Navy until around 1810 when he retired to Teignmouth. His remarkable output amounted to some 3000 paintings and many of these were engraved.

Medland, Thomas *(1755-1822)* English draughtsman and aquatint *(qv)* engraver of landscapes, topographical views and naval subjects, who taught drawing at the East India College.

Mezzotint A type of engraving *(qv)* in which the engraving plate is first roughened with a tool known as a rocker. The rough surface holds the ink and appears as a black background and the design is then burnished onto it by scraping away the rough burr to create lighter tones and by polishing the surface for highlights. Thus the artist works from dark to light, creating a tonal effect which was particularly suited to reproducing paintings and had its heyday in eighteenth-century England.

Milton, Thomas *(1743-1827)* English aquatint *(qv)* engraver of landscapes and portraits after his own designs and those of his contemporaries, and son of a marine painter.

Orme, Daniel *(fl late eighteenth and early nineteenth centuries)* English aquatint *(qv)* engraver of decorative, military and naval subjects after his contemporaries.

Owen, Samuel *(1768/69-1857)* English marine painter, principally of watercolours of coastal and fishing scenes, some of which were produced in W B Cooke's *Thames* of 1829. His few large battle pieces, painted in oils, include a depiction of Jervis's action off Cape St Vincent, 1797.

Owen, William *(1769-1825)* English landscape and society portrait painter, who died from accidental opium poisoning.

Ozanne, Nicholas Marie *(1728-1811)* French draughtsman and painter of marine subjects and brother of Pierre Ozanne. He was made draughtsman to the French Navy in 1762 and is remembered chiefly for his accurate recording of maritime and naval events.

Pass, J *(fl late eighteenth and early nineteenth centuries)* English line engraver of topographical views, portraits and rural subjects after his contemporaries.

Pocock, Nicholas *(1740-1821)* Foremost English marine painter of his day. He was apprenticed in the shipbuilding yard of Richard Champion in Bristol before being appointed to command the barque *Lloyd*, setting sail to Charleston in 1768. This was the first of a number of voyages for which there are illustrated log books, some of which are at the National Maritime Museum. He was present at the West Indies campaign in 1778 or '79, and completed an oil painting in 1780, receiving helpful criticism from Sir Joshua Reynolds. Thereafter he devoted himself to his art and painted numerous depictions of the struggles with Revolutionary France

Pocock, Lt William Innes *(1783-1863)* English marine painter and a son of Nicholas Pocock *(qv)*. Like his father he went to sea in the merchant service before spending ten years in the Royal Navy from 1805 to 1814, during which time he recorded incidents in sketch books, many of which are held by the National Maritime Museum. His oil paintings are very much in his father's style and suggest that he spent time as his pupil.

Pollard, Robert *(1755-1838)* English line and aquatint *(qv)* engraver of naval and historical subjects, as well as of portraits and architectural scenes. He set up business in London in 1781 and is known to have collaborated with Francis Jukes *(qv)*.

Pringle, James *(fl late eighteenth and early nineteenth centuries)* English marine painter, mainly based in Deptford, who exhibited a number of naval works at the Royal Academy. The National Maritime Museum has a series of small drawings of warships which demonstrate skilled technical draughtsmanship.

Reynolds, Sir Joshua *(1723-1792)* Foremost English portrait painter whose early reputation was made with his portrait of Keppel with whom he sailed to Italy in 1749. He returned to London in 1753 and established himself as the leading portrait painter of his day. He was made President of the Royal Academy upon its foundation in 1768 and in his 'Discourses' —lectures—he endeavoured to create an intellectual foundation for English art.

Robertson, Archibald *(1765-1835)* Scottish portrait painter who studied at the Royal Academy under Joshua Reynolds *(qv)*. He moved to America in 1791 where he painted Washington and his family and acquired a considerable reputation. He was the author of *Sketches of America*.

Sayer, Robert and Bennett, John *(fl mid-late eighteenth century)* London publishers, based in Fleet Street, of sporting subjects, topographical views and maps.

Schouman, Martinus *(1770-1838)* Dutch marine painter who is credited with reviving the tradition of marine painting in Holland in the nineteenth century. As well as dramatic seascapes, he painted a number of naval subjects.

Serres, Dominic the Elder *(1722-1793)* French marine painter, born in Gascony, who, after running away to sea, was captured by a British frigate in 1758 and taken to England. He became a pupil of Charles Brooking and was a founder member of the Royal Academy. Though a Frenchman he became one of the most successful marine painters of the Seven Years War and of the American Revolutionary War.

Serres, John Thomas *(1759-1825)* English marine painter and elder son of Dominic Serres, the Elder *(qv)*. Though he painted a number of dramatic naval battle scenes in the manner of de Loutherbourg *(qv)*, whom he greatly admired, his main activity was drawing the coasts of England, France and Spain in his capacity as Marine Draughtsman to the Admiralty. A selection were subsequently published in *Serres Little Sea Torch* (1801). He died in debtors' prison as a result of the pretensions and wild extravagances of his wife,

the self-styled 'Princess Olive of Cumberland'.

Sewell, J *(fl late eighteenth century)* English publisher and founder member of the short-lived Society for the Improvement of Naval Architecture.

St John, Georgina *(fl mid nineteenth century)* English land- and seascape painter.

Streatfield, Reverend Thomas *(1777-1848)* English topographical painter whose lasting monument is his fifty-volume history of the county of Kent held in the British Museum.

Stothard, Thomas *(1755-1834)* English history painter and one of the most important and prolific book illustrators of his day, completing some 5000 subjects.

Sutherland, Thomas *(fl late eighteenth and early nineteenth centuries)* English aquatint *(qv)* engraver of sporting, naval and military subjects and portraits after his contemporaries.

Tardieu, Ambroise *(fl late eighteenth century)* French engraver who did plans of harbours and fortifications, and published a number of atlases.

Tobin, J *(fl late eighteenth century)* English line engraver of figures and landscapes after his contemporaries.

Tomlinson, John *(fl early nineteenth century)* English engraver of landscapes who left England to work in Paris where he drowned himself in the Seine when drunk.

Turner, Charles *(1773-1857)* English aquatint *(qv)* and mezzotint *(qv)* engraver of portraits, military and sporting subjects and topographical views. His engraving of J M W Turner's 'A Shipwreck' in 1805 was the first one made after a Turner painting.

Vernet, Antoine Charles Horace called **Carle** *(1758-1836)* French painter and son of Claude Joseph Vernet *(qv)*. Though he painted battle scenes and history subjects, he is best known for his equestrian paintings.

Vernet, Claude Joseph *(1714-1789)* French landscape painter who is probably best known for his series of paintings of the ports of France which he painted in the 1750s and 60s and which were engraved at the same time.

Vinkeles, Reinier *(1741-1816)* Dutch engraver of portraits and landscapes.

Wells, J G *(fl late eighteenth and early nineteenth centuries)* English aquatint *(qv)* engraver of landscapes and topographical views and naval and military subjects after his own designs and those of his contemporaries.

West, Benjamin *(1738-1820)* American painter who is now regarded as the founding father of the American school. He settled in London in 1763, and though he retained his contacts with his native land, he remained there for the rest of his life. His history paintings, as personified by 'The Death of General Wolfe', became an inspiration for young American painters depicting the history of their young nation.

Westall, William *(1781-1850)* English painter of landscapes and an illustrator and engraver of topographical views who was appointed by the Admiralty as draughtsman to accompany Captain Flinders in *Investigator* on an exploratory voyage around Australia between 1810 and 1813. On the return journey their ship was wrecked on a coral reef and marooned for eight weeks while his heroic captain sought help in an open boat.

Whitcombe, Thomas *(born c1752)* English marine painter who, like Nicholas Pocock *(qv)* and Luny *(qv)*, was celebrated for his huge output of paintings depicting the French Revolutionary Wars. He contributed some fifty plates to the *Naval Achievements of Great Britain* and also painted numerous works for engravings. There is no record of his death.

Wilkins, William *(fl early nineteenth century)* English landscape painter who ventured into naval subject matter with his 'Battle of Cape St Vincent, 14th February 1797'.

Williamson, Thomas *(fl early-mid nineteenth century)* English engraver of portraits and decorative works after his contemporaries.

Yates, Lt Thomas *(c1760-1796)* English marine painter who entered the Royal Navy in 1782, leaving a few years later to become a painter. With the outbreak of the French Revolutinary Wars he began to engrave and publish from his drawings of celebrated naval actions. He was shot in a family dispute and few works remain from his short life.

INDEX

All ships are British unless otherwise indicated in brackets following the name

Abbreviations
Cdr = Commander
Cdre = Commodore
Fr = France

GB = British merchant ship
Lt = Lieutenant
Lt-Col=Lieutenant-Colonel
Lt-Gen=Lieutenant-General

Neths = Netherlands
R/A = Rear-Admiral
RM=Royal Marines
Sp = Spain

US=United States
V/A = Vice-Admiral
